THE THEORY OF
FREE COMPETITION

Nothing, it may be said, is more familiar to Englishmen than competition, whether as a scientific conception or as a feature of our social life. The fact of competition sums up a large part of our economic activities, and on the concept is built up most of our economic theory. Yet we shall find that very opposite opinions are held as to the nature of the competitive struggle, and that very few careful attempts have been made by economists to define the term in its scientific use.

HERBERT SOMERTON FOXWELL

THE THEORY OF FREE COMPETITION

By
C. J. RATZLAFF, Ph.D.
Professor of Economics
Lafayette College

UNIVERSITY OF PENNSYLVANIA PRESS
Philadelphia
1936

LONDON: HUMPHREY MILFORD
OXFORD UNIVERSITY PRESS

Manufactured in the United States of America

To

L. N. R.

PREFACE

IT IS remarkable that a term which signifies not only so important a concept in economic philosophy but also so dominant an institution in human activities as "free competition" conveys such uncertain meaning. Economic thought presents essential differences of opinion on *any* aspect of the subject of "free competition." It seems to me that it is necessary to state more clearly the nature, the operation, and the limitations of competition and the competitive order. To this end this book directs attention.

Although the work is not so divided in the table of contents, it contains four rather distinct parts. These are: first, a statement of the problem (Chapter 1); secondly, the analysis and statement of the nature of "economic competition" (Chapter 2); thirdly, the critical examination of the use of "free competition" in the writings of some leading economists (Chapters 3, 4, and 5); and fourthly, the limitations of competition as seen in the economic doctrine and in the programs of control of competition proposed by those writers who have concerned themselves almost solely with this aspect of the subject (Chapters 6, 7, and 8).

This book traces the development of the theory of free competition as it is found in those economic treatises which economists regard as permanent contributions to economic doctrine. The period considered is from Adam Smith down to the beginning of the present economic depression. In a sense, it may be said that this period constitutes an era of free competition which culminated with the world-wide industrial collapse of 1930. From that time on there has been a phenomenal development of regulation and planning of the competitive order. Beginning with such devices as national economic councils (which antedated the depression) in various European countries, an increasing amount and kind of social control has been undertaken.

It is not the purpose of this book to consider the evaluation and criticism of free competition and the competitive order which have been so sharply expressed during the economic crisis since 1930. Sufficient time has not passed to permit one to consider this evaluation and criticism with true perspective. Nearness tends to produce distortion and over-emphasis. Nevertheless, a body of economic doctrine with respect to social control is rapidly accumulating. I shall treat this in a forthcoming volume under the title of *The Theory of Controlled Competition.*

June 1935 C. J. RATZLAFF

CONTENTS

I

INTRODUCTION

Sec. 1. Existing confusion in the use of free competition in economic writing. p. 1.
Sec. 2. Terms used interchangeably: "laissez faire," "individualism," "free competition," the competition of business parlance. p. 3.
Sec. 3. Scope of study. p. 5.

I

FEW terms in economic writing have been more widely and vaguely used than that of "free competition." Although it is to be expected that writers who are interested in economic art will use the term according to the various ends that they may seek to attain, it is peculiar, indeed, that the writers who are interested in economic science can differ so widely in their usage of a postulate so fundamental in economic reasoning as that of free competition. In so far as economics is to serve as a science, that is "to establish certain general propositions, either positively or hypothetically true, respecting the coexistence and sequence of facts,"[1] the assumptions under which the propositions were derived must be clearly stated. If these general propositions are to serve in economic art, in formulating practical rules, the assumptions under which the general propositions have been stated must be understood in order that if any assumption was hypothetical the proposition must be qualified in its appli-

[1] Henry Sidgwick, *Principles of Economics* (3rd ed.; London: Macmillan, 1901), p. 13.

cation to the actual condition.[2] Certainly it is obvious that to use a term, which denotes a definite and restricted assumption, in any other sense throws light neither on the soundness of the economic proposition nor the application of such a proposition in drawing up practical rules for the attainment of certain ends.

What has been said applies to "free competition." The wide diversity in the uses of this term is remarkable and, strangely enough, no writer, to my knowledge, has given more than passing attention to this important subject. Economic literature is replete with diverse uses of free competition in the reasoning of different writers on the same subject, with the result that diametrically opposed conclusions are arrived at.[3] That particular uses of terms to serve particular purposes are necessary in a social science is readily admitted, but this does not deny that it is incumbent upon the writer to state clearly what his use may be. Not to do so places him open to the charge of carelessness or intellectual dishonesty.

It is interesting to note that the same writer upon a single subject may use "competition" in such a way as to involve essentially totally different ideas. This is very well illustrated in the statements which follow:

> The essential nature of competition, then, is rivalry in efficient service to the consuming public. . . .[4]

[2] This point has been exceedingly well discussed by W. Cunningham in his Inaugural Lecture at King's College, London, in 1892, under the title of "The Relativity of Economic Doctrine," *Economic Journal*, II (1892), 1-16.

[3] Instances of these will be given at some length in the following chapter on "Free Competition and Economic Competition" in connection with the discussion of competition in the economic sense.

[4] J. M. Clark, *Social Control of Business* (Chicago: University of Chicago Press, 1926), p. 38.

And further:

> But what if the new producer, once he is in the business, chooses to combine or agree with those who are already there, or they with him, and so extinguish the competition as fast as it starts up? Even under these conditions competition would have some effect, though not what its advocates intend it to have; but "free competition" in the usual sense bars out such combinations or agreements. It exists only when each competitor follows his own financial interests absolutely independent of the others, with no collusion or concerted action of any sort. Competitors are free—except to combine.[5]

Also in speaking of "grades of competition" this writer states that "Cutthroat competition and predatory competition differ from ordinary competition . . . ."[6]

It is unnecessary at this point to pause for an analysis of the foregoing. In passing one might note that the brief statement regarding the "essential nature of competition" has three different ideas, none of which the author elucidates.

2

Enough has been said regarding the diversity in the usage of the term "competition" or "free competition," per se. We now turn for a brief consideration of various terms with which competition has been used interchangeably. Most notably these have been "laissez faire" and "individualism." The erroneous reasoning and conclusions to which this interchangeable usage leads will be developed in the following chapter. It will suffice here to point out that these terms are not synonymous with competition. "Laissez faire," or the absence of state intervention, has never existed in absolute form in any one phase of economic activity, that is, in production, exchange, dis-

[5] *Ibid.*, p. 146.
[6] *Ibid.*, p. 152.

tribution, or consumption, and is the expression of governmental *policy* differing both as to time and place. This policy may be extended with the consequent increase of competition in the economic sense or a decrease of such competition—depending entirely upon the circumstances of time and place of the application of the policy of laissez faire.[7]

Even more frequently have "individualism" and "competition" been used interchangeably. What has been said regarding laissez faire we shall see applies to individualism—the system of industrial organization in which all initiative is originated by private individuals, and all organization to their voluntary agreement.

Passing now to the interchangeable use of the "competition" of common business parlance with that of "competition" in the economic sense, or, what comes to the same end, namely, the failure to point out the precise connotation of the latter, we find as a result obviously fallacious views. This has been very well stated by one writer who says:[8]

> The word "competition" is in constant use in common speech to designate a great variety of efforts on the part of those engaged in like occupations to secure some advantage over each other. . . .
>
> The competition which prevails in business is oftentimes very different from that contemplated in economics and may be directly hostile to it in results. The business man assumes that he has, in his methods, the justification of fundamental social laws simply because, using the same language as the economist, he designates his relation to his rivals as that of competition. For this error the economist is frequently at fault. He fails to distinguish between the use and abuse of competition, and between the very different modes of business that go by that name.

[7] *Cf. post*, Chap. II.

[8] John Bascom, "Competition, Actual and Theoretical," *Quarterly Journal of Economics*, XIV (1900), 537-542. This article is exceptionally lucid and concise.

He gives no definition of competition. He employs the word of such wide and familiar use as to require no definition. It is this very breadth and familiarity which make definition necessary, if we are not to confound under the same word forms of business as wide apart as they can well be, and utterly dissimilar in their social and ethical bearings. The competition involved in the reconciliation of productive processes is definite and restricted, and cannot be left, without great confusion, to slide into the forms of rivalry which common practice and common speech bundle together under this convenient and apologetic word.

3

This book purposes to be in part analytical and in part historical. It has been prompted by the feeling that much of the confusion of thinking, especially in such fields as, for example, socialism, labor problems, and the trust problem, is caused by a lack of understanding as to some of the assumptions upon which such reasoning was based. Particularly true is this of the basic assumption of free competition. The significance, to take but one instance, of the pronouncements of writers so widely read as the Webbs[9] (if their sweeping indictment of the present capitalistic civilization were taken seriously) is apparent. The social significance referred to is not necessarily to be measured only by a growth of revolutionary spirit that a book such as *The Decay of Capitalist Civilisation* might cause, but more so by the growth of the invidious, destructive industrial unrest.

The whole of the socialistic doctrine—both Marxian and utopian—with the tremendous loss of human energy and satisfactions as a result of the misdirection it sponsors, is largely due to the socialists' failure to conceive competition in the economic sense.

Again (and more apparent) one can see the significance

[9] See their *The Decay of Capitalist Civilisation* (London: The Fabian Society, 1923).

of competition in the reasoning involved in formulating trust legislation. The American criteria of the existence of competition have been size and numbers of competitive units. Does competition, in the economic sense, require the repression of the trust, amalgamation, and cartel? The European answer has been distinctly different from the American. The former view is reflected in the following:[10]

> . . . It appears how misdirected is the American policy (as to trusts), when for instance it endeavors in every way merely to maintain the competitive struggle, and to suppress every effort toward monopoly, every larger concentration of enterprises. This is simply impossible of execution, because each competitive struggle is itself an endeavor to secure monopoly, and the more violent it is the more surely does it lead to monopoly. The monopoly of the Kartell and trust is therefore nothing more than the competitive conflict pushed to its limit. . . . A rational policy toward monopoly . . . should not clumsily seek to prevent every attempt to monopolize, nor attempt to establish a state of continued competitive warfare. That is uneconomical, leads to continual upheaval, stimulates speculation, and after all is simply furthering the effort to monopolize.[11]

Here, too, the problem calls for a statement of what constitutes the essence of economic competition. With this we, as Americans, have not concerned ourselves; size—the control of seventy to eighty per cent of the output—in itself constituted the lack of competition.

The foregoing indicates the nature of the analytical work which will fall within the scope of this book; the distinctions which need to be made in the understanding

[10] Robert Liefmann, "Monopoly or Competition," *Quarterly Journal of Economics*, XXIX (1914), 308-325.

[11] In this view, Liefmann suggests (although he does not express or develop) a consideration regarding competition which the present writer regards as of primary importance, viz., the importance of distinguishing "form" and "results" in competition. (See next chapter.) The American policy places importance with the former (the number and size of the competing units), the German policy is concerned not with the competitive struggle, per se, but rather the "results."

of free competition and economic competition. Excepting for a summary chapter on the Classical School, the historical phase of this work will be concerned with the use of free competition in the important economic writings beginning with Cairnes's work in 1875. Confining myself to the period since 1875 has been dictated, primarily, by the fact that a thorough analysis of the classical economic literature would open a field much too broad for the present volume. Secondarily, Cairnes may be said to close the Classical Period, and his work marks a convenient beginning point for the study of recent economic writing. This is true not only because of Cairnes's change of emphasis in the reasoning of his predecessors, but also the forces which were operating at that time—particularly Parliamentary legislation, the criticism of the German Historical School, and the growth of humanitarian interest—opened a new era in economic thought.

II

FREE COMPETITION AND ECONOMIC COMPETITION

I HAVE indicated the diversity of usage of "free competition" in economic writing. The confusion in thinking in which this has resulted, we have seen, is accentuated by the synonymous use of other terms, such as "laissez faire" and "individualism." Particularly misleading is the use of "competition" in the business sense, which writers frequently and unintentionally drift into, notwithstanding their purpose and effort to maintain their writing on a critical and scientific basis. At this point it is necessary to state my own views upon the subject of "free competition" before undertaking a critical examination of the sense in which "free competition" is used in the writings of those economists which I shall consider. It may be contended that one's own views should, more properly, be stated at the close of such an examination as I propose to make. With this contention I do not agree. If my purpose were to set forth a purely historical development of the use of "free competition" in economic reasoning, it would not only be true that my own views should not be expressed at the outset, but indeed they would be quite irrelevant at the close as well. Inasmuch, however, as this is a *critical* examination, the grounds upon which the criticism rests should be as clearly stated at the outset as the rather general purpose of this work permits. Such is the aim of the following sections of this chapter. They will develop the distinctions, the propositions, the prerequisites which pertain to "free competition" when used in the economic sense, or, in other words, to set forth the nature of "economic competition."

We turn, first, to the consideration of fundamental distinctions that need to be made in the use of "competition" in economic thinking.

I

Possibly the most important distinction is that of competition as to form and competition as to result. By the former is meant the number and size of the competing units; by the latter is meant the satisfactions which flow from the activities of these units. The principle expounded by Bentham and John Stuart Mill is apropos, namely, that the justification of every human institution must be found exclusively in its social utility.[1]

Economic history is, of course, the story of the evolving, changing form of our economic institutions. To identify the results of competition, in its creation of products or services, with a particular form of competing units, either as to their size or number, is obviously fallacious. Changes in human wants, in the environment, and in the state of the arts, necessitate changes in the structure of our economic institutions. Since these institutions are only means to an end, the result—satisfactions of wants or "social utility"—is the primary consideration.

Failure to distinguish competition as to its forms from competition as to its results accounts, in large part, for the different conclusions reached by different writers on the same subject where the central issue involved is that of competition. This failure of distinction is very well seen in many writers[2] who point to the decreasing competition in our present industrial organization. As evidence of this decreasing competition they would cite the

[1] One must be aware, however, of the intimate relation of "form" and "results"—they have reciprocal influence. That is to say, the results or satisfactions which flow from economic institutions are not separate entities in themselves. These results are greatly affected by the conditions under which the results (or satisfactions) are brought about. This, of course, is clearly illustrated by sweating industries and child labor. Such industries and labor create satisfactions, but considering a period longer than that of the immediate or short run, the social cost is greater than the social gain.

This particular phase of competition has received elaborate treatment at the hands of such writers as Hobson and Veblen, although they do not make the distinction which I have made here, i.e., "competition as to form" and "competition as to results." Able, discriminating analysis of this problem has been made by Pigou in his *Economics of Welfare*. It will be given consideration in Chap. VI.

[2] For example, Sidney and Beatrice Webb, *The Decay of Capitalist Civilisation, passim.*

concentration of ownership and control of capital and the diminishing number of producing units. The increasing competition as to results—the larger number of products and services produced, or the larger products in terms of quality—this competition is ignored.[3]

The following writers are clearly not making the distinction to which I have called attention:

> . . . in the world of capital and in the world of labor, individual freedom of contract leads inevitably to *combination*, and this *destroys free competition* between individuals. If we desire to maintain free competition between individuals, the only conceivable way would be such a state interference with contracts as would prevent, not only *every kind of association, but also* every alienation of land and every transfer of small businesses to larger ones which would in any way cause or increase inequality of wealth or power.[4]

The fallacious view that the sole, or the important criterion of competition is that of form (the size and number of the competing units) is seen in the foregoing quotation. The clarity with which this error is avoided by Professor Liefmann is seen by his statements that

> Competition . . . is not merely the presence of several sellers in the market. . . . One does well to distinguish between free competition . . . and the competitive *struggle*, the mutual underbidding, which has been regarded as the essential characteristic of the competitive system.[5]

Again, this is, in part, what Marshall had in mind, in stating the view of economists, when he said, "In order

[3] At this point we are confining our attention merely to the distinction of competition as to form and competition as to result. Without considering the latter it could be easily shown that competition has increased enormously in the former. But this is anticipating our discussion in the fourth section of this chapter.

[4] Sidney and Beatrice Webb, *Industrial Democracy* (London: Longmans, Green, 1897) II, 689. Italics mine.

[5] Robert Liefmann, "Monopoly or Competition," *Quarterly Journal of Economics*, XXIX (1915), 316-317. Italics mine.

to preserve what is *essential* in the benefits of free competition, they are willing to have a great extension of public control over private and semi-public undertakings. . . ."[6]

The form and nature of competition, as well as other social institutions, are relative to time and place. With expanding industrial environment free competition of individuals has been greatly modified. The competing unit has passed from the personal to the partnership, from the partnership to the corporate, and from the corporate to the associative form.[7] That this transition has necessarily modified the relation of employee to employee, of employee to employer, of employer to employer, and of producer to consumer, is true. And, indeed, these relations would also have been altered by changes in social institutions other than that of economic organization.

Since the competitive relation is a fourfold one, the general observation that the "free competition of individuals has been destroyed" conveys very uncertain meaning. We may readily grant that the transition from personal proprietorship to the large corporate organization has meant an increased bargaining and reserve power not equally shared in by the individual worker.[8] Has not,

[6] See *Memorials of Alfred Marshall*, Edited by A. C. Pigou (London: Macmillan, 1925), p. 290. Italics mine.

[7] This has been the dominant trend in manufacturing and commercial enterprises, although, to be sure, many activities still are concerned with personal services and work which calls for the expression of individuality. The individual proprietorship or partnership is particularly suited to render such services and remains an important form of organization. In agriculture, also, the economic unit is primarily the individual or family unit. Interesting recent developments point to some important changes in the producing unit in this large field of activity.

[8] That is, unless he is a member of a trade or labor union whose growth in strength has equalled that of their employers, as, for example, the Railway Brotherhood. It is my opinion that we, as Americans, are prone to overlook the increasing number of "closed shops" and unions sufficiently open to include, for the particular locality, so many of the total number

however, this loss of bargaining, competitive strength been much more than offset by increased competition in the other relations pointed out above? Increasing division of labor, enabling the individual worker to acquire proficiency quickly over a wide range of the industrial field, has added remarkably to the mobility of workers. This has resulted in increased competition of producer with producer. The rapid growth of welfare work, pensions, seniority clauses, profit sharing, stock distribution, etc., on the part of employers is in large part due to their recognition that labor is increasingly mobile and that producers are increasingly competing not only with other producers in their own industry but almost all other industries.[9] In sharp contrast to the conditions of the handicraft period, increased division of labor (increased simplification) has relieved the employee of dependence upon a limited number of employers, of a particular locality, or of an industry. The individual turns his hand to diverse activities; a few weeks, or a month, suffices to acquire skill.[10]

Increased competition has also occurred in the relation

of workmen as to give the employees bargaining power approaching the power enjoyed by the employer. My opinion is based upon observations made in Chicago at more than a dozen of the large industrial plants in entirely different industries.

Apropos of this point, see the discussion of Professor Taussig on "Labor Unions" (*Principles of Economics*, Vol. II, 3rd ed., Chap. 57). He states, "in many British trades, it no longer occurs to any one that the individual workman shall bargain with the employer; all is done through the union."

[9] This has not been sufficiently recognized. Welfare work has been belittled, commended, and condemned for diverse, and frequently superficial reasons. In a survey which I made in 1923-1925 of some twenty large plants located in various parts of the country, it was clear that *the* major motive of these companies was the desire to reduce "labor turnover."

[10] At this point we are not interested in the mobility of labor, as such, but merely because such mobility throws into clearer relief one of the fourfold competitive relations to which I have referred. The particular question of the *mobility* of labor, and also of the other factors of production, will be discussed fully in Section 4 of this chapter, pp. 28 ff. (As to mobility of labor, in particular, see pp. 37 ff.)

of producer to consumer. Augmented productiveness of labor, as a result of technological progress, has created a larger "reservoir" of commodities and services. In the disposal of these, producer has vied with producer in a very real sense. New commodities, the public demand for which has not yet been awakened, have brought ever increasing competition of producers with consumers. Rising above the subsistence level, the masses have constituted an ever expanding market. A small profit per unit of product, elastic demand, increased output, decreasing cost —these have been the driving forces of increasing competition of producers with the consumers. With free competition (that is, unrestricted consumers' choice in the market place)[11] the relation of producer to consumer has been increasingly free and competitive.

Those who point to the decrease of "free competition between individuals" have undoubtedly failed to see this competitive relation. A particular phase of the mechanics of competition, of which the money wage is a part, is not the only significant consideration. An enlarging reservoir of consumable products and services, freedom of consumers' choice in drawing upon this reservoir—these are the significant considerations. The increasing competition of producers with each other and of producers with consumers is measured, in part, by the rise of real or commodity wages since the middle of the nineteenth century.

We may conclude, therefore, that the distinction of competition as to form and competition as to results is essential. The former—the size and number of the competing units—is not in itself a criterion of the latter—the utility, satisfactions, and opportunities which these com-

[11] Excepting for those commodities—and services—which consumers themselves have elected to prohibit, such as narcotics and formerly intoxicating liquors.

peting units produce. To hold that competition is decreasing because the size of the competing units is increasing and the units are growing fewer in number—this is to mistake medium for substance.

2

We proceed now to a second group of distinctions in the term "competition" that are absolutely prerequisite to the understanding of the reasoning in which the term has been used. Competition as a postulate, competition as a precept, competition as an institution—these are the uses to which the term may be employed, and these are the distinctions to which we refer. It is curious that controversy upon controversy has occurred because of a failure to recognize that the uses of competition as a postulate, as a precept, and as an institution are directed toward essentially different purposes. This section proposes to examine the purposes which have necessitated this threefold sense of "competition."

As to competition in the sense of a postulate: The very nature of social science is such as to require a process of simplification in order that the causal relations of social phenomena may be set forth. Two reasons explain this procedure of abstracting from a highly complex situation (and one becoming increasingly so) a few of the basic factors.

In the first place, social phenomena are numerous and undergo continuous variation. It suffices only to point to those of an industrial and commercial sort to appreciate the tremendously rapid changes which have occurred not only since the English Industrial Revolution but also during the American industrial revolution of the post-

Civil War period. One need only call attention to the changes in transportation, markets, division of labor, storage, financing, industrial organization, immigration, and so forth.

Economics can lay claim to being a science only because, out of this rapidly changing picture, it has isolated the forces which approach universality and permanency. It is obvious, of course, that economic reasoning and principles can be *exact* only if two conditions are completely obtained: first, that all forces which are universal and permanent be used in the formulation of economic principles; and second, that transient forces be measured, and allowances be made for them in their effect upon the permanent forces. Since social life contains no forces which are either absolutely universal or permanent—and certainly the multitude of local or transient counter influences are only partly measurable—it must follow that economic principles are statements of *tendencies* rather than "undeviable" laws.

It has become necessary, therefore, in our economic reasoning, to use postulates, that is, to assume positions as true. One of these is competition. It is John Stuart Mill who says, " . . . only through the principle of competition has political economy any pretension to the character of a science."[12] That the conclusions we reach in our economic reasoning are absolutely true only to the degree that our premises are universal in their scope, and further, that such premises include all of the forces which are operative—these are the provisos that must be kept in mind.[13]

[12] *Principles of Political Economy* (Ashley ed., London: Longmans, Green & Co., 1926), p. 242.

[13] Cf. W. Cunningham, *op. cit.*, pp. 1-16.

It is equally clear that, although our conclusions are not true in toto, they are very useful if one bears in mind *to what degree* the postulates fit actual conditions. If such postulates are more true to actual conditions than they are false, then it must follow our economic reasoning is more right than wrong. This calls for discrimination in the formulating of economic principles and also in their use; it adds difficulty, and at the same time interest, to the subject. It is precisely the failure on the part of critics of economic theory in general, or of the "orthodox economics" in particular, to use this discrimination and to recognize the usefulness and limitations of deductive reasoning that has led to much dissipation of energy and humor.

We see, therefore, that the use of competition as a postulate is due to the needs of methodology. The purpose of deduction—simplification—per se, is to throw into sharp outline the operation of basic forces in economic life. The purpose is the same as that in which economists assume a dominant force in human motivation as exemplified by the "economic man"; it is not to create a *homo oeconomicus* as a true representation of man in reality. That this process of using competition as a postulate bears no necessary relation to use of competition as a precept should be quite clear. In a great deal of economic literature a direct relation is erroneously implied or expressed.

As to competition in the sense of a precept: Use of competition in this sense manifests itself in an advocacy of laissez faire, laissez passer. "In its original sense the former referred to the freedom to adopt whatever trade one would and manufacture whatever one would" and the latter to the "freedom to send goods whithersoever one would and fetch them whencesoever one would."[14] Laissez faire in its original meaning and also in its more recent usage expresses a relation not of individual to individual but of the individual to the government. The advocacy of a relation of any sort between the people and the government tacitly or expressly presupposes an objective to be desirable. Laissez faire is a "policy"—a program of action—and perforce involves considerations quite aside from the investigation of the laws that determine production, exchange, and distribution of wealth so far as these depend on the free competition of individuals. This is clearly stated by Sidgwick who says:

It must be obvious, however, as soon as it is pointed out, that the investigation of the laws that determine actual prices, wages, and profits, so far as these depend on the free competition of individuals, is essentially distinct from the inquiry how far it is *desirable* that the action of free competition should be restrained or modified—whether by the steadying force of custom, the remedial intervention of philanthropy, the legislative or administrative control of government, or the voluntary combination of masters or workmen. So far as the purely scientific economist studies primarily the results that tend to be produced by perfectly free competition, it is not because he has any predilection for this order of things—for science knows nothing of such preferences—but merely because its greater simplicity renders it easier to grasp. He holds that a knowledge of these simpler relations precedes, in the order of study, the investigation of the more complex economic problems that result from competition modified by disturbing causes. But the adoption of competition perfectly free and perfectly active as a scientific ideal—as a means of simplifying the economic facts which actual society presents, for the convenience of general reasoning—does not imply its adoption as a *practical* ideal, which the statesmen or philanthropists ought to aim at realising as completely as possible.[15]

[14] Alfred Marshall, *Industry and Trade* (3rd ed.; London: Macmillan, 1919), p. 84.

[15] Sidgwick, *op. cit.*, pp. 23-24. Italics are mine. Cf. also the exceptionally well-stated view of Dunbar on the necessary distinction of economic

Much misunderstanding of economic writing has arisen because of the central position which free competition and the absence of government interference has held in economic doctrine since the time of Adam Smith. "Free competition" in economic doctrine is due to the fact that the striking characteristic of modern economic societies is that of increasing absence of authority and an increasing degree of voluntarism—rational self-direction. A movement from "status" to "contract" was Sir Henry Maine's description of progressive societies. Free competition is not only restricted by government intervention but also, as pointed out by Sidgwick, very largely from the force of custom, and other factors.[16] Although one should grant that an extension of government interference has occurred, the net balance may still be in the direction of increased freedom of competition owing to a greater decrease in authoritative control of inertia and custom.[17] Economic reasoning based on the assumption of free competition undoubtedly has more nearly corresponded to actual facts of modern industry than conclusions obtained from other equally simple hypotheses which could have been used.

This central position which competition as a postulate has held in economic doctrine has frequently led to the inference that a necessary connection exists between free competition as a postulate and free competition as a precept.[18] For this mistaken relation the economists have

law and legislative policy in his article "The Academic Study of Political Economy," *Quarterly Journal of Economics*, V (1891), 411.

[16] Cf. T. N. Carver, *This Economic World and How It May Be Improved* (Chicago: A. W. Shaw, 1928), pp. 131-137. Also Jacob H. Hollander, *Economic Liberalism* (New York: Abingdon Press, 1925). See especially the interesting chapter on "The Meaning of Economic Liberalism."

[17] This conclusion is more fully supported in the note to this chapter. See pp. 53-54.

[18] This point has been particularly well discussed by J. M. Keynes, *Scope*

been largely responsible. Imbued with Adam Smith's attack on mercantilism and with John Stuart Mill's "Essay on Liberty," many economists have not been satisfied with the investigation of economic phenomena and the formulation of economic principles, but they have also concerned themselves with government policy; "things as they are" and "things as they ought to be" have often been fused.

As to competition in the sense of an institution: Competition used in this sense finds its expression in drawing the analogy of evolution through selection and survival of biological life with progress in social life. This view is clearly seen in the statement:

> Progress everywhere from the beginning of life has been effected in the same way, and it is possible in *no other way*. It is the result of selection and rejection.[19]

And again:

> The law of life has been always the same from the beginning,—ceaseless and *inevitable struggle and competition*, ceaseless and inevitable selection and rejection, ceaseless and inevitable progress.[20]

Especially well is this idea of competition brought out by Kidd's further views—those on socialism—in which he says:

> Underneath all socialist ideals, there yawns the problem of population. The condition of selection being suspended (through deviating from a policy of laissez-faire and assuming a policy of protection of the weak), such a people could not in any case avoid progressive degen-

and Method of Political Economy (2nd ed., London: Macmillan, 1897), pp. 67-72.

[19] Benjamin Kidd, *Social Evolution* (New York: Macmillan, 1898), p. 36. Italics mine.

[20] *Ibid.*, p. 41. Italics mine.

eration even if we could imagine them escaping more direct consequences.[21]

Here we have competition used as a social institution in a bold, clear-cut manner. Not only this, but it is directly related to the government policy of laissez faire.

Spencer's use of competition is also in the sense of the biological institution. Here again the identity of competition in economic life and biological life is maintained. He says:

> Placed in competition with members of its own species and in antagonism with members of other species, it [the animal] dwindles and gets killed off, or thrives and propagates, according as it is ill-endowed or well-endowed. Manifestly an opposite régime, could it be maintained, would, in course of time, be fatal to the species.
>
> . . . *Does anyone think that the like does not hold of the human species?*
>
> Society in its corporate capacity, cannot without immediate or remote disaster interfere with the play of these opposed principles under which every species has reached such fitness for its mode of life as it possesses, and under which it maintains fitness.[22]

Social progress occurs, of course, at the cost of human energy. Strange as it may seem, the Spencerian argument does not recognize the wastefulness, in terms of human energy, of progress as a result of biological struggle. The economy of conscious direction to the struggle, which, of course, the human species are capable of and the animal species are not, is entirely neglected.

The biological argument of Spencer and his followers is not, in itself, of much interest to us in this book, but the importance of Spencer's view is due to its pervasive influence on much economic writing regarding competition.

[21] *Ibid.*, pp. 222-223.

[22] Herbert Spencer, *The Man versus The State* (New York: D. Appleton, 1884), pp. 65-66. Italics mine.

In its naïve form it finds expression in an *unqualified* support of laissez faire and the argument of the survival of the fittest; in its subtle form an author may be reasoning from the premise of Spencerian competition as follows:

> But Individualism, the full freedom of each individual, limited only by the equal freedom of all others, has never yet been reached, and the social injustice now prevailing exists, not on account, nor in spite, of Individualism, but through limitations of individualism, imposed or acquiesced in by the state.[23]

It is extraordinary, indeed, that this use of competition as referring to the force of biological struggle—selection and rejection—was ever regarded as related to the free contractual, economic relations of individuals. It is this fallacy which is the root of the view that any directing or restricting of free contractual economic relations is perforce a decrease of economic competition. Certainly the fact that the very essence of economic competition[24] requires restriction and direction of an increasing number of activities could not be understood when approached from the view of competition as an institution.

We conclude, therefore, that each of the threefold uses of competition—as a postulate, as a precept, and as an institution—have no necessary relation to each other; they must be clearly distinguished.

[23] Max Hirsch, *Democracy versus Socialism* (London: Macmillan, 1901), p. 251. Hirsch's discussion is a curious mixture of Mill's view as expressed in his *Essay on Liberty* and Spencer's view as seen in his *Man versus the State.*

Cf. also John Harvey, et. al., *Competition, a Study in Human Motive* (London: Macmillan, 1917).

The few sources quoted here (Kidd, Spencer, and Hirsch) are selected to bring out clearly the use of competition in the sense of a biological force or institution. These authors have but one criterion of competition (and they make no distinction of intensity and duration), namely, uninterrupted struggle.

[24] See Section 4 of this chapter.

3

We continue now and consider a third group of distinctions to be made in the use of competition. These are competition as applied to each of the four main phases of economics, namely, consumption, production, exchange, and distribution. In much economic reasoning and writing it is not made clear whether the conclusions arrived at in regard to competition in one phase of economic relations—for example, distribution—hold for the others.

As to consumption: It is a notable fact that free competition (that is, freedom of choice by the consumers) in consumption has been either ignored or taken for granted by most writers. That freedom of consumers' choice need not prevail is obvious and, as a matter of fact, such freedom differs considerably according to the time, the place, and the nature of the satisfactions one considers.

Free competition of consumers for consumption products and services has been, in the large, an ever increasing one as time has gone by. Less and less restricted by legal authority and governmental officialdom, custom, or pressing needs of a subsistence level, individuals have experienced a widening range of choice which they themselves might exercise unrestrictedly.[25] This holds for material

[25] Cf. R. G. Hawtrey, *The Economic Problem* (London: Longmans, 1925), Chap. XVIII, "Consumer's Choice." This is a suggestive, interesting (but brief—13 pages) chapter concerned chiefly with the difference in the range of consumers' choice of the wealthy as compared to that of the poor at the present time. The particular point we are considering, namely, the increasing choice of consumers as a whole, with the *passing* of time, due to the factors we have mentioned—this Hawtrey does not consider. It is the present writer's opinion that Hawtrey does not substantiate either of two important contentions. These are: "His [the consumer's] choice of products is doubly limited. It is limited to the things actually produced and put on sale, and among those things it is limited to the things brought to his notice by advertisement or otherwise" (p. 204) and "On the whole large-scale production reinforces the consumers' inertia. It stereotypes pat-

goods especially. In consumers' choice for "intangibles," such as, for example, education and sanitation, this possibly is not the case. At least minimum "amounts" or standards have been fixed, and within these standards free competition, or choice, has not been permitted although for *more* than the prescribed minimum amounts the consumers' choice is not restrained. Most of these requirements, however, the consumers themselves have chosen to bring about through the exercise of their electoral privilege.

It is important to notice that even pronounced socialists would apparently leave the demand of the consumer free as a general rule.[26] This is concisely stated by the Webbs:

> To obtain for the community the maximum satisfaction it is essential that the needs and desires of the consumers should be the main factor in determining the commodities and services to be produced.[27]

Again this same view is expressed by Schäffle who says, in discussing demand in a socialistic state:

> A complete and officially organized system of collective production could undoubtedly include at least as thorough a daily, weekly, monthly, quarterly, or yearly statistical registration of the *free wants* of individuals and of families, as under the present system these effect, each for themselves, by their demand upon the market; and the national

terns, and makes any departure from accepted styles more exceptional and therefore more eccentric." (p. 205).

His conclusion also is that "the consumer's preferences have a very slight relation to the real good of the thing he chooses. Market value is so far from being a true measure of ethical value that it is hardly even a first approximation to it" (p. 215) is certainly not supported.

It is my opinion that while what Hawtrey has said may be perfectly true for a *particular* time and place, it is most assuredly too narrow a view to take regarding consumers' choice.

[26] Cf. J. S. Nicholson, *Principles of Political Economy* (London: Macmillan, 1901), pp. 190-193. Also, J. S. Furnivall, "Organization of Consumption," *Economic Journal*, XX (1910), 24.

[27] *Industrial Democracy* (London: Longmans, 1897), II, 818.

production could thus both in respect of quantity and of quality adapt itself to this *free* demand.[28]

As to consumption, therefore, both critics and exponents of the present economic order agree. Free play of consumers' choice, free competition—at least as to material things—this is desirable.[29] True, the socialists look toward changing of wants, but this shall be brought about not through interference with wants directly but through the influence of the leveling of incomes.

Regarding free competition as applied to production there is great diversity of opinion. The range of reasoning includes the full scope from complete free trade (free

[28] *The Quintessence of Socialism* (Translation from 8th German ed. by Bernard Bosanquet; New York: Humboldt Pub. Co., 1894), p. 43. Italics are mine.

[29] Or at least they would hold, in general, that consumption is an *individual* act (although, to be sure, it has social *consequences* as irrational, harmful consumption clearly demonstrates) whereas production, exchange, and distribution are necessarily *social acts*. Since consumption is of this nature it does *not* lend itself to "classification," "averaging," and orderly arrangement, upon the basis of which, principles can be drawn. Hence statements regarding consumption must, in the large, be regarded as personal observations or opinions. When, however, cause and effect relation can be *demonstrated* between the act of consumption and consequence, then such *particular* forms of consumption lend themselves to evaluation through the *measurable* social influence of the consequence.

For example, it was stated to me that a large wing of the Cook County (Chicago) Hospital given to the treatment of cases of liquor insanity was closed (about 10 years after the Prohibition Amendment was enacted) because of the decreased number of such cases. Assuming the information to be reliable (which I have no reason to doubt) a cause and effect relationship is established between the act of consumption and the consequence. The statement of this relation becomes then not that of a personal opinion but that of a principle.

Disagreement upon whether "consequences" are good, bad, or indifferent (unless the consequence is one of physical deterioration) makes many demonstrable causal relationships in consumption of no practical import and precludes the restricting or encouraging of various forms of consumption. This is the real basis of critics and exponents "agreeing" that free competition in consumption is "desirable"; the agreement is arrived at *negatively* rather than positively.

competition, or at least what is regarded as such by many using the term) in all factors of production to practically the complete absence of free trade. The same range of diversity is manifested in the advocacy of complete laissez faire to complete state socialism; free competition to full regulation; thoroughgoing voluntarism to absolute authoritarianism.

Unlike the discussion in consumption, no unanimity of opinion exists as to the desirability of free competition. More than this, no agreement prevails as to when free competition may be said to exist, what it essentially is, or the conditions prerequisite to its operation. To many writers a laissez faire policy means free competition; to others such a policy means precisely the opposite. To many, the movement of industry and trade has been distinctly away from free competition and as special support for their argument they point to the development of trusts and monopolies. Directly opposed to this view is that of Nicholson who holds that in the modern world as a whole the progress in the direction of free trade is astonishing. He maintains that we lay too much stress on particular tariffs and overlook free trade in immense areas, for example, the United States and Germany. Even as regards Great Britain the foreign trade is but a small part of the whole. And continuing, Nicholson states that it is "A grave historical error to suppose that at present, even in the United States the proportion of 'monopoly' to 'competition' is greater than at any former period."[30]

We see, therefore, that free competition applied to consumption, upon the existence and desirability of which there is, in the main, common consent, tells us nothing regarding production. With respect to the latter, both as

[30] *Op. cit.*, pp. 204-207.

to desirability of free competition and existence of it, there is widest of disagreement.

Concerning distribution, it was John Stuart Mill who held that:

> The laws and conditions of the Production of wealth partake of the character of physical truths. There is nothing optional or arbitrary about them. . . . It is not so with the Distribution of wealth. That is a matter of human institution solely. The things once there, mankind can place them at the disposal of whomsoever they please, and on whatever terms.[31]

In spite of this dictum it is possible to say, with Henry Clay:

> In no department of economic policy is the principle of laissez-faire so complete as in distribution of wealth. Before the 18th century the right and the expediency of Government interference were hardly questioned; in the 19th century not only the expediency but the morality of any attempt on the part of Governments to determine the distribution of wealth came to be rejected with equal unanimity. The valuation of services, like that of commodities were left to be determined by the relations of supply and demand in a free market. . . . In the present century public opinion has changed; laissez-faire is discredited, any a priori objection to State interference with distribution, or with any other problem of economic organisation, has gone. It might have been expected, therefore, that there would have been a corresponding change of policy, and that Governments would actively participate in fixing wages and prices, the regulation of profits, and the distribution of wealth generally. There has been a change, but it has not taken the lines of a reversal of laissez-faire. . . . The central problem of distribution—the determination of wages, salaries, interest and profits—is still left to private contract without Government interference.[32]

[31] *Op. cit.*, pp. 199-200.

[32] "The Authoritarian Element in Distribution," *Economic Journal*, XXXVII (1927), 1-18.

The misleading way in which "free competition" is used is clearly seen when it is related to distribution. Factory acts, child-labor laws, minimum-wage legislation, and so on, have been put forth as a diminution of free competition. This contention involves a double fallacy. In the first place, such regulatory legislation does not vitiate free competition except when we refer to the Spencerian competition of physical struggle. Competition in the economic sense can only exist *because* of such regulation.[33] In the second place, it is implied, if not expressed, that such "decrease" of competition or "individualism" in this (distributive) phase of economic activity is indicative of what is true of economic relations in general. This is obviously false. While increased regulation—authoritarianism—has occurred in one set of social relations (say, production) it has usually resulted in even greater increase of freedom—voluntarism—elsewhere. Regulation of conditions of work resulting in increased efficiency of the worker, and hence greater freedom to select more work and also work of another kind, illustrate what has been said.

We conclude, therefore, that this third group of distinctions in the use of competition—that is, competition as applied to consumption, to production, to exchange, and to distribution—should be recognized. Competition applies to each of these phases of economics in different degrees. The reasoning and conclusions which hold for one need not hold for another.

4

The purpose of the discussion thus far has been twofold. This was, first, to present the varied and vague

[33] This point will be developed in the next section of this chapter.

usage of the term "competition" and, second, to state the distinctions which must be kept in mind if confusion is to be avoided. Attention will now be given to the central problem of this chapter, namely, the consideration of what constitutes competition in the true economic sense. I shall proceed by stating the generally accepted propositions upon which the explanation of this section is based.

In the first place, economic terminology should be defined in relation to the general purpose of economic science. Definition of a particular term should be limited to the function which the phenomenon, included within this term, performs. The phenomenon of competition bears a definite relation to the general purpose of the science of economics; the definition of competition should be limited to the part which this phenomenon plays among productive and distributive forces.

The general purpose of the science of economics is, of course, the explanation of consumption, production, exchange, and distribution of wealth. The wealth contemplated is not the wealth of the individual but the collective wealth of the community. The fact that collective human wants are greater than the wherewithal to satisfy these wants gives rise to a *relation* of individuals and groups to each other which one may term "conflict," "rivalry," or "competition." The entire multiplicity of forms which such conflict takes is not concerned with the scarcity of those things which fall into the category of wealth. Competition in the economic sense does not, therefore, include such forms of conflict as the militant, recreational, or political;[34] it relates to "those rivalries which grow out

[34] For a discussion of human conflict see T. N. Carver, *Essays in Social Justice* (Cambridge: Harvard University Press, 1925), Chaps. 2, 3, 4, and 5.

of the desire to possess those things which are classed under the name wealth."[85]

Secondly, we assume that individuals are rational and that everyone strives to exchange the products of his labor for as much as possible of the products of the labors of others. If this process is general, then similar exchange will take place on similar terms. Granting that all are striving for maximum return and that labor and capital go where return is highest, then ultimately an equality of return will be the result. The *basis* of competition in the economic sense is this process or unrestricted movement to places and activities where return is highest; the *result* of competition in the economic sense is the equality of return which at the same time means the maximum of return or satisfaction of wants of all.

The latter has been very well stated by Liefmann, who says:

> For each economic person the greatest satisfaction of wants is obtained when he expends so much effort upon each satisfaction that the marginal returns, i.e., the returns secured with the last unit expended, are of the same size for the different satisfactions.
>
> . . . Maximum satisfaction of the wants of all is attained when so much capital and labor flow to each branch of industry that, with due regard to the differences in risk, the marginal returns, the returns of the last and most expensive enterprises, in all branches are equal.
>
> . . . In this way the economic principle of the greatest conceivable provision for wants is fulfilled.[86]

It follows from what has been said that the essence of economic competition is mobility of the factors of production. That which increases mobility increases economic competition; that which decreases mobility decreases economic competition. Biological struggle, the number and

[85] *Ibid.*, p. 95.
[86] *Op. cit.*, pp. 313-314.

size of competing units, or the organization and ownership of such units increase or decrease competition in the economic sense *only* in so far as the *mobility* of the factors of production is increased or decreased. Mobility is to be understood as applying not only to the present moment but also to the future.

The validity of this explanation of economic competition is based upon the general proposition which I have stated, namely, that economic terminology should be defined in relation to the general purpose of the science. Economics is concerned with the increase of general wealth, and the maximizing of satisfactions which flow from this wealth. Individuals being rational, mobility adds to the product which they produce, since an opportunity to produce more would (being mobile) cause them to go into that in which they are most productive. Inasmuch as production and distribution become one and the same process, in a society of division of labor, through the mechanism of exchange, it is, of course, true that what increases production increases satisfaction.[37]

Since mobility of the factors of production is the very essence of competition, the sense in which mobility is used must be clearly understood. There is, in the first place, the general sense in which the term is used with regard to the relation of the social quantum of the factors of production to each other. In this general sense the meaning given to mobility is tacitly or expressly that of physical mobility of land, labor, and capital. In this usage, mobility is not associated with the organization of the factors of

[37] This is true only in so far as satisfactions flow from that which is produced, i.e., wealth. Economic analysis is confined to this merely because other sources of satisfactions ("intangibles") are incommensurable.

production in individual economic production units, such as in a farm, a factory, a railroad, and so forth. There is, therefore, in the second place, this latter sense, that is, mobility associated with the organization of individual producing units.

The mobility in this more special, definite meaning consists of two phases. These are: (1) mobility relating to the shift of land, labor, capital, and management from one product to another, or from one industry to another; and (2), mobility relating to the increase or decrease in quantity of any one of these factors.[38]

The usage of mobility in this more special sense is far more accurately conveyed by such terms as "variability" and "shiftability." Are the *proportions* in which land, labor, capital, and management *freely variable* by the *individual* producing unit? If so, mobility (and competition) exists. The general usage tells us little or nothing about mobility in the sense of variability of the organization or constitution of the producing unit. And we shall see that it is precisely *this* variability (or mobility) which affects the relations of individuals or classes to each other.[39]

Now what may be said to be the basic prerequisites of mobility?

First, the most basic of these is the phenomenon of scarcity.[40] This is the prime motivating economic force.

[38] This second phase of mobility is essentially a corollary of the first.

[39] The reader's attention is called to the two general classes of problems with which competition is concerned, namely, those of "economic sociology" and those of "pure theory." This is discussed on pp. 39 ff.

[40] "Scarcity" is not used here in the sense of "rarity" with which it is frequently confused. The former is a purely relative term, i.e., the means of satisfying wants in relation to the number of wants. Scarcity may be much greater in one country than in another although both countries possess the same number of people and like amount of resources, if the people in one country have developed wants (due to such institutions as

If scarcity did not exist mobility would cease, since satisfactions could not be increased by the expenditure of energy necessary to moving. It is very apparent that new wants, in large part as a result of the expansion of three fundamental institutions, namely, public education, transportation, and communication, have multiplied more rapidly than the wealth to satisfy those wants. In this sense scarcity has increased and added tremendously to mobility.

Second, as a corollary of the prerequisite of scarcity to a condition of mobility, is the factor of the occidental, utilitarian philosophy of life, that is, satisfaction of wants rather than the oriental philosophy of repression. A religion of ignoring the material wants and the deification of other wants[41] can alone explain much of the oriental immobility.

Third, a more direct prerequisite to complete mobility is that of complete knowledge. No unrestricted movement can occur unless the differences in return in different activities and places are known. This applies not only to existing differences but also to potential differences. Uncertainty as to the present or as to the future tends to be cumulative in its effect.[42] With respect to knowledge of

---

public education, democratic government and churches, easy communication, and other social institutions) which the people of the other country have not developed.

"Rarity" is an absolute term having only the objective connotation—the amount of resources as against the number of people. Its meaning is best understood when used as opposed to "density."

[41] For example, the religious obligation, on the part of everyone, to have a male descendant at the earliest reproductive age. Also the Buddhist doctrine that spiritual conditions (*not* material conditions) are the only concern, and that spiritual life would flourish as well in poverty and starvation as in comfortable environment, and in fact, much better than in luxury.

[42] The uncertainty element as a cause of imperfect competition has been stressed by F. H. Knight, *Risk, Uncertainty, and Profit* (Boston: Houghton, Mifflin; 1921).

existing differences there can be little doubt regarding the remarkable increase which has occurred because of the educative, communicative, and governmental agencies. Concerning knowledge of the future, the question is more difficult. While it is true that the art of forecasting both in the physical and social sciences makes the future less uncertain than it has been, yet from another important factor the future has become somewhat more uncertain. This is due to the fact that consumers' demands have changed more rapidly, as years have gone by, with reason and knowledge supplanting tradition and habit. Uncertainty of the future, from this cause, may have increased with a consequent decrease in mobility of the factors of production in the sense of movement to the places or activities where the return is the greatest.[43] Here again, the *net* balance is the significant question, that is, the greater information of the present has, we may reasonably suppose, more than offset the uncertainty of the future.

Fourth, complete mobility presupposes complete divisibility of the factors of production. In the case of labor, divisibility and mobility do not require homogeneity as some economists have held. Inborn qualities, as well as those acquired, cause differences of capacity in individuals. Requirements of tasks (no matter whether industrial or professional) for labor and management vary over a wide range. It is a commonly observed fact that the individual is most efficient when the requirement of the task for labor or management is just equal to the capacity of the laborer or manager for the work under consideration. This can be more simply put by saying that anyone gets most

[43] The question may be raised as to whether the uncertainty from changes in consumers' demand is not, in part, decreased by the degree to which consumers' demands are created, controlled, or directed by advertising in its manifold forms.

return (efficiency) for his effort if he applies himself to work that is neither too difficult nor too easy for his ability. Mobility can only exist where divisibility of the factors of production permit such adaptations of capacities.[44]

And fifth, mobility in its fullest sense requires what I choose to call a neutralizing or elimination of those social institutions which retard the unrestricted movement of the agents of production to places and activities where return is the greatest. These "social institutions" are varied—some, tangible and objective, and others, intangible and psychological. Among the former are legislative barriers such as immigration restrictions, tariff legislation, and obligations of citizenship; among the latter are such factors as custom, religious requirements, and bonds of race, nationality, or kinship.

It is on this very point, namely, that mobility of the factors of production—economic competition—requires a neutralizing or elimination of certain social institutions, that fallacious reasoning so frequently arises. To many writers competition means a policy of "hands off" on the part of the Government. To them a state of free contract means that government regulation is reduced to enforcement of contract and maintaining law and order. This sort of "free competition" is the very antithesis of competition in the economic sense. Paradoxical as it may seem, such a negative governmental policy is most *positive* in

[44] English land tenure is such as not to permit this adaptation, and it illustrates very well the existence of immobility. It is not only the large size of the operating unit but also the lack of a *diversity* of sizes of farms that takes the rungs out of the English agricultural ladder. Many English farm laborers have capacities which would give them greater returns as tenants. Again many (although fewer) have capacities to give them still larger returns as owners or part owners. The lack of sufficient divisibility of land and capital (in the field of agriculture) in England, therefore, results in marked immobility of English agricultural workers.

destroying mobility and economic competition. In the very nature of social organization no governmental policy can be "neutral." As Professor Carver has emphatically put it:

> The term free or unrestricted competition is a misnomer. There is no such thing in any civilized country and never was. The thing which distinguishes *economic competition* from the brutal struggle for existence *is regulation*, standardization, or the determination of what may be done and what may not be done in the pursuit of self-interest. The suppression of violence and fraud even if nothing else is done, is a regulation of competition.[45]

Competition in the economic sense is dependent upon the elimination of those social institutions which restrict free movement, and it is likewise dependent upon the *creating* of institutions which increase free movement. I have mentioned instances of the former; of the latter, the most important include compulsory public education, furthering of communication and transportation, and the elimination of activities and practices which fall into the general category of "fraud" and "unfair trade practices." Where this cannot be accomplished if left to the individual, government regulation and expenditure are not only consistent with competition in the economic sense, but the failure to undertake such regulation is a policy of destruction of competition. The policy of *caveat emptor* is no more consistent with a policy of economic com-

[45] *This Economic World and How It May Be Improved* (Chicago: A. W. Shaw, 1928), p. 139. Italics are mine. It is also precisely the point which Nicholson, *op. cit.*, p. 211, has in mind when he states that "industrial freedom" is wider than "competition." He points out that voluntary associations "though in respect of their regulations they limit the independence of their members, by increasing their power may add to their personal freedom on the whole. In these voluntary associations the individual limits his freedom of action by consenting to obey certain rules, or it may be the will of a majority, or of an arbiter, or even a dictator." Cf. also Woodrow Wilson, *The New Freedom* (New York: Doubleday, Page; 1913), pp. 177, 222, and especially his interesting Chap. 12, "The Liberation of a People's Vital Energies."

petition than a policy of *caveat vendor*. Whether a government chooses or no, its policy *is* directive. If the result is an increase of unrestricted movement of the factors of production, economic competition has increased; if the result is the reverse, then economic competition has decreased.

I have said that the essence of economic competition is mobility of the factors of production. The prerequisites to such mobility have been stated. In applying what has been said, the question now arises: Has competition in the economic sense increased or decreased?

As to labor: That competition has tremendously increased with regard to this factor of production is very evident.[46] Not only have laborers improved their knowledge of returns in different places and activities, but even more notable has been the effect of division of labor in fitting the task to the man. Creating diversity of tasks is the very essence of division of labor. The concentrated ownership of the capital used, in itself, has no bearing upon this

[46] It is of course true that great immobility of labor still exists in many industries, as, for example, the English cotton industry where a high proportion of women workers and close personal relations of employers and employees are the causes. (Cf., J. Jewkes and H. Campion, "The Mobility of Labor in the Cotton Industry," *Economic Journal*, XXXVIII (1928), 135-137.)

If to this is added the lack of financial reserve and the pernicious requirement that legal residence must be established before unemployment doles can be claimed, the result is obvious. Workers cannot move, not only because of the lack of means, but also because the discontinuance of the dole while establishing legal residence elsewhere (which they are now receiving if unemployed) makes movement out of the question. (Cf. *infra*, Chap. VIII, Sec. 3, pp. 273-274. See footnote 35 of that chapter.)

Here then we have social, economic, and legal influences combining to cause immobility. But this does not deny the fact that the *historical trend* has been, in general, toward increased mobility of labor. And even in the particular industries where labor is now quite immobile it might still be true, of course, that labor is more mobile than it has been in the past.

at all. The failure to recognize that fact leads to the following reasoning, which I should regard as fallacious:

> Inasmuch as industrial concentration involves a sacrifice of economic freedom, it can only be judged as one of the many factors that in our days restrict economic mobility. In fact, it is the diminished mobility itself and its effect upon the productivity of the world's economic organisation that in the first instance deserve our attention.[47]

Industrial concentration, in my opinion, may or may not restrict mobility, depending upon the circumstances under which such concentration occurs. Given the prerequisites of mobility which we have discussed in the preceding pages (and in particular the fifth prerequisite —that of neutralizing or eliminating certain social institutions), we may say that industrial concentration has *aided* rather than restricted mobility. As a matter of fact, hand in hand with industrial concentration have gone further development of specialization, division of labor, and accessory industries. The consequence is an increased demand for labor and a wider field of choice for the worker. And even more has this extension of demand for labor and the field of his choice been due to the fact that with the growing industrial concentration has occurred, *pari passu*, increased compulsory public education, communication, and trade-school advantages.[48]

[47] Gustav Cassel, "Recent Monopolistic Tendencies in Industry and Trade," *League of Nations, Int'l. Econ. Monographs*, Geneva 1927; Preface, p. 2.

[48] It is quite obvious that *only* in cities of industrial concentration is it possible for the workers and their children to secure the advantages of the public and private (endowed and profit) trade and technical schools. The magnificent Dunwoody Industrial Institute at Minneapolis, open to everyone of any age, offering training in *all* conceivable trades from common blacksmithing to electrical engineering at nominal fees, is an example of dozens of endowed or profit schools in all large cities.

The Superintendent's office of the Boston School Committee informs me that there are five schools of high-school rank which give training in commercial, practical, and mechanical arts in Boston (proper) alone.

As to capital: Before considering the question what has been the change in mobility and competitiveness of capital, it is necessary to state in what sense we use the term "capital." The defining of economic terms and their adaptation to the particular problem which is being studied is necessitated by the fact that any one term includes a wide range of economic phenomena. To avoid confusion, in many cases it is essential to indicate the particular nature of the problem in hand. This, it seems to me, is particularly necessary in stating one's views regarding capital.

There are two general classes of problems toward which the use of economic terminology is directed. The first, that of economic sociology (also referred to by various terms such as "social ethics," "welfare economics," and "social philosophy"); the second, that of pure theory.

Our problem, concerned as it is with the changes in fourfold relations of employee to employee, employee to employer, employer to employer, and of producer to consumer—this problem is one of economic sociology. These are relations of individuals to each other, and in *our* use of "capital" we have the individual's point of view. To a producing unit (as well as to any one industry) capital is *purchasing power.*[49] Purchasing power—loanable funds

There are also two schools of grade-school rank (for boys and girls), of a similar character. These schools charge no tuition. Each of the suburbs has its private or public trade schools, an example of the latter being the Rindge Technical School of Cambridge.

In addition to these there are, of course, actually dozens of classes or schools maintained for profit or supported in response to civic or altruistic motives.

I have discussed Cassel's contention (quoted above) at some length since it is typical of many conclusions drawn in regard to "competition." In no place is it my intention to have my discussion become of a polemic nature, but rather to use the quoted material to set in clearer outline my own views upon *economic* competition.

[49] This capital concept is expounded by such writers as, for example,

(money and credit)—gives to the individual direct and absolute control over the problem which to the individual is the *only* problem of capital. This problem is the variation in the *proportions* of the factors of production (as well as the aggregate amount of all the factors) which he finds it advantageous or necessary to make with the changes occurring in the value of the factors he uses and also in the value of the product he produces.

In the second general class of problems, that of pure theory, "capital" is not to be understood as I have just defined it. "Capital," for the major problem of pure theory, namely, that of the analysis of the equilibrium of the forces of demand and supply (the phenomena of value), can have but *one* meaning. "Capital" used for a problem of this sort means produced goods used in production. These goods (*not* "purchasing power") are, of course, the source from which comes the "flow" of commodities against the "flow" of demand in the market place. The social quantum of commodities at any one time is directly a function of the goods (capital) employed in production. We see, therefore, that the twofold usage of the term "capital" (purchasing power and physi-

(1) R. G. Hawtrey, *Currency and Credit* (London: Longmans, Green & Co., 1919). He says: ". . . the word capital is a dangerous one. . . . On the one hand, it means . . . stocks of goods . . . fixed plant; on the other, it means . . . *purchasing power*. . . . The employment of the country's productive resources is governed by effective demand in the form of *purchasing power*, and the accumulation of the desired surplus of production over consumption can only be accomplished insofar as the holders of *purchasing power* choose to apply it" (p. 348). Italics mine. (2) D. H. Robertson, *Banking Policy and the Price Level* (London: King & Son, 1926). See especially Chapter 5, "Kinds of Saving."

This view of capital is also the one held by Professor Schumpeter who stated in one of his lectures, at Harvard, on economic theory (Oct. 4, 1927): "This real thing [capital] is money paid into the firm giving command over means of production." This same view of capital is expressed by Schumpeter in his *Theorie der Wirtschaftlichen Entwicklung* (Leipzig: Duncker & Humbolt, 1912).

cal goods) is useful for the analysis of different problems; the definitions are not conflicting but rather supplementary.

To return to the central issue: What may be said of the mobility or competitiveness of capital? Can the *proportion* of any factor of production used by any plant or any given industry be quickly *increased* or *decreased*?

Possibly one of the most remarkable economic phenomena as years have passed is the increasing degree to which the variation in the proportion of the factors employed in any plant or industry can be accomplished. This is largely because of two important factors. These are: first, the marked growth in knowledge, both present and future (for reasons already stated) of returns in different places and products; and, second, the increased divisibility of capital. The latter has been brought about by means of the multitude of types and denominations of financial instruments. From common stock of no par value to registered, closed first mortgage bonds with protective sinking fund provisions and "after-acquired property clauses" present almost complete divisibility and range of the three basic dimensions of capital commitment, namely, amount, risk, and duration.

Not only has flexibility in control of capital (purchasing power) been facilitated by the development of investment securities, but increased mobility has also been given to capital by a perfected banking structure and an improving credit control. This, of course, the Federal Reserve System illustrates with its elastic note issue, centralized control and liquidity of reserves, and its creating of a discount market.

Not only has increased mobility of capital occurred (from the causes just discussed) by the *increase* in the quickness and the amount of the purchasing power that can be commanded by any one plant or industry, but increased mobility of capital is also seen in the rapidity with which capital in any plant or industry is *decreased.* It is frequently said that every machine, from the first day of its use, is on a continuous and rapid march to the scrap-pile. Improvement in the state of the arts, engendered in part from within the plant but largely from the field of science, is shortening the length of time over which it is profitable to use a machine before supplanting it with a more perfected one.[50] Reserves for depreciation and obsolescence are, and must be, built up for the purpose of "writing off" drastically and promptly assets which advance in technique has made ineffective.

We come to the conclusion, therefore, at least for the problem of the relationships with which our analysis of competition is concerned, that capital has become increasingly mobile and competitive. With augmented elasticity of purchasing power—loanable funds—in the hands of a producer or an industry, the rate of expansion of a company or of an industry has grown notably.[51] Likewise the

[50] This is reflected in the reply to a question asked of one of the most enterprising New England manufacturers whether his company took out patent rights upon the numerous devices which this company was constantly introducing. His answer was that they did not do so since the life of these improvements was short and before competitors adopted them his company would have perfected other devices.

The same, of course, is increasingly true in all industries. Research departments are employed to study desirable changes in the product even where such changes necessitate altering or scrapping equipment now used.

[51] What seems to me very interesting substantiation of this statement appears in Chap. 2, "Industry" by Dean D. S. Kimball, College of Engineering, Cornell University, in *Recent Economic Changes* by the Nat'l Bur. of Ec. Research. Kimball says, "The magnitude of some of these new industries is impressive. Thus the automotive industry, *not mentioned* in the 1900 Census, is credited in the 1925 with employing over 400,000 with an output valued at over $4,000,000,000. Rayon *mentioned specially* for the *first* time in the Census of 1925 employed *19,128* workers, and the product of radio manufacture, an enterprise only a few years old, was valued in 1927 at about $191,200,000. . . . The chemical industry, a

rate of replacement of capital, through depreciation or obsolescence, has been greatly accentuated as a result of the increasing rate of change in the state of the arts and the accelerated rapidity with which producing plants are adopting such changes in technology.

As to land: Here again it is well to repeat that in speaking of competition I have reference to the unrestricted movement of a factor of production to places and activities where return is greatest. As in the case of the other factors, in speaking of competition with reference to land I refer to the movement of individual units and not to the total fund or quantum of the factor of production. Has land mobility in this sense? In other words can two "shifts" or "variations" of this factor be brought about, namely, from one product to another, and, secondly, an increase or decrease in its quantity for individual producers or industries? Not only *can* these changes occur but, for example, in agriculture, every producer (whether enterprising or not) is constantly varying his combination of the factors of production, land, as well as labor and capital, in an attempt to arrive at the greatest profit combination.[52] In this variation, the producer is guided by the changes in the cost of his input factors and the changes in the market value of the products to which his producing unit can be

---

new growth and difficult to classify, employed 38,075 workers, with an output valued at $6,438,027,000." Italics are mine.

[52] For a study of the variation in the combination of the factors of production see, for example: (1) Henry C. Taylor, *Agricultural Economics* (New York: Macmillan, 1919), especially Chap. XII, "The Choice and Combination of the Grades of the Factors of Production"; Chap. XIII, "The Proportions of the Factors of Production"; Chap. XIV, "The Size of Farms." (2) John D. Black, *Introduction to Production Economics* (New York: Henry Holt, 1926) Part III, Chaps. XI-XVII, "The Elements of Production and their Combination." (3) T. N. Carver, *Principles of Rural Economy* (Boston: Ginn & Co., 1911) pp. 155 ff.

adapted.[53] In the midwest diversified farm the range of adaptation is wide because of the numerous products to which the farmer may turn his land.[54] With furthered exploitation of by-products the industrial plant may shift its land (as well as capital, labor, and management) to different uses. It is equally apparent that it may decrease the proportion of land it employs by using its site more intensively. By the process of renting more land it can increase the proportion of land it uses. This, of course, is what a company chooses to do in decentralizing rather than concentrating at one point.

As to management: Mobility here, as in the other factors of production, depends upon the free movement of managers to places and activities where return is the greatest. Heightened public esteem to those who are successful in the "trades," growing knowledge available regarding present and future opportunities, broadening range in the diversity of managerial tasks, furthered reduction of the art of management to a science, increased teaching of this science at the communities' expense (for example, the state universities' schools of business)—these are some of the notable factors in giving mobility to management. To these must be added the large amount of published material concerned with various phases of management. It is important to note that the expense of this information,

[53] A particularly well-organized, succinct study is that of John G. Thompson, "Mobility of the Factors of Production As Affecting Variation in Their Proportional Relation to Each Other in Farm Organization," *Journal of Political Economy*, XXIX (1921), 108-137. He points out that mobility of land occurs through the methods of: (1) Simple reorganization of the individual farms in large estates, (2) Ordinary sale and purchase, (3) The settlement of estates, (4) The renting of additional land by owners, (5) Changing to a less intensive type of farming. He also discusses the mobility of labor and capital in farm organization.

[54] To mention some of these—dairying, livestock, grain, vegetables, forestry, and poultry. Each of these is, of course, a general class including several products.

also, is borne in large part by the community that purchases the products, the advertising of which supports the circulation of these trade journals. And, finally, of accumulative significance to mobility of management is the recent growth of local, national, and international associations in an increasing number of trades and industries.

In the foregoing discussion I have set forth the meaning of competition in the economic sense, the essence of which is mobility of the factors of production, and mobility being a product of certain existing conditions and influences. Economic reasoning is frequently vitiated as a result of using a term as self-explanatory or as being adequately understood by its popular usage. The great social import of such reasoning and the conclusions arrived at by prominent writers can be appreciated when one realizes that it is this reasoning that very largely is directive in such social control as, for example, trust legislation and social insurance. A statement of the problem involved can be seen most clearly in diametrically opposed views upon the same subject. The first subject I shall consider is the more general one of "capitalism," and the second, the more specific problem concerned with "trusts."

5

Possibly in no statements can more clearly be seen the failure to comprehend competition in the economic sense, as I have developed it, than in those frequently made against "Individualism" and "Capitalism." It would probably be difficult to find, in short space, so complete a misconception of economic competition as one finds in Sidney Webb's indictment of individualism. None of the fundamental distinctions which I have pointed out as being necessary in the use of competition are made, nor is competition in the economic sense of mobility of the factors of production seen in the slightest degree. He says:

The mere worker, qûa worker, is necessarily working, as far as its own remuneration is concerned, on the very worst land in economic use, with the very minimum of industrial capital. Every development toward a freer Individualism must, indeed, inevitably emphasize the power of the owner of the superior instruments of wealth production to obtain for himself all the advantages of their superiority. Individualists may prefer to blink this fact, and to leave it to be implied that, somehow or another, the virtuous artisan can dodge the law of rent. But against this complacent delusion of the philanthropist political economy emphatically protests. So long as the instruments of production are in unrestrained private ownership, so long must the tribute of the workers to the drones continue: so long will the toilers' reward inevitably be reduced by their exactions. No tinkering with the land laws can abolish, or even diminish economic rent, however much it may result in the redistribution of this tribute. The *whole* equivalent of every source of fertility or advantage of all land over and above the worst in economic use is under free competition abstracted from the mere worker on it (p. 368).

. . . The growth of capital has been so vast, and is so rapidly increasing, that any hope of the great mass of the workers ever owning under any conceivable Individualist arrangements the instruments of production with which they work can only be deemed chimerical. . . .

Hence it is that irresponsible personal authority over the actions of others—expelled from the throne, the castle, and the altar—still reigns, almost unchecked, in the factory and the mine (p. 374).

Moreover competition, where it still exists, is in itself one of the Individualist's difficulties, resulting under a system of unequal income, not merely in the production as we have seen, of the wrong commodities, but also of their production in the wrong way and for the wrong ends (p. 377).[55]

[55] Sidney Webb, "The Difficulties of Individualism," *Economic Journal*, I (1891), 360-381. This quotation has been given at some length since throughout it illustrates the failure to make the distinctions which I hold to be necessary in an understanding of competition. Not only does his inexact use of competition in his reasoning lead him to erroneous conclu-

With special reference to "Capitalism"[56] Webb contends:

Roughly, it was not until the middle of the nineteenth century that the more penetrating observers began to urge that the dictatorship of the capitalist had not only hopeless limitations in wealth production, but was actually producing a great deal that was the very reverse of wealth. From that time onward, as is now evident, profit-making became increasingly subject to malignant growths and perverted metabolisms, which created their own poisons and lessened the advantages of the system itself.[57]

---

sions, but he is also inaccurate in his value theory. As to the latter, a basic error in Webb's reasoning is that which Henderson (See his *Supply and Demand* (New York: Harcourt Brace, 1922), pp. 59-60), calls a "misinterpretation of the margin." The margin may be conceived either as applying to the marginal *producer* or to the marginal *output* of any producer. In agriculture when speaking of a marginal farm, it is true, we have in mind the least fertile and worst situated farm which it is just worth while to cultivate (as Webb says), *but* we do *not* mean that the other (reproducible) factors of production are the worst. As to these factors they are "representative" in quality. To fail to see that competition would result in the increasing of the reproducible factors of production with a consequent lowering of price to a return adequate to cover the cost of the *representative* firm (not the "worst in economic use")—this is the error in an indictment such as Webb's.

Again the same general use of "free competition," with none of the distinctions which I have indicated as being necessary in the use of the term, and also with no conception of what has been developed in my discussion of *economic* competition is obvious in Sidney and Beatrice Webb's *Industrial Democracy* (Vol. II, p. 688). They say, "One thing is clear. Those capitalist dykes and . . . artificial floodings, have become so *constant* and general a feature of the whole debatable land of economic bargaining, that any discussion of the relation between consumers and producers, or between capitalist and brainworker, and manual laborer, which is based on the assumption of . . . freely competing individuals . . . is, from a practical point of view, *entirely obsolete.*" (Italics mine.)

[56] Whether Webb would make any distinction between "Individualism," "Competition," and "Capitalism" he does not state. (His definition of "Capitalism," however, becomes quite useless for the problem with which he is concerned, i.e., the "Decay of Capitalism" (See his *The Decay of Capitalist Civilisation* [London: George Allen and Unwin, 1923]). He begs the question by defining "Capitalism" as he does. See p. 2.)

[57] *Ibid.*, p. 85. One should notice that Webb does not speak of the decay of capitalism in the same sense that Veblen does. The latter is concerned with "cultural gains of the past" and "the indirect or incidental cultural bearing of business principles and business practice is wide reaching and

It is interesting to turn from Webb's view, which is typical of the implications found in many other writers, to the diametrically opposed view of Henry Clay. This he states as follows:

They [the Webbs] date its [capitalist civilisation's] decline from about 1850; one would have thought that the decade that saw the extension to industry in general of the principle of limited liability joint stock, and the foundation of an effective system of public control by Factory Acts and trade unionism, marked the true beginning rather than the decline of modern capitalism. . . . The argument constantly seems to assume that the ownership and control of capital are still united, or, at any rate, that their separation means the end of capitalism. . . all of which may have been accurate in 1840, but is not the industrial organisation of today.[58]

We pass now from the divergent views on the general question of competition to divergence in views concerning competition in a more specific question as seen, for example, in discussions on the trust problem.

What may be termed a "trust" has been the subject of controversy. The three most usual tests are: first, the control of supply, by one company, to give control of price; second, not only the possession of such control but its use; and third, the manner in which the control was obtained. It is the first of these, exclusively, which is pointed out by Professor Elliot Jones as the essence of the trust. He says:

A trust (industrial monopoly) may be said to exist when a person, corporation, or combination owns or controls *enough* of the plants producing a certain article to be *able* for all practical purposes to fix its price . . . it seems fairly certain that as a general rule the pro-

forceful." See Veblen's *Theory of Business Enterprise* (New York: C. Scribner's Sons, 1923), Chap. X, "The Natural Decay of Business Enterprise."

[58] "Review of Sidney and Beatrice Webb's, 'The Decay of Capitalist Civilisation,'" *Economic Journal*, XXXIII (1923), 215-220.

duction of from 70 to 80 per cent of the national supply, and possibly even less, is quite ample for price control.[59]

In keeping with the spirit of American anti-trust legislation, Jones holds that trusts were organized primarily for the purpose of suppressing competition. Where the trust form of organization has been successful it is not due, he insists, to the economies of such organization. Anti-trust legislation has been necessary to remove "impediments to the free play of competitive forces."[60]

This is sufficient to state the general issue: The size of the competing unit determines the existence of a trust; the existence of a trust destroys competition. Strange as it may seem, it is not clearly stated whether the existence of a trust (in the sense of size) per se, destroys competition, or whether the power of a trust makes such destruction *potentially* possible! It is obvious that the social control called for is essentially different.

Opposed to the view held by Jones, the broader reasoning of Carter is as follows:

The continuous progress of industry and commerce, their organization and administration under the pressure of the law of economy of forces, has tended toward the concentration of enterprise and production. As the investment of fixed capital increased, a tendency toward over-production and crises arose. The difficulty of adjusting supply to demand becomes all the more difficult as industry becomes more concentrated and markets more extended. Industrial combination seems to arise as a natural resource intended to relieve the situation, as a means of establishing some degree of equilibrium between supply and demand. Thus it may be stated that the combination movement is due not to

[59] *The Trust Problem in the United States* (New York: Macmillan, 1921), p. 1. Italics mine.

[60] *Ibid.*, Cf. especially Chap. XIX, "The Anticipated Economies of the Trust," and Chap. XXI, "Conclusion."

chance or to mere intentions of organizers but rather to a "dominant, over-mastering tendency" acting within modern industry.[61]

Even more emphatic in opposition to the view that size determines the existence of a trust is the statement by Hadley, who says:

It is commonly assumed that the more competitors you have, the greater will be the intensity of competition. But in actual experience there is *no competition* in the world so *intense* as that which prevails between two highly organized bodies that stand opposed to one another. In the old days of small concerns there was much more slackness of management, and much larger profit per unit of product than we find to-day. It is proverbial that the largest houses can make the closest calculations in selling goods at a slight margin above expense; and competition is generally strong enough to force them to make closer calculations than would have been deemed possible a half century ago.[62]

I have pointed out that a trust (monopoly) has not only been defined as the possession of control but also the *use* of such control. The latter is upheld by Clark, whose statement is:

Size, then, does not make a monopoly. Conceivably a corporation might make *all* the goods of a given class and yet be held completely in check by merely potential competitors. . . . Monopoly is that monopoly *does*; and the typical act which identifies the unlawful power is the crushing of rivals by the means described above.[63]

[61] George P. Carter, *The Tendency Toward Industrial Combination* (London: Constable & Co., 1913), pp. 349-350.

[62] A. T. Hadley, *Economics* (New York: G. T. Putnam's Sons, 1896), p. 117. Italics mine. It is interesting to note that although Hadley states his view clearly, he does not consider whether with the increased intensity of competition it follows that competition will be equally *permanent*. *Intensity* and *duration* are not the same.

[63] J. B. Clark, "Monopolies and the Law," *Political Science Quarterly*, XVI (1901), 471. Italics mine. Cf., H. W. Macrosty, *The Trust Movement in British Industry* (London: Longmans, Green; 1907). See especially, pp. 344-345, where exactly the same views are expressed.

6

To recapitulate: The opposed views cited above place before us in clear-cut fashion the widely diverging opinions on what constitutes competition. The purpose of this chapter has been to set forth the meaning of competition in the economic sense.

In my analysis, I have developed certain distinctions which are fundamental in the use of the term "competition" in economic meaning. These are, first, competition as to form should be distinguished from competition as to results. The change from personal competition to corporate, and from corporate to associative competition are the products of economic development. The failure to distinguish form from result has led to the conclusion that the supersession of personal competition by the corporate, and especially of the corporate by the associative competition has necessarily meant a decrease in competition. Thinking in terms of results in competition—free movement of the factors of production, with a consequent increase of satisfaction through the increase in the production of wealth—the growth in competition has been remarkable.

Second, the use of competition as a postulate, competition as a precept, and competition as an institution must be distinguished. The use of complete competition as a postulate in reasoning is a mode of simplification necessitated by the complexity of our social life. Such a postulate bears no relation to competition as a precept (the advocacy of a policy of laissez faire). The use of competition in the sense of an institution finds expression in drawing the fallacious analogy of biological evolution and social development. These uses of competition should be clearly differentiated since they are in no manner related.

Third, the use of competition in the four phases of economic life, namely, consumption, production, exchange, and distribution, should be distinguished. To speak of competition as applied to economic activities in general, and draw conclusions in one phase of such activities with the tacit or expressed inference that such conclusions hold for the other departments of economic life is false. Proof of this is seen in the unanimity of opinion as to the desirability of free competition in consumption, whereas the widest divergence of opinion exists in regard to production.

The definition of competition in the economic sense should be in accord with the general purpose of the science. This purpose is the increase of satisfactions. Mobility of the factors of production is prerequisite to increased satisfactions. Hence, mobility may be said to be the essence of competition. The basic prerequisites to mobility are scarcity, utilitarianism (greatest satisfaction of wants), complete knowledge of present and future differences in returns in different places and activities, complete divisibility of the factors of production, and the neutralizing of diverse and numerous social institutions. The existence of these prerequisites is dependent upon a positive policy on the part of the government. Contrary to the usual belief, competition in the economic sense does not prevail because of a "let alone" policy but rather because of a program of regulation.

All of the factors of production have enjoyed increased mobility and may, therefore, be said to be more competitive. The sense in which this applies to capital is from the point of view of the individual producing unit or industry.

Purchasing power (loanable funds), which financial organization and instruments have made more flexible, has added enormously to the variability in the proportions of the factors of production used by the individual firm or industry. This variability has meant that two "shifts" are facilitated, namely, from one product to another, and an increase or decrease of the quantity of any factors of production used. The result is but one, and that is that the relation of individual to individual, and industry to industry, is more competitive.

NOTE TO CHAPTER II

Many who hold that individualism and laissez faire have ceased, overlook that economic life is a composite of counteracting forces or "pulls." Having a narrow view of individualism and laissez faire in mind, and defining their use of the terms in this particular, *limited* sense, such writers may be precisely right. But this reasoning, even when such terms are not used in an undefined, general sense, is very misleading.

Reasoning in every phase of economics calls for a balancing of counteracting forces or "pulls," and it is the *net* balance of *all* these forces (which operate simultaneously and cannot be isolated individually) that is of real significance when one evaluates *actual* economic life. What I have said is very well illustrated in some important problems in the discussion of value. Extractive industries are usually classed as industries of diminishing returns. This is true if one takes a sufficiently long-time view and bears in mind that diminishing returns apply to the *net* balance of opposing forces. This has not been adequately emphasized and often misleads the student in not seeing that for some time there may be distinctly increasing returns in these industries owing to important "input," (cost), elements not being used at present to full capacity, and which can be used to more complete capacity. Of course this is the phenomenon of increasing returns under conditions of joint costs and the internal and external economies that develop from the more complete utilization of expensive "input" elements. The midwestern *diversified* farm, not only for the individual farmer but also for the social fund of such land, there is reason to believe is an industry (although extractive) of distinctly increasing returns due to the fact that the input elements that have become the expensive ones are *management* and *labor* rather than land. Both of these input (cost) factors have been, and are, utilized distinctly below their capacity.

The reasoning above applies in the question as to the net balance of opposing forces in the general nature of our economic life. Although such influences or forces are hard to measure, it is safe to say that the development, at least until the recent emergence of political dictatorships, has been toward increasing individualism, self-direction, voluntarism. No statement could have been more accurately or succinctly stated than that of the historian of English Liberalism who states:

> Paradoxical as it may appear to say that a positive policy of constant interference is the same as a negative policy of constant abstention, it is true that the mental habit at the back of one is *identical* with that at the other. *Both* aim at emancipating the individual from the thing which prevents him from developing his natural capacities.[64]

[64] W. Lyon Blease, *A Short History of English Liberalism* (New York: 1913), pp. 7-8, 328. Quoted by Hollander, *op. cit.*, p. 14. Italics mine.

III

THE CONCEPT OF COMPETITION IN THE PHILOSOPHY OF THE CLASSICAL WRITERS[1]

[1] This chapter makes no claim to completeness of the analysis of the works of the classical writers. In planning the present volume I had arranged to deal with the classicists' use of competition in a much more exhaustive manner. This included four chapters in Part II treating the classical writing and four chapters in Part III concerned with the utopian socialists' and the nationalists' viewpoints, before coming to Part IV dealing with the subject of the restatement of the doctrine of free competition, the discussion of which would begin with J. S. Mill.

It is my opinion that insufficient attention has been given to the influence of socialists on economic thinking. And when attention is directed to them it is to the Marxian (scientific) school rather than to the utopians. Strangely enough this is true although the fallaciousness of the Marxian doctrine has been so clearly and frequently demonstrated as to warrant no serious thought, whereas unquestionably the human appeal and also the persuasiveness of utopian writers such as Saint Simon, Fourier, Blanc, and Proudhon had direct influence upon J. S. Mill (and through him upon the economic writing of the whole generation which Mill dominated) and even more so upon the general reform movement and legislation that, at least in part, embodied utopian ideas.

This treatment of the classical period, however, opens a field much too broad. It has seemed advisable, for the purpose of this book, to place the emphasis upon more recent writers and their use of the concept of competition. For this reason I have confined myself in this chapter to the analysis of the important economic treatise (*Principles of Political Economy* in each case except, of course, Smith's *Wealth of Nations*) of the writers who shaped economic thinking in the time in which they wrote, namely, Smith, Ricardo, McCulloch, and J. S. Mill. I am fully aware that such a limited treatment of these writers is inadequate, but I have felt that it is possible, even in limited space, to analyze their use of the concept of competition sufficiently to indicate the misleading or absolutely false points of view often presented by those who have apparently read the classical writers only in part.

I

HAVING now stated my own views regarding competition, the reader's attention is directed to the use of competition in the works of the classical writers. With these writings have usually been associated such terms as the natural order, laissez faire, individualism, complete and free competition. Calling attention to statements as, for example, ". . . by directing that industry in such a manner as its produce may be of the greatest value he (every individual) intends only his own gain, and he in this, as in many other cases, is led by an invisible hand to promote an end which was no part of his intention,"[2] and "All systems either of preference or of restraint, therefore, being thus completely taken away, the obvious and simple system of natural liberty establishes itself of its own accord,"[3] some writers would hold that these statements reflect the mode of reasoning, not only of Smith in particular but classical economists in general, by which logical deductions are reached from premises of perfect competition and hedonistic human nature.[4]

Further, it is emphatically contended by many writers (who have extracted these and similar statements from the whole body of doctrine of which they are only a part) that the classical writers were necessarily supporters of "laissez faire," and it is still further alleged that the deviation, by governments, from the policy of laissez faire marks the "decline" of the "orthodox" or classical school.

As opposed to this view it has been held with equal emphasis that:

> English statesmen and economists have *never* entertained the rigid aversion to Government interference that is vulgarly attributed to them, but with all their profound belief in individual liberty they have *always* reserved for the Government a concurrent sphere of social and economic activity. . . . Our [English] economists are continually reviled as if they sought to leave the world to the play of self-interest and competition, unchecked by any ideas of social justice or individual

[2] Adam Smith, *Wealth of Nations* (Everyman's Library edition; New York: E. P. Dutton) Vol. I, p. 400. All references in this chapter to the *Wealth of Nations* are to this edition.

[3] *Ibid.*, Vol. II, p. 180.

[4] This, Thorstein Veblen holds, characterizes classical economics in general. See his "The Preconceptions of Economic Science," *Quarterly Journal of Economics*, XIII (1889), 396-426.

human right. But in truth the doctrine of laissez-faire has *never* been held by any English thinker, unless, perhaps, Mr. Herbert Spencer.[5]

And it is further maintained by those (for example, John A. Hobson) who hold the view in common with Rae, that the use of the classical economists' statements as social precepts can be laid at the door of the journalists and politicians who had special interest to further.

Finally, it is also generally contended, or implied, that English classical economists are alike in their use of free competition, and what may be said of one holds, in the large, for the other writers of this "school."

These are some of the views in general concerning the place of competition in the writings of the group of economists who have since their time dominated our economic thought, namely, the English classical writers. It is the purpose of this chapter to throw light upon the manner in which competition was actually employed by these writers.

2

Among the general considerations which must be kept in mind in an attempt to understand the economic doctrine of a particular time, I would place, first, the economic conditions under which the writing occurred. Particularly important is this factor in shaping the economic philosophy of the various members of the English classical group. This, of course, in a *general* way has always been recognized by economic students, but the very fact that the writers of the period we are now considering are commonly referred to as the Classical "School" conveys the misleading attitude held regarding this first consideration.

Classical economic writing reflects three rather distinct

[5] John Rae, *Contemporary Socialism* (London: Swan Sonnenschein, 1890), p. 351.

stages of industrial development. Especially true is this of the four authors to be considered, namely, Smith, Ricardo, McCulloch, and J. S. Mill.[6] Adam Smith lived on the eve of the industrial revolution, Ricardo in the midst of it, and J. S. Mill in a time when the stresses and strains of that revolution had created a social outlook and spirit vitally different from the earlier periods. It is significant to note that McCulloch's writing overlapped the period of Ricardo with its industrial revolution in full swing, and also the period of Mill's writing with its changed social outlook. This, no doubt, accounts in part, for McCulloch's statement in his last edition (1849):

> In this edition . . . a still greater extension has been given to the practical parts, or to inquiries respecting the real or probable influence of different systems of economical legislation, over the wealth and well-being of society. The work, indeed, is no longer to be regarded as a mere attempt to trace and exhibit the principles of Political Economy; but also as an attempt, however imperfect, to exhibit their more important applications.[7]

The three stages of industrial development alluded to are set in clear relief if one points to some familiar historical facts. These are frequently forgotten by those who speak of the classical writers as a "school."

As to the first stage of industrial development, what was the economic condition under which Smith wrote? It was seven years before the publication of the *Wealth of Nations* that Arkwright patented his water-frame and James Watt his steam engine; and it was a few years after the appearance of the *Wealth of Nations* that Cartwright

[6] Cf. Arnold Toynbee, *Lectures on the Industrial Revolution of the 18th Century in England* (London: Longmans, 1884—9th Impression 1927). It is a very helpful, concise source. See especially Lecture VII, "The Mercantile System and Adam Smith," pp. 73 et seq.

[7] *Principles of Political Economy* (Edinburgh: A. and C. Black, 1849), p. vi.

invented the power loom and Crompton, the mule. While it was true that the internal commerce of England was free—so far as provincial custom barriers were concerned—this is not what Smith observed in contemporary France and Prussia.[8] Although in England the movement of commodities was free, there still existed a network of restrictions on mobility of labor and capital.[9] Some of these were: (1) no person could follow any trade until he had served seven years; (2) whenever there was a municipal corporation, the restriction which it imposed made it generally impossible for a man to work unless he was a freeman of the town, and this he could as a rule only become by serving his apprenticeship; (3) corporations supervised the prices and quantities; (4) the medieval idea of state guarantee of the genuineness of wares continued; (5) regulations of wages by Justices of the Peace; and (6) the external trade was entirely carried on by great chartered companies (whether joint stock companies, as, for example, the East India Company, or "regulated" companies like the Turkey Company).

This brief description of the economic environment of Smith's *Wealth of Nations* of 1776, would not fit Ricardo's *Political Economy* of 1817. The forty-one years

[8] Restriction of industry he saw on the Continent as a whole but especially in Germany with its medieval regulation and lack of economic unity, which, of course, continued long after Smith's time, since the industrial development of Germany became perceptible only after the creation of the Zollverein (1834).

For a particularly well-ordered, concise, and interesting discussion of German and French industrial conditions during the classical era see J. H. Clapham, *The Economic Development of France and Germany, 1815-1914* (London: Cambridge University Press, 1923), especially Chap. III, "Industrial Conditions in France 1815-1848," and Chap. IV, "Industrial Conditions in Germany 1815-1848."

[9] It is not clear how far such restrictions were operative. There were, even at that time, many free towns like Birmingham and Manchester which flourished.

that had passed brought about what one might call the second stage of industrial development in the classical era. In this stage the scarcely perceptible industrial movement of Smith's time had accelerated to a whirlpool momentum. To use the words of Toynbee, ". . . The steam-engine, the spinning-jenny, the power-loom, had torn up the population by the roots; corporation laws, laws of settlement, acts of apprenticeship, had been swept away by the mere stress of physical circumstances."[10]

More than a quarter of a century passed before J. S. Mill's *Political Economy* of 1848 and McCulloch's fourth and last edition of *Political Economy* in 1849. It was inevitable that the stresses of a phenomenal transitory period should be productive of what might well be called a third stage of development in this classical period—a stage characterized in general by a new spirit of dissatisfaction and unrest reflected by the work and writing of such utopian, associationistic, realistic, and revolutionary socialist critics as Saint Simon, Robert Owen, Charles Fourier, William Thompson, Louis Blanc, Pierre Proudhon, Karl Robertus, and Karl Marx. Indeed, the environment which produced Marx's *Communist Manifesto* (1848) would necessarily leave its imprint prominently on Mill's *Political Economy* of the same year.

Coming to another general consideration which must be kept in mind in an attempt to understand the economic doctrine of a particular time, one can place second the political and social condition under which the writing occurred. With regard to the former, Smith, especially, had good reason to place very little trust in the competence or

[10] *Op. cit.*, p. 5.

good faith of the government.[11] In my opinion, this consideration alone, rather than idealism or optimism, goes a long way to explaining the "individualism" of Smith, and the other classical writers as well. In fact, to one who had written the *Theory of Moral Sentiments*, the irresponsiveness of government officials to the individuals they were governing, which at that moment was causing revolution of the American colonies and also revolution of the French people—this governmental irresponsiveness was an important factor in shaping Smith's regard for the incompetence of the government and the competence of individual initiative.

And finally, the nature of the general problem, in which the writers were interested, is significant in comprehending the economic doctrine and the distinctions between writers usually regarded as a "school." Especially important is this consideration in a very dynamic period, such as the last quarter of the eighteenth century and the first half of the nineteenth century was with its inevitable maladjustments.

To Smith, inquiring into the nature and causes of the increase of wealth, the central issue was practices or activities which directly affected production. Being interested in this problem and being a keen observer of the effectiveness of division of labor, Smith's *Wealth of Nations* naturally became a specific attack upon certain types of governmental activity which clearly retarded personal, local, national, and international division of labor. Bounties, duties, and prohibitions on foreign trade; apprenticeship and settlement laws; legal monopolies; laws hindering

[11] Cf., Jacob Viner, "Adam Smith and Laissez Faire," *Journal of Political Economy*, XXXV (1927), 232.

free trade—these were the activities he attempted to eliminate.[12]

To Ricardo production of wealth was not the problem of special interest. In a letter to Malthus he said:

> Political Economy you think is an enquiry into the nature and causes of wealth; I think it should rather be called an enquiry into the laws which determine the division of the produce of industry amongst the classes who concur in its formation. Every day I am more satisfied that the former is vain and delusive, and the latter only the true object of the science.[13]

That each of the writers we shall examine differed with regard to the economic condition under which he wrote, the political and social condition under which the writing occurred, and also the problem with which each was concerned, can be clearly shown. These are general considerations which must be kept in mind in our attempt to understand the use of competition by the classical writers.[14]

3

It is frequently pointed out that the fundamental idea of the *Wealth of Nations* is the efficacy of self-interest and the desirability of an order of "natural liberty." Inasmuch as the order of natural liberty, according to Smith, "establishes itself of its own accord" when "all systems either of preference or of restraint" have been "completely taken

[12] *Ibid.*, p. 218.

[13] Quoted by L. L. Price, *A Short History of Political Economy in England* (11th ed., London: Methuen, 1922), p. 65.

[14] Possibly no better illustration can be found of the failure to keep these particular considerations in mind and the unwarranted or fallacious views into which this leads than in J. K. Ingram's interpretation of the *Wealth of Nations* (see his *History of Political Economy*, London: Macmillan, 1894, p. 108). With due regard to the excellence of Ingram's book, I cannot agree with this authority. After an examination, in the next section, of Smith's use of competition and "natural liberty" I shall quote Ingram's conclusion to set in sharp relief my own analysis. Vide post, p. 72.

away," it has been contended that Smith "described and analyzed these [economic] processes not only to show what they were, but also to show that they were not likely to be improved by human restraints and regulations."[15] It is usually held that the basis of the economic reasoning of Smith (and also his followers) is "free competition." Further, it is contended that "orthodox Political Economy in England . . . has generally included an advocacy of Laissez Faire."[16]

It has been suggested in the preceding section of this chapter that three general considerations should be kept in mind in my analysis of the classical writers' use of competition, namely, the industrial condition of the time, the political administration, and the problem in which the writer was interested. This has particular force in regard to Smith's writing. His Book I, which considers the improvement of the productive power of labor—so far as his writing is directly concerned with competition—brings out clearly the condition of the time under which he wrote (economic and political) and also the problem in which he was interested. The latter centered about the evil of *certain* types of government activity, and Smith's attack on these particular governmental restrictions is interesting in its frankness and naïveté.

The statutes of corporations and apprenticeship, "and all those laws which restrain, in particular employments, the competition to a smaller number that might otherwise go into them, have the same tendency," namely, to create a monopoly price, which is "upon every occasion the highest which can be got."[17] Such enhancement of the market

[15] Sidgwick, *op. cit.*, p. 19.
[16] *Ibid.*, p. 22.
[17] *Wealth of Nations*, pp. 54-55.

price could endure only as long as "the regulations of police which give occasion to them." Smith hastened to add, however, that such statutes worked to the disadvantage of the laborers as well as to their advantage. The former would be the case when a manufacturer was not in prosperity and the statutes (which in prosperity had resulted in a raise of a worker's wages) now would exclude the laborer's entrance "to many employments."[18]

Interspersed in the attack upon certain government restrictions and regulations is clearly a refutation of the usual assertion that Smith's view regarding the natural order made him a supporter of free competition and laissez faire.[19] As in the case of his attack upon the government regulations which were not conducive to increase of wealth, Smith, in pointing out that the natural order if left to its own course would not work always in favor of the general welfare, uses *specific* cases.[20] The interests of workmen and masters are "by no means the same. The workmen desire to get as much, the masters to give as little as possible."[21] There being fewer masters, combination is easy, and no acts of parliament forbid it as in the case of laborers. The former are always and everywhere in a "sort of tacit" combination, and they "never cease to call aloud for assistance of the civil magistrate."

We have observed that the problem of Smith's Book I was particular instances of restriction of competition brought about by government statute. I have referred to corporation, apprenticeship, and combination laws. Smith

[18] *Loc. cit.*
[19] Cf., Viner, *op. cit.*, p. 218.
[20] Indeed, I venture to suggest that few students who read Smith but once appreciate the keen observer Smith was of industrial circumstances about him.
[21] *Wealth of Nations*, pp. 58-59.

next directs his criticism against the evil of chartered companies. The "want, famine, and mortality" in the East Indies is due to the "mercantile company which oppresses and domineers in the East Indies"; the favorable condition of North America being attributable to the absence of control by such chartered companies.[22]

Turning again to the inadequacy of natural liberty, Smith points to the force of custom entering in to hinder free play of competition, as seen in great differences in wages in various localities separated but a few miles.[23] Also, liberal payment of wages by the piece is very apt to cause workmen to "over-work themselves, and ruin their health and constitution in a few years."[24] Furthermore, equality of wages may not occur "even where there is the *most perfect freedom*" since such equality requires "first, the employment must be well known and long established in the neighborhood; secondly, they must be in their ordinary, or what has been called their natural state; and, thirdly, they must be the sole or principal employment of those who occupy them."[25]

Inequalities are also occasioned "by obstructing the free circulation of labor and stock, both from employment to employment and from place to place." This restraint of competition is due to "the exclusive privileges of corporations."[26] The by-laws regulating the number of apprentices and the years of service violated the sacred right of each man in his own labor. This restraint of competition is an evil, since the public loses by keeping the "work of all artificers" from coming to the market cheaply. "High du-

[22] *Ibid.*, p. 65.
[23] *Ibid.*, p. 66.
[24] *Ibid.*, p. 73.
[25] *Ibid.*, p. 103. Italics mine.
[26] *Ibid.*, p. 107.

ties upon foreign manufactures" tend to the same purpose as corporation laws.[27]

Again, however, Smith sees no correction in free competition of a natural order or natural liberty since "People of the same trade seldom meet together, even for merriment and diversion, but the conversation ends in a conspiracy against the public, or in some contrivance to raise prices."[28] In fact, competition may be increased in some employment to such a point as to occasion disadvantage. The public stress placed upon training for the church causes a "much smaller recompense than what such an education would otherwise have entitled them to."[29]

It was, however, the "absurd" statute of apprenticeship and the laws of settlement which brought about the very unequal price of labor. The latter was particularly detestable to Smith, and with specific information he supports his conclusion that "The unequal price of labor which we frequently find in England in places at no great distance from one another is probably owing to the obstruction which the law of settlements gives. . . ."[30]

In Book II Smith turns his attention to the "Nature, Accumulation, and Employment of Stock." Here he is interested, again, in attacking certain types of governmental activity. He centers his attack upon only a few of these and does so with all that force and effectiveness which were peculiarly Smith's. There is no *carte blanche* adherence to laissez faire or free competition. Regulation of competition is clearly suggested, or where such restriction of competition does not seem advisable, it is often due to

[27] *Ibid.*, p. 116.
[28] *Ibid.*, p. 117.
[29] *Ibid.*, p. 118.
[30] *Ibid.*, p. 127.

the "profusion of government" at *that time*, and not government as such. It was "the highest impertinence and presumption, . . . in kings and ministers, to pretend to watch over the economy of private people, and to restrain their expense, either by sumptuary laws, or by prohibiting the importation of foreign luxuries. They are themselves . . . the greatest spendthrifts in the society."[31]

In so far as Smith's further discussion in this Book (II) touches on competition he deals with the evil of another political institution. This is the law of primogeniture which, "in order to enrich one, beggars all the rest of the children."[32] He pointed out that "perhaps more than one-third, part of the whole lands of the country [Scotland] are at present supposed to be under strict entail."[33] This was undesirable to Smith, *not* because it ran counter to his views on natural liberty but simply on the grounds of unfavorable *results* of extensive land holdings. "Compare," he says, "the present *condition* of those estates with the possessions of the small proprietors in their neighborhood, and you will require no other argument. . . ."[34] In fact, through the greater part of Europe population did not double in less than five hundred years, whereas in the North American colonies population was doubling in twenty or twenty-five years. This was due, in large part, according to Smith, to the law of primogeniture.[35]

[31] *Ibid.*, p. 309. In this connection it is interesting to note that the view, frequently expressed, to the effect that the classical writers did not deal with the economics of consumption is misleading. It is true that McCulloch was the only one who devoted a separate part of his book under that title, but the economics of consumption is scattered through Smith's writing. Cf., for example, pp. 305-312. See especially his illuminating discussion of the advantageousness of expenditure for "durable commodities" as against the expenditure in things which are consumed immediately (pp. 310-312).

[32] *Ibid.*, p. 342.

[33] *Ibid.*, p. 342.

[34] *Ibid.*, p. 344. Italics mine.

[35] *Ibid.*, p. 370.

Before passing to the next book, it is significant to note that Smith again recognizes the exception to the principle of natural liberty. To regulate bank-note issues when people are willing to accept them is "in some respects a violation of this principle. But those exceptions of the natural liberty of a few individuals, which might endanger the security of the whole society, are, and ought to be, restrained by the laws of all governments, of the most free as well as of the most despotic."[36]

In Book IV, on "Systems of Political Economy," Smith's discussion, so far as it bears on competition, is a plea for unrestrained competition in foreign commerce. His major premise is clearly and directly stated, that is to say "the quantity of every commodity which human industry can either purchase or produce naturally regulates itself in every country according to the effectual demand, or according to the demand of those who are willing to pay the whole rent, labour, and profits which must be paid in order to prepare and bring it to the market."[37] Government regulation to increase the balance of trade was fruitless since domestic trade, which created most employment, was more valuable. Smith would reply that upon "every individual . . . continually exerting himself to find out the most advantageous employment for whatever capital he can command" is to be found the proper direction of production. This is not only most advantageous for him but also for society.[38]

Strange as it may seem, the passage which has just been quoted and the similar statement by Smith of the "invisible hand" (appearing on the very next page) have been

[36] *Ibid.*, p. 289.
[37] *Ibid.*, p. 381.
[38] *Ibid.*, p. 398.

continually used in support of the contention that Smith was an advocate of free competition, natural liberty, or laissez faire. Nothing could be more fallacious. Such views illustrate again the danger of reading a treatise in part. Nowhere else[39] in Smith do these passages occur, and their use is directed to the particular problem in hand, namely, the fallacy of regulation of foreign trade. They furnish the basis of the well-known maxim which he states immediately: "What is prudence in the conduct of every private family can scarce be folly in that of a great kingdom."[40] If foreign countries can supply us with a commodity cheaper than we can make it, it is wise to buy it from them. This, it seems to me, is an empirical observation. Smith was not expounding political philosophy in general and creating "laissez faire" or "invisible hand" economics as some writers have insisted.

And again in this book (IV) Smith enunciates notable exceptions to the system of natural liberty. The navigation acts are justifiable, "as defense . . . is of much more importance than opulence."[41] In fact they were the "wisest of all commercial regulations of England." Also an import duty equal to the domestic tax upon the same commodity is advisable. This Smith would not extend further than to the precise foreign commodities which could come into competition with those which had been taxed at home. Retaliatory import duties should be practised when they bring results. Again, bounties given "to artists and manu-

[39] It is true that analogous reasoning (although not the term "invisible hand") appears in Smith's refutation of the alleged advantages of bounties. "Without intending the interest of the people, he [the inland corn dealer] is necessarily led, by a regard to his own interest, to treat them, even in years of scarcity, pretty much in the same manner as the prudent master of a vessel is sometimes obliged to treat his crew." (*Ibid.*, Vol. II, p. 24.)

[40] *Ibid.*, p. 401.

[41] *Ibid.*, p. 409.

facturers who excel in their particular occupations are not liable to the same objections as [other] bounties"—the effect of the latter merely being that of forcing trade into a disadvantageous channel.[42]

It is true that Smith holds that "the natural effort of every individual to better his own condition" under freedom and security can carry society to prosperity. But here again it is not natural liberty, per se, but clearly the *results* obtained from unobstructed individual action as compared to the social results in the midst of a "hundred impertinent obstructions with which the folly of human laws too often incumbers its operations."[43] The consideration of competition in itself is secondary; the ineffectiveness of bounties to *increase trade* was of primary importance.

In the colonial trade competition also should rule. The monopoly of colony trade was "like all the other mean and malignant expedients of the mercantile system." It was depressing in its effect upon the industry of all countries and chiefly the colonies.[44] To support his view, however, Smith puts an amusing stress upon the contention that the raising of profit in the colonial trade would "destroy that parsimony natural to the character of the merchant," and "if the master is dissolute and disorderly" so would be the servants.[45]

At the close of his attack upon the Mercantile System, Smith sets forth the three duties of the sovereign. These are, as is well known, protection against violence and invasion, protection of every member of society from the injustice or oppression of every other member ("an exact administration of justice"), and erecting and maintaining

[42] *Ibid.*, Vol. II, p. 23. References from here on are all to Vol. II.
[43] *Ibid.*, p. 40.
[44] *Ibid.*, p. 107.
[45] *Ibid.*, p. 109.

such public works and institutions as it is not profitable for individuals to erect and maintain. These have frequently been abstracted from Book IV (of which they serve as an emphatic conclusion) and set forth as an enunciation of a general policy of restriction of government activity and regulation to a limited range. It would hardly seem that this view is possible to one who had read even Book IV, as a unit, and certainly not if the *Wealth of Nations* had been read, as a whole, with the considerations in mind of which I spoke in the preceding section of this chapter.[46] If the latter has been the approach, that is, if we see that Smith was concerned with particular types of obsolete governmental regulation, with the particular industrial circumstances of his time, and with governmental administration which was utterly void of ability or vision, we come to the construction of Smith's threefold governmental function, which has been so aptly stated by Nicholson:

> Thus, according to the actual teaching of Adam Smith, if competition, leads to injustice or oppression, the State *ought* to intervene, and if self-interest is inadequate to provide various institutions for the satisfaction of social needs, the State *ought* to provide for their erection and maintenance. It would be impossible to state more precisely the general position that the State may be called on to *interfere*—on various grounds—with the liberty of individuals in the production and distribution of wealth; and it would be easy to show by particular

[46] The failure to keep these particular considerations in mind leads one into views which are unwarranted or absolutely false. This is illustrated by J. K. Ingram's interpretation of the *Wealth of Nations* (see his *A History of Political Economy*, London: Macmillan, 1894, p. 108): "Smith justifies the individual attitude and its consequences, presenting the optimistic view that the good of the community is best attained through the free play of individual cupidities, providing only that the law prevents the interference of one member of the society with the self-seeking action of another. . . . He assumes . . . that every one knows his own interest and will pursue it, and that the economic advantage of the individual coincides with that of society. To this last conclusion he is secretly led . . . by a priori theological ideas, and also by metaphysical conceptions of a supposed system of natural right and natural liberty."

references that Adam Smith was himself prepared to *advocate* such *interference* in many cases, and that in the natural course of progress this list of cases for interference has been largely extended.[47]

Again, to those who contend that a system of natural liberty, free competition, and laissez faire is *implicit* in the *Wealth of Nations* (although not explicit) it is safe to say that such a contention usually reflects either insufficient attention to the threefold consideration of which I have spoken or reading into the economic doctrine of Smith (his *Wealth of Nations*) the general philosophical doctrine of Smith (his *Theory of Moral Sentiments*). Indeed, one of the duties with which Smith charges the Government, namely, the "exact administration of justice," to the end of protecting "every member of society from the injustice or oppression of every other member of it," would alone give almost unlimited scope to governmental activity! The latter view is as implicit in the *Wealth of Nations* as the view of "natural liberty." Especially true is this, it would seem, if one bears in mind the numerous instances of shortcomings even in the non-regulated ("natural liberty") relations of individuals or groups to each other, which Smith himself pointed out and to which the preceding analysis has referred.[48]

[47] *Principles of Political Economy*, Vol. III, pp. 179-180. Italics mine. Cf., Viner, *op. cit.*, pp. 213-218.

[48] What is a most naïve and false misinterpretation of Smith's *economic* doctrine is seen in Thomas Chalmers, *Political Economy in Connexion with the Moral State and Prospects of Society*, Vol. II (Edinburgh: Sutherland and Knox, 1850), pp. 317-318. The following is quoted at length since it was (and possibly *is*) typical of the views frequently held regarding Smith's use of natural liberty and free competition.

"He [Smith] throws the whole matter altogether open to the free and unshackled operation of the great principles of Nature. . . . He stops short with the assertion, that it were better for trade and for the interest of the country, that every positive interference on the part of Government were done away; and he escapes all the hazards of the theorist, by leaving the whole concern to the free operation of Nature, and presuming no aggression whatever on any of her provisions, or on any of her tendencies.

Further, Smith's assigning to the State the duty of erecting and maintaining public works and institutions which it can never be to the interest of individuals or groups of individuals to erect and maintain leaves an enormous field open to the regulatory power of the Government, inasmuch as Smith does not suggest the limitation of such public works. That this throws additional doubt upon Smith's adhering to a system of natural liberty or a policy of laissez faire cannot be denied. Indeed, one might well ask, with Rae:

> Now in these ideas about truck and usury, as in the proposal previously touched upon for checking the growth of disease or ignorance, is not the principle of social politics that is applied by Smith precisely the principle that runs through our whole recent social legislation—factory, sanitary, and educational . . .[49]

Smith's Book V, on the "Revenue of the Sovereign," throws very little additional light on his views regarding competition. In so far as his discussion does so it affirms the conclusions which have been indicated in this chapter. That he would advocate increased scope of governmental activity is clear in his statement that the expense of the sovereign would be "very different in the different states of society, in the different periods of improvement."[50] And again Smith admitted the advisability of encouragement through administration of taxation, for he says the administration of a tax "could be managed to give, not

. . . We would, in short, raise no positive apparatus whatever for the direct object of meeting and alleviating the ills of Poverty . . . we satisfy ourselves with simply asserting, that unfettered Nature, working in individuals, can do the thing better than regulation can; and, on the obvious principles of human nature, verified by the actual result, in a way most striking and triumphant, throughout all the parishes of the kingdom, do we aver, that it would have been the wiser part in our Legislature to have let the matter alone."

[49] *Op. cit.*, p. 357.

[50] *Wealth of Nations*, Vol. II, p. 182.

only no discouragement, but, on the contrary, some encouragement to the improvement of land."[51]

This section has attempted to present the view of Smith on competition as one finds it by an examination of his *Wealth of Nations* with regard to the time in which he wrote and the problems in which he was interested. As we turn to Ricardo, in the following section, we shall see that in both respects a marked difference should be recognized.

4

The forty-one years which passed between the publication of the *Wealth of Nations* and Ricardo's *Principles of Political Economy* brought tremendous social and economic changes. Of the former the French Revolution was most prominent in creating a spirit of eliminating hindrances to the movement of people and goods. In England equally great were the social consequences of non-enforcement of obsolete legislation. As to economic changes, the development of land and water transportation was most far-reaching in its widening of the market and in turn the division of labor and competition. The reciprocal effect of these changes brought about what has been referred to, in Section 2 of this chapter, as the second stage of industrial development in the classical era. This was a stage in which "the immediate environment of Ricardo's life embraced circumstances in which, if ever, competition was almost perfectly and perhaps beneficially realised, its remoter environment had in it much that could explain and condone any apparent harshness in the results of economic analysis."[52] He wrote at a moment when competition in industry was pronounced. Not only was there non-enforcement

[51] *Ibid.*, p. 315.

[52] F. W. Kolthammer, Introduction to Everyman's Edition of Ricardo's *Political Economy*, p. ix.

of obsolete statutes, as has been suggested, but also no factory acts had yet been passed[53] and trade combinations of workmen were still illegal.

Again, the threefold considerations pointed out (in Section 2) as essential to an understanding of classical writers, namely, the economic environment, the problem in which the writer was interested, and the political administration of the time are equally important to an understanding of Ricardo's use of competition. This is what Patten had in mind when he said that Ricardo's

> . . . famous propositions are all the result of concrete studies of English conditions in *his* time. In his reasoning he always had *these* conditions before him as a picture, and he returns to them for the facts and premises upon which any new conclusion is based. He naturally reasoned from the particulars of a concrete illustration to some general conclusion. . . . Bold generalizations are drawn directly from the facts of some *concrete problem* which attracted his attention in his *immediate* environment.[54]

Ricardo's use of competition in the various phases of his discussion and the conclusions which he reaches are frequently misinterpreted by those who do not bear in mind that Ricardo was not dealing with "the temporary effects." These are left "entirely out of our consideration whilst we are treating of the laws which regulate natural prices, natural wages, and natural profits, effects totally independent of these accidental causes."[55]

[53] The Health and Morals of Apprentices Act of 1802 with its chief provision of limiting the working day to 12 hours was utterly ineffective, due to the reliance of inspection on the justices of the peace. (Cf., B. L. Hutchins and A. Harrison, *A History of Factory Legislation* (2nd edit., rev.; London: P. S. King, 1911), pp. 14-29.

[54] "The Interpretation of Ricardo," *Quarterly Journal of Economics*, VII (1893), 345-346. Cf. C. F. Dunbar, "The Reaction in Political Economy," *Quarterly Journal of Economics*, I (1887), 12. Italics mine.

[55] Ricardo, *Principles of Political Economy and Taxation* (Everyman's Edition; New York: Dutton, 1911), pp. 50-51. All references in this chapter to Ricardo's *Principles* are to this edition.

At the same time, nevertheless, Ricardo was perfectly aware of short-time effects and the economic problems which they presented.[56] He holds that like all other contracts, wages should be left to the fair and free competition of the market, and should never be controlled by the interference of the legislature. While he held that "the poor laws are in direct opposition to these obvious principles" he also held that if "it be desirable to prevent the most overwhelming distress to those for whose benefit they were erroneously enacted, their abolition should be effected by the most gradual steps."[57]

In Ricardo's reasoning involving the concept of competition we are conscious that his primary interest is to determine the ultimate results of the competitive process and that the economic problems of a transient and immediate nature are of secondary interest. He explained this to Malthus, when Malthus, at considerable length, held

[56] Professor Ely in speaking of the "few hypotheses" of the Old School states that one of the four hypotheses is the *absolute* lack of friction in economic movement. "Not only do capital and labor move with *perfect ease* from place to place and from employment to employment, but this, it was implicitly maintained, is accomplished without the *slightest loss. . . .*" (See his "The Past and Present of Political Economy," *Johns Hopkins University Studies in Historical and Political Science*, Second Series, March 1884, pp. 5-64). Italics mine.

This statement, I believe, is, in general, absolutely misleading, and the implication which Professor Ely holds is present, is, in particular, erroneous. It seems to me that the penchant to reduce economic reasoning to "hypotheses" and "postulates" usually leads to false conclusions; it conveys but a part of the full scope of a writer's thought.

In regard to Ely's contention one might say (which Ely did not bring out) that it is true that Ricardo's reasoning was to the effect that *given time* labor and capital would respond to differences in "rates of profits." This transference of capital and labor due to the "restless desire on the part of all the employers of stock to quit a less profitable for a more advantageous business has a strong tendency to equalise the rate of profits of all." (Ricardo, p. 48.) This, however, makes *no* contention regarding the *absolute* lack of friction, nor *perfect* ease of movement, nor that no loss is involved. To insist that Ricardo makes such contention is positively erroneous, as we shall see.

[57] Ricardo, *Principles*, p. 61.

that "the desire to simplify has occasioned an unwillingness to acknowledge the operation of more causes than one in the production of particular effects."[58] In a letter to Malthus (1820) Ricardo says,

> Our differences may in some respects, I think, be ascribed to your considering my book as more practical than I intend it to be. My object was to elucidate principles, and to do this I imagined strong cases, that I might show the operation of these principles.[59]

In discussing foreign trade Ricardo held, of course, that "under a system of perfectly free commerce, each country naturally devotes its capital and labor to such employment as are most beneficial to each." He points out also, however, that the reluctance of men to leave their native land together with the feeling of insecurity which exists when capital is not under the immediate control of its owner checks the emigration of capital.[60] He was, therefore, merely expressing a long-time *tendency* in his view of free competition bringing about equality of profit and in fact he says, "These feelings (patriotism), which I should be sorry to see weakened, induce most men to be satisfied with a low rate of profits in their own country." Further, the equilibrium in foreign trade is made impossible, he asserts, by the influence of improvements in arts and machinery as well as the introduction of bounties and taxes.[61]

Ricardo urged free transfer of land through the abolishing of "the duty by stamps, with which the transfer of

[58] T. R. Malthus, *Principles of Political Economy* (Boston: Wells and Lilly, 1821), pp. 4-14.

[59] Quoted by Luigi Cossa, *Introduction to Political Economy* (London: Macmillan, 1893), p. 213. The same view Ricardo had also expressed elsewhere three years *before* Malthus published his *Principles*. See Ricardo's *Principles*, p. 72.

[60] Ricardo, *Principles*, p. 83.

[61] *Ibid.*, p. 87.

landed property is loaded."[62] This, he believed, would place such property into the most productive hands. Such taxation, and the indefinite nature and value due to it, would cause land to go into the hands of speculators rather than sober-minded proprietors.[63] In addition, regulation in the form of taxes on land falls on the consumer since the reduction of profits would cause the farmer to remove his capital to some other trade.[64] The result would be a raising of the price of the farmer's produce.

It is, as is well known, usually emphasized (typified in the statement of Ely's which has been cited above) that the very basis of Ricardo's reasoning was free or pure competition—unrestricted movement of labor and capital. From this it is inferred that Ricardo not only failed to realize the obstacles to such free movement but, further, he did not concern himself with economic problems due to the absence of complete mobility. Apropos of this Toynbee says:

> . . . with all that visible movement before his eyes, with that ceaseless tossing and eddying of the liberated industrial stream ever before him is it to be wondered at that, with a strong native bias of

[62] On this point of free trade in land (as upon certain other points) Malthus' discussion reflects more grasp of the economic significance involved in the point under discussion. Malthus said, "It will be found, I believe, true that all the great results in political economy, respecting wealth depend upon *proportions* . . . there is no part of the whole subject [political economy] where the efficacy of proportions in the production of wealth is so strikingly exemplified, as in the division of landed and other property; and where it is so very obvious that a division to a certain extent must be beneficial, and beyond a certain extent prejudicial to the increase of wealth." (*Principles*, p. 334.)

This, the present writer believes, is the most notable point in Malthus' whole book, and it is stated with remarkable clearness. Unfortunately he did not see the basic significance which proportionality has in all phases of economics, and did not develop his point. He veers off into a discussion of the danger of abolishing primogeniture inasmuch as English political liberty had been due to the existence of a landed aristocracy.

[63] Ricardo, *Principles*, p. 131.

[64] *Ibid.*, p. 171.

his mind already in this direction, he should make *without hesitation* that postulate of *pure competition* on which all the arguments of his treatise depend? . . . he was *unconscious* of the *character* of his own logical method. . . .[65]

This view of Ricardo's reasoning is misleading. I have already noted that Ricardo called attention, for example, to the effect of patriotism, improvements in the arts and machinery, and the effect of bounties and taxes. To these should be added his direct statement:

Commodities, however, of all descriptions can be reduced in quantity, and capital can be removed from trades which are less profitable to those which are more so, *but with different degrees of rapidity*.[66]

And again he says:

The commencement of war after a long peace, or of a peace after a long war, generally produces considerable distress in trade . . . much fixed capital is unemployed, perhaps wholly lost, and labourers are without full employment. The duration of this distress will be longer or shorter according to the *strength of that disinclination which most men feel to abandon that employment of their capital to which they have long been accustomed*.[67]

That Ricardo was conscious of the sense in which he used the concept of competition is further indicated when he says that

In rich and powerful countries, where large capitals are invested in machinery, more distress will be experienced from a revulsion in trade than in poorer countries where there is proportionally a much smaller amount of fixed, and a much larger amount of circulating capital. . . .[68]

And what has equally current interest to us is Ricardo's statement that war induced capital to be transferred to

[65] Toynbee, *op. cit.*, pp. 5-6. Italics mine.
[66] *Principles*, p. 122. Italics mine.
[67] *Ibid.*, p. 176. Italics mine.
[68] *Ibid.*, p. 177.

agriculture from which it cannot be withdrawn, at the termination of the war, without the sacrifice of a great part of the capital.

From what has been said, it is clear that Ricardo's use of competition was not merely that of complete or free competition as a postulate in reasoning. It is true that he was primarily interested in the ultimate consequence when the force of competition had run its course, but he was not unaware or disinterested in temporary effects. As is the case of Adam Smith, so also Ricardo's economic doctrine cannot be said to constitute an argument for laissez faire.

While indeed Ricardo, like Smith, did attack specific instances of government activity and regulation he would in other instances extend the hand of the Government. In regard to the former he attacked (as has been mentioned above) the poor laws, holding that "like all other contracts, wages should be left to the fair and free competition of the market, and should never be controlled by the interference of the legislature," but in this he was expressing agreement with the views of his outspoken critic, Malthus.[69]

In regard to regulating competition it is seldom brought out that Ricardo would advocate extending governmental regulation. That he would do so has been very well stated by one writer who says:

> Ricardo himself touches only incidentally on the functions of the state but he then does so to defend interventions, such as minting

[69] Sympathetic as Malthus was with the laboring people (who he felt worked too hard for their health, and that it was more desirable to have less national wealth and more leisure) still he held, "To interfere generally with persons who are arrived at years of discretion in the command of the main property which they possess, namely their labor, would be an act of gross injustice; and the attempt to legislate directly in the teeth of one of the most general principles by which the business of society is carried on, namely, the principle of competition, must inevitably and necessarily fail." (*Principles*, p. 366.)

money, marking plate, testing drugs, examining medical candidates, and the like, which are meant to guard people against deceptions they are themselves incompetent to detect. Moreover, he was a strong advocate for at least one important extension of the State's industrial rôle—he would establish a National Bank of issue with exclusive privileges; and it is not uninteresting to remember that in his place in Parliament he brought forward the suggestion of a system of Government annuities for the accommodation of working men; which was introduced by Mr. Gladstone half a century later, and has been denounced in certain quarters as that statesman's first step in Socialism, and that he [Ricardo] was one of a very small minority who voted for a Parliamentary inquiry into the social system of Robert Owen.[70]

Enough has been said, in this summary chapter, regarding Ricardo's use of competition. He, as well as other writers since his time, used the term without defining in what sense he was using it. The economic condition of the time in which he wrote, together with the problem with which he was concerned, must be borne in mind. His was a treatise which was clearly delimited by the latter and he himself definitely stated this (as we have seen) when he said that he was not dealing with "temporary effects" and when he wrote to Malthus that the latter had considered his (Ricardo's) book "more practical" than it was intended to be.

In coming to the discussion of the next section we turn to one who held first place in the field of economics from 1820 to 1850. This was John Ramsay McCulloch, to whom James Mill wrote at the death of Ricardo, "As you and I are his two and only disciples, his memory must be a point of connection between us," and to McCulloch is usually attributed the narrowest and most direct following of Ricardo's economic reasoning.

[70] John Rae, *op. cit.*, p. 360.

5

I have suggested that McCulloch's writing began in the environment of the second stage of the industrial revolution (that of its full momentum) and the last edition (the fourth) of his *Principles* appeared in 1849 when the stresses of this tremendous change had brought about a new social attitude.

Certainly not the least effective of the forces to create this attitude were the utopian (and other) socialistic writings. To these should be added the maladjustments brought about by the enclosure and consolidation systems in agriculture, the decay of the domestic system, the concentration of a non-disciplined laboring element, and the widespread social and political unrest manifested by the revolutions of 1848. That these maladjustments brought evils which were cumulative in their effect is obvious, and the growth of factory legislation was but one manifestation of an awakened social consciousness of those evils.

Factory Acts of 1819,[71] 1825,[72] 1831[73] were ineffective due to supervision by local justices. The Factory Act of 1833 corrected this inefficacy by creating an inspection department of the central government.[74] Then came the ten-

[71] Robert Owen, the English contemporary of the French utopians, supported a bill for a twelve-hour day for children under sixteen, prohibiting child labor under ten years of age, and the appointment of paid and qualified inspectors. The Act, as passed, however, merely forbade persons under sixteen to be employed more than twelve hours, and left the inspection to the local justices.

[72] Reduced the average working day by a half-hour.

[73] Night work prohibited to all persons under twenty-one (limited to cotton mills).

[74] The Act prohibited night work to all under eighteen in cotton, woolen, worsted, hemp, flax, tow, linen, or silk. No person under eighteen to be employed more than twelve hours per day. Hutchins and Harrison, *Factory Legislation* is a brief and very useful treatment of the subject. Also very usable is the short chapter (fifty pages), entitled "The Historical Development of the Factory Acts" by Miss Hutchins in the interesting little

hour day with the Act of 1847. The light which the agitation for each of these acts threw upon the economic conditions of the time in general, and the evils of child labor in particular, was certain to call forth economic treatises of a different nature than that of the earlier classical period. It would be strange, indeed, if we should find in McCulloch, who wrote in the midst of this and was removed in time a whole generation from the writing of his teacher, Ricardo, merely a restatement of the early masters. This is, however, the contention of Ingram, who said of McCulloch:

> He adopted too hastily the theoretic exaggerations of some of Smith's successors, and exhibited in full measure their habitual deadness, in the study of social questions, to all but material considerations.[75]

Because of the general agreement that McCulloch is the staunchest follower of the early classicists it is especially interesting to examine his *Principles of Political Economy* of 1849 with a view to determine what classical economics became in a stage of industrial development essentially different from that in which it had its early development. So far as his reasoning involves competition, is it that of unrestricted competition, "perfect freedom," "natural liberty"? Is there the advocacy of laissez faire usually attributed to Smith and Ricardo?

Discussing the interference of government with the pursuits and property of individuals, McCulloch says,

> An idea seems, however, to have been recently gaining ground, that the duty of government in regard to the domestic policy of the country

book *The Case for the Factory Acts* (edited by Mrs. Sidney Webb; London: Grant Richards, 1902). The arrangement of the chapter is topical, with the inconveniences inherent in such an arrangement. The topics are: extent of application, limitation of hours, health and safety, and methods of administration.

[75] *Encyclopedia Britannica*, 9th Edit., XV, 134-135.

is almost entirely of a negative kind, and that it has merely to maintain the security of property and the freedom of industry. But its duty is by no means so simple and easily defined as those who suppose this opinion would have us to believe. . . . *Freedom is not* as some people appear to think, *the end of government: the advancement of the public prosperity and happiness is its end*; and freedom is valuable in so far only as it contributes to bring it about. . . .

However disinclined, it is *obliged* to *interfere*, in an *infinite variety* of purposes.[76]

After an enumeration of some classes of objects requiring interference (among which he asserts that government must frequently engage, or authorize individuals to engage, in various sorts of undertakings deeply affecting the rights and interests of others, and of society) he concludes, "It is, indeed, obvious that no solution of this problem [to determine what duties the state ought to perform] can be applicable at all times, and under all circumstances."[77]

It seems to me that it would be difficult to state in general terms, briefly and concisely, the underlying principle guiding enlightened legislation regarding the extent to which competition is desirable more accurately than the foregoing expressions of McCulloch's. Here is a recognition of the need of increased security of property and production (materialism) to be tempered with welfare and happiness (idealism); the need of government authorization (regulation) of various sorts of undertakings (public service industries) to be supplemented with government itself engaging in such enterprises (government ownership and operation); and the need of extending government activity as time and conditions vary. And these views

[76] *Principles of Political Economy* (4th edit.; Edinburgh: A. and C. Black, 1849), pp. 262-263. Italics mine. All reference to McCulloch refer to this edition.

[77] *Ibid.*, p. 264.

McCulloch did not state as abstractions to be promptly forgotten. To Senior's contention that the function of an economist was not to advise, McCulloch retorted that an economist who confines himself to mere abstractions "may as well address himself to the Pump in Aldgate as to the British Public."[78]

McCulloch attributed progress to the instruction of the masses[79] and held that furnishing an elementary education for *all* classes of persons is a foremost duty of the Government.[80] In this connection it should be added that he held that children were employed at too early an age, and "parental affection is not always to be depended upon." He desired the education of children employed in factories, but denied the contention that factory employment caused stupidity.[81]

Having in mind, no doubt, Smith's distinction concerning the advantageousness of agriculture, manufacture, and commerce, McCulloch differed from Smith and regarded these as equal. Where the death rate was high (Manchester and Liverpool) this was not due to the evil of competition but to the carelessness of police regulation.[82] But such a view was assuredly not to be construed as a *carte blanche* approval of competition, for "perhaps it may, in the end, be found that it was unwise to allow the manufacturing system to gain so great an ascendancy as it has done in this country, and that measures should have been early adopted to check and moderate its growth," although we are too far advanced to think of retreating.[83]

[78] *Ibid.*, Preface, p. x.
[79] *Ibid.*, p. 123.
[80] *Ibid.*, p. 263.
[81] *Ibid.*, p. 186.
[82] *Ibid.*, p. 184.
[83] *Ibid.*, p. 191.

Nevertheless, we must "*do all* that is possible by *judicious legislation* to give stability to industry, and to avert or modify the influence of revulsions."[84]

In his chapter on "Causes of Gluts" (Part I, Chap. 7) especially, McCulloch's discussion goes far beyond the assumption of simple and complete competition. Denying Malthus' contention that there may be general overproduction, McCulloch held that there may be gluts in particular industries with resultant serious hardship. He did not argue for "free competition" but rather that "*every* practicable means should be tried that may seem most likely to abridge and facilitate the painful state of transition."[85]

It is true that McCulloch holds that the maxim *pas trop gouverner* should never be overlooked; non-interference should be the guiding principle. In all ordinary cases individuals should be left to shape their conduct according to their own judgment. Legislators should stop, indeed, when they are not impelled by a strong sense of public duty, but where this sense of duty is felt "they should never hesitate in their course. There are many cases in which government must and many more in which it should interfere. And, it is the duty of the legislature, having once fully satisfied itself, by a careful inquiry, of the expediency, all things considered, of any measure, resolutely to carry it into effect."[86]

To arrive at cost of production being the "grand regulating principle of exchangeable value," McCulloch states that we must "*assume* that the wages earned by the labourers engaged in the different branches of industry are,

[84] *Ibid.*, p. 191. Italics mine.
[85] *Ibid.*, p. 210. Cf. p. 225.
[86] *Ibid.*, p. 308.

all things considered, nearly equal. . . ."[87] This holds only where capital can be easily withdrawn and not, for example, in agriculture. Consideration is also given to the influences of variation of demand and supply, and of speculation on price.

McCulloch's writing occurred contemporaneously with the indescribable suffering of the Irish due to famine. It took place with particular force in 1821. He points out that a considerable fall in wages brings about a lower standard of living, and this "is perhaps the most serious of all evils that can befall them [the laborers]. . . . Everything should be done to make such apathy [that is, submitting quietly to wage reductions] seem discreditable." To bring about security of property and freedom of trade is all that government can do directly, although government may also exercise its influence *indirectly*. Still what it (and employers also) "can do for labourers is but as the dust of the balance, compared with what the latter can do for themselves."[88]

While this may seem to be an advocacy, with a vengeance, of the direct check of Malthusianism, the economic condition under which the discussion occurred (as I have mentioned before) is an important consideration. The striking accompaniment of the Industrial Revolution seen in the unprecedented rise in population, manifested itself in Ireland, which had no industrial revolution at all, as well as in England. The low standard of living, coupled with a direct dependence on the potato crop, made only two consequences possible at every crop failure, namely, increased deaths or migrations. Both developed to a marked degree, particularly after the potato blight of

[87] *Ibid.*, p. 328. Italics mine.
[88] *Ibid.*, pp. 415 et seq.

1846-47, after which numbers fell rapidly from eight million to less than five million. Because of geographical nearness, Irish migrations fell with particular severity upon the crowded English industrial centers,[89] with their festering spots of disease and conflict, and with less severity upon American communities.[90] It is hardly surprising that McCulloch should come to the conclusion that improvement of the Irish people should occur *in Ireland*. Immigration restriction should prevent British labor from being dragged "down to the same hopeless abyss of pauperism and wretchedness in which she [Ireland] is sunk." In spite of "great difficulty and expense," McCulloch advocated directing these paupers to colonial possessions.

Although McCulloch held that all measures regarding wages would only aggravate evils unless they are founded, on the one hand, on the principles of giving new vigor to industry, opening new markets, and enlarging the amount of capital; and, on the other hand, on the restraining of numbers of laborers, still he held that unemployment relief was "indispensable." Regulation of hours of work for women and children (already accomplished) is "proper"; public education is "most promising"; providing of elementary instruction for *all* classes is "most pressing"; friendly societies and savings banks are "desirable"—these are the views of McCulloch, expressed with a high degree of judiciousness and a keen sense of practicableness.

To the other classical writers, freedom of consumers' choice—free play of competition in the market place—was taken for granted, and consumption was not regarded

[89] Cf., for example, G. M. Trevelyan, *History of England* (London: Longmans, 1926), *passim*.

[90] Although later, we had our "Molly Maguires" in the sixties and early seventies!

as coördinate with other departments of economics. Scattered throughout their works are discussions which constitute a theory of consumption. Questions concerning poor and poor laws, the advisability of protecting resources, the ultimate effects of certain enterprises and trade, the effects of taxation, and so forth, are not brought together. McCulloch proposed to deal, in Part IV of his *Principles*, with the economics of consumption as such. To this particular phase of competition, however, his discussion adds very little.

One important generalization he did make which, in the views regarding regulation of consumption, has not been adequately recognized. Not all sorts of consumption are equally advantageous but "to decide as to this, we must look at the *results* of the consumption, and at them *only*. By fixing the attention on the *species* of consumption carried on, and not on its results, this part of the science has been encumbered with *imaginary* distinction. . . ." Surveillance and sumptuary laws are oppressive. Because of inequalities in incomes, what would be "ridiculous extravagance in one man may be well-regulated moderate expenditure in another."[91]

In closing my examination of McCulloch I may say that his writing reflected a third stage in the industrial development of the time—a stage in which had emerged a critical attitude and spirit of dissatisfaction with the unequally distributed stresses of a transitory period. His use of the concept of competition was never that of assuming the free and immediate movement of labor and capital generally attributed to Ricardo. Nor did McCulloch use competition as a maxim of legislative conduct in advocat-

[91] *Ibid.*, pp. 572-573. Italics mine.

ing laissez faire. Quite the contrary: From the second edition, in 1830, onward to the author's last edition in 1849, he not only devotes a special chapter to the limits of government interference, but he also begins the discussion of the chapter with an *explicit* repudiation of the doctrine of laissez faire. Notwithstanding his maxim *pas trop gouverner* he was desirous of extending government regulation and activities over the competitive process. In his discussion, especially of the subject of wages and labor, there was not the "habitual deadness" attributed to him by Ingram, but rather a high degree of common sense largely tempered by social sympathy.

In regard to consumption he saw that which is so frequently not seen and beclouds even our current discussion, namely, that the useful criterion of social control is results and not the criteria of types of expenditures and motives involved.

6

John Stuart Mill's *Principles of Political Economy*, published in 1848, was written in the same economic environment—the same stage of industrial development—as that of McCulloch's *Principles*. Again, it must be emphasized that the causes which brought about this (third) stage of industrial development and new social attitude must be borne in mind if one is to understand Mill's use of the concept of competition. The human appeal of utopian socialistic writing, the ruthlessness of the enclosure-consolidation movement in agriculture, the suffering involved in the decay of the domestic system, the evil of concentrating non-disciplined laborers in congested urban centers, the agitation of the revolutions of 1848—these are vital influences in accounting for the wider range of

Mill's reasoning than that of the more limited scope of Ricardo, in whose school he was trained.

The key to Mill's reasoning concerning competition is found in the point which he justly claims distinguishes his work from previous expositions. This is:

> . . . in making the proper distinction between the laws of the Production of Wealth, which are *real laws of nature,* . . . and the modes of its Distribution, which subject to certain conditions, *depend on human will.* The common run of political economists confuse these together, under the designation of economic laws, which they deem incapable of being defeated or modified by human effort; ascribing the same necessity to things dependent on the unchangeable conditions of our earthly existence, and to those which, being but the necessary *consequences* of *particular* social arrangements, are merely *coextensive* with these. . . .[92]

In the beginning of Mill's discussion of distribution, a chapter is devoted to elucidate that the right of private property rests on the grounds of "general expediency." Socialism in its various forms "cannot be truly said to be impracticable."[93] And it naturally follows that "the power of bequest may be so exercised as to conflict with the permanent interests of the human race."

Mill's chapter "Of Competition and Custom" is particularly significant in one's attempt to understand the use of competition in his economic reasoning. The principle of competition, he holds, is necessary if political economy is to lay claim to being scientific. "Assume competition to be their *exclusive* regulator, and principles of broad generality and scientific precision may be laid down . . . but it would be a great misconception of the *actual* course of human affairs, to suppose that competition exercises in fact

[92] *Autobiography* (London: Humphrey Milford; 1873), pp. 174-175. Italics mine.

[93] *Principles of Political Economy* (Ashley Ed.; London: Longmans, 1926), pp. 204 ff. All references in our discussion refer to this edition.

this unlimited sway."[94] Causes disturbing to competition, such as monopolies, have always been allowed for, but competition may be counteracted by custom. Prices generally are less affected by the latter than are rents, although retail prices in particular feel very slowly the effect of competition. After illustrating the pervasive influence of custom in various activities, Mill states very significantly, "These observations [regarding custom] must be received as a general correction to be applied whenever relevant, whether expressly mentioned or not, to the conclusions contained in the subsequent portions of this treatise."[95]

Mill, therefore, *fully* recognized that his use of competition was that of a postulate, and this process of simplification and conclusions reached by this process were not to be misinterpreted as fitting actual condition, nor as suitable for drawing up precepts of legislative conduct (that is, laissez faire).

Chapters then follow regarding economic orders "in which competition has *no part*." These chapters are concerned with slavery, peasant proprietors, and metayers.[96]

In the discussion of cottiers the element of competition is interesting as being operative, but nevertheless the majority of a population of eight millions had "long grovelled in helpless inertness and abject poverty under the cottier system."[97]

Mill's distribution theory has been the phase of his writing upon which attention has usually been centered.

[94] *Ibid.*, p. 242. Italics mine.

[95] *Ibid.*, p. 247.

[96] *Ibid.*, Bk. II, Chaps. 5-8.

[97] *Ibid.*, p. 329. With Mill's suggestions for "Means of Abolishing Cottier Tenancy" (Book II, Chap. 10) cf. his parliamentary speeches on the subject in his "*The Irish Land Question*" (London: Longmans, 1870), pp. 97-125.

Unfortunately in the treatment of a writer's whole distribution theory, coupled with the practice of referring to the English writers from Smith to Cairnes as a "school" (Classical), a very misleading impression has developed that a close uniformity of reasoning characterizes the work of these writers. This we have seen is not true in the use of the concept of competition by the writers we have already examined with the difference in the industrial environment in which they wrote and the problems in which they were interested.

Particularly true is this of Mill's use of competition, already noted in his discussion of the competitive order, in which he emphasizes social expediency as its basis. In his explanation of the distributive shares Mill very clearly brings out the limitations of competition. This is not brought out once and for all, and then to be forgotten, but these limitations are, rather, something to which constant references are made.

Holding, as Mill did, the Wages Fund doctrine with its explanation of wages depending "upon the demand and supply of labour; or as it is often expressed, on the proportion between population and capital," he nevertheless refers to "custom or individual character" as "a modifying circumstance."[98] The effect of legal restraint and custom on numbers and hence on wages is given lengthy discussion by Mill, with his keen interest in the Malthusian explanation.[99]

After giving attention to Adam Smith's chapter[100] on differences of wages which Mill says "as far as it goes

[98] *Principles*, p. 343.

[99] Not only is this seen in the chapter on "Wages," where ten of the eighteen pages are devoted to Malthusianism, but also in the two chapters which follow that are concerned with "Remedies for Low Wages."

[100] *Wealth of Nations*, Book I, Chap. 10.

. . . is tolerably successful," the latter again points out that "law or custom may interfere to limit competition."

As to profits: Following a particularly lucid explanation of the mode in which profits tend toward equality and the statement that the "equalizing process, commonly described as the transfer of capital from one employment to another is *not* necessarily the onerous, slow, and almost imperceptible operation which it is very often represented to be" (because of "the numerous and multifarious channels of credit"[101]), it is remarkable, indeed, that in spite of this explanation Mill says "that even in the countries of most active competition *custom* also has a considerable share in determining the profits of trade."[102]

Thus far, I have considered Mill's use of competition in that phase of economics which he has termed the "Statics" of the subject, that is, economic phenomena in their causal relation. In the "Dynamics" of the subject—the economic laws which have to do with the changing society—Mill's use of the concept of competition is, in some respects, interesting and unique. Because of Mill's thesis that the rate of "profits" (when a country has long possessed a large production and saving) "is habitually within . . . a hand's breadth of the minimum," due to the strength of the "effective desire of accumulation," he holds that this "materially alters many of the practical conclusions which might otherwise be supposed to follow from the general principles of Political Economy."[103]

[101] Cf. my definition of capital, *Vide supra*, pp. 39 ff.

[102] *Principles*, p. 415. Mill states, however, that competition, at least in England, is breaking down the customary notion of a "suitable rate of profit." In some parts of the Continent such standards (or "suitable rates") are as high as a hundred per cent (mark-up of retail prices over wholesale —Mill is not speaking here of return on capital).

[103] The discussion of this view is found in Bk. IV, Chaps. 4 ff.

The Government's relation to the competitive process—regulation and direction in the use of capital—is affected by virtue of the fact that the "tendency of profits to a minimum is constantly operative." Mill held that the argument "against the expenditure of public money for really valuable, even though *industriously unproductive*, purposes" was weakened. Such unproductive expenditure would not affect national wealth.[104] Also in spite of the evil effects of sinking great sums in railways this was not to the detriment of the productive resources of the country since it was "mostly a mere appropriation of the annual overflowing which would otherwise have gone abroad, or been *thrown away unprofitably*. . . ."[105]

From our present-day point of view it seems strange that Mill should not have given sufficient weight to the elasticity of demand (due to a rising standard of living) and the accelerating rate of improvement in the arts with its ever increasing channels for the use of capital. Also interesting, in the same connection, is his expression of the desirability of the stationary state as against the present state. This is but another instance of Mill's general philosophy pervading his economic philosophy. How far, if at all, Mill would have social control of the competitive process to check "the struggle for riches" and bring about the "Art of Living" he does not say. That we can agree with Mill the economist, in his advocacy of limiting the amount of inheritance is clear; that we cannot agree with Mill the philosopher, that "hitherto (1848) it is questionable if all the mechanical inventions yet made have lightened the day's toil of any human being" is equally clear![106]

[104] *Principles*, p. 741. Italics mine.
[105] *Ibid.*, p. 743. Italics mine.
[106] *Ibid.*, p. 75. What I have especially in mind in referring to Mill's

Possibly nowhere is my point that in McCulloch and Mill you have economic thought reflecting a third stage of industrial development (one characterized by a critical social attitude due to accumulated stresses of the industrial revolution) better seen than in Mill's long expatiation concerning the possibilities of laborers' associations in general, and coöperative societies in particular.[107] His discussion can be understood only in light of it being contemporaneous with French utopianism and Owenism. It is important to remember also that Mill wrote at the moment when the revolutions of 1848 were placing this coöperative-socialistic subject in the center of the stage. Whether he would have given the same amount of emphasis to this discussion in the absence of the stirring events of the time and if his consideration rested upon ground of economic analysis per se we do not know. At any rate, for the particular purpose of our analysis, his view of competition in the dynamics of economics is interesting and significant.

By means of "associations," Mill asserted that capital could become the joint property of all, and if this transformation was effected it would give us the nearest approach to social justice.[108] Still he utterly dissents from

general philosophy is also seen in his *Essay on Liberty*. Then too, one may observe his emphasis on the strength of the theory of self-dependence as opposed to the weakness of "the theory of protection," and likewise the inequality of legal, industrial, and social rights of the sexes as being the greatest hindrance to moral, social, and even intellectual improvement. (See his Book IV, Chap. 7, "On the Probable Future of the Labouring Classes." This chapter Mill states "had a greater influence on opinion than all the rest" of the chapters of his *Political Economy*. He attributes the chapter entirely to Mrs. Mill. *Vide Autobiography*, p. 174.)

[107] More than thirty pages, much of it in fine print. See pp. 760 ff. of his *Principles*. In the excellent editorial work which Professor Ashley has given us in his edition, the changes in Mill's views, from one edition to another as years went by, regarding the possibilities of the associationistic movement (as opposed to the competitive order) can be partly seen.

[108] *Principles*, pp. 791-792.

the socialists' "declamations against competition"! At least one can say Mill was fully aware of the shortcomings of competition, and while it was not the "best conceivable stimulus" it was "at present a necessary one."

The indispensable functions which Mill would assign to the Government are not the simple duties of affording protection against force and fraud: the requisite functions are multifarious.[109] And these are susceptible to wide interpretation. The ground of justification of interference with unregulated competition is "general expediency," and the only rule curtailing governmental activity is that the case of expediency should be strong. The necessary functions are of an "extremely miscellaneous character." Mill's limiting his discussion to laws of taxation, property and contracts, and police is due to the fact that these are of "principal importance."

Mill was not in favor of unrestricted right of property. The right of bequest he would limit to the amount necessary to care for the persons who were concerned and also "that no one person should be permitted to acquire, by inheritance, more than the amount of a *moderate* independence."[110]

Improper interferences of the Government with competition are based upon the false doctrine of protection, says Mill. This includes protection to industry, Corn Laws, and Navigation Laws.[111] Next to the protectionist doctrine are certain fallacious interferences with contracts, of which usury laws and regulation of food prices are instances. The conferring of rights which lead to monopolies (except patents) is detrimental. Finally, among evil inter-

[109] *Ibid.*, pp. 797 ff.
[110] *Ibid.*, p. 889.
[111] *Ibid.*, pp. 916 ff.

ferences of government are seen the laws against combinations of workmen.

In completing our examination of Mill's use of the concept of competition we come to his chapter on the limits of the province of government.[112] Government intervention, he holds, is of two types—authoritative and advisory, the latter including the promulgation of information. The former is "much more limited" and in fact "there is a circle around every human being which no government . . . ought to be permitted to overlap."[113] Mill's opposition to authoritative intervention is based upon general philosophical ground rather than economic reasoning as such. Every increase of government functions increases its power, the government is already overcharged with duties, the great disadvantage of government administration is due to "an inferior interest in the result, and, finally, the individuals carrying on these functions themselves are thereby trained for the "business of life,"—such are Mill's views on governmental participation in competitive, economic activities.

[112] *Ibid.*, Bk. V, Chap. II.

[113] This thesis of Mill's is, of course, expanded fully in his *Essay on Liberty* (London: Longmans, 1874). In it he lays down two maxims. These are, "first, that the individual is not accountable to society for his actions, insofar as these concern the interests of no person but himself. Advice, instruction, persuasion, and avoidance by other people, if thought necessary by them for their own good, are the only measures by which society can justifiably express its dislike or disapprobation of his conduct. Secondly, that for such actions as are prejudicial to the interests of others, the individual is accountable, and may be subjected either to social or to legal punishment, if society is of the opinion that the one or the other is requisite for its protection." (See pp. 168-169.)

To me, it seems that these "maxims" merely indicate a "desirable attitude" regarding the free action (competition) of individuals. In a complex, closely interdependent society such as ours, all that one would need to point out is that scarcely any act of an individual, from his first breath to his last, concerns but himself. One might maintain, therefore, that according to Mill's own maxims there should be almost complete *regulation* of the individuals' actions rather than almost complete, unrestricted competition.

His opinion that laissez faire "should be the general practice" must be interpreted in light of the exceptions which he makes to his statement.[114] It does not hold where the consumer is not a competent judge of the commodity or service (elementary instruction should, for example, be compulsory); where the mental or physical capacity of the individual is lacking (as in the case of an infant or idiot); where an individual irrevocably decides now what is best for him at a distant time (the individual cannot comprehend the latter); where individuals delegate the management of concerns to others (greater publicity should be required); where individuals acting alone cannot give effect to their judgment (hours of labor); where the acts of individuals are for the interests of other people (charity); where the consequences extend beyond the life of individuals concerned (colonization); and, where important public services are not performed because no individual is specially interested. Finally, as if to further nullify (if such, indeed, is necessary!) his practical maxim of laissez faire, Mill makes the significant statement:

> In the particular circumstances of a given age or nation, there is *scarcely anything* really important to the general interest, which it may not be *desirable, or even necessary*, that the government should take upon itself. . . .[115]

This closes our examination of the use of the concept of competition by a writer whose views are extraordinary in the breadth of their scope and in the flexibility with which those views can be interpreted and applied. John Stuart Mill felt the influence of the writing of the past and was equally attuned to the agitation which characterized the period in which he wrote.

[114] *Principles*, pp. 953-979.
[115] *Ibid.*, p. 978.

7

To sum up: The economic reasoning of the classical writers has usually been characterized as that of natural order, laissez faire, and free competition. It is, further, frequently contended these writers were supporters of a negative—laissez faire—policy on the part of the Government. Also, as a result of referring to these writers as the Classical "School," it is commonly inferred that what may be said of the views of one, regarding competition, holds in general for all.

It has been the thesis of this chapter that certain general considerations must be kept in mind if one is to understand the economic writing of a particular writer and of a particular time. They are frequently overlooked as a result of our misleading practice of classifying writers into "schools" and "periods." The considerations referred to are threefold, namely, the economic condition under which the writing occurred, the political and social conditions of the time, and the nature of the general problem in which the writers were interested. For the classical writers we have examined, a marked difference existed regarding the first, and greater or less difference regarding the other two considerations.

To Adam Smith, who lived in the economic environment of the eve of the Industrial Revolution, the problem was the removal of specific instances of government regulation of competition. His was not the use of competition as a legislative precept to support a general policy of laissez faire. In so far as a doctrine of natural liberty is to be inferred from his writing, it may well be contended that Smith was suggesting a constructive program to give effect to his attack upon the specific instances of government regulation he wished to remove. He was, undoubtedly, aware of the inefficacy of a purely negative attack. And, indeed, Smith may with equal reason be interpreted to give support to wide extension of government interference with free competition.

Ricardo wrote under changed social and economic conditions—a second stage in industrial development of this era of classical writing. The two decades since Smith's writing had added greatly to the mobility of labor and capital. Although interested in the ultimate consequences when the assumed force of free competition had run to its full conclusion, Ricardo was fully aware of "the temporary effects" and, in fact, pointed out specifically that unrestricted movement of labor and capital does not hold in actual life. Though his problem was not the question of the efficacy of unrestrained competition, and hence, he touched only incidentally upon the advisability of government interference with competition, his writing cannot be construed to propose a policy of laissez faire. Merely two reasons, as we have seen in my analysis, need be given in support of this assertion, namely, that Ricardo himself specifically stated he did not intend his book to be "practical" (which is but another way of stating that he did not formulate precepts to be applied to social problems) and also Ricardo (again specifically) advocated extending government regulation along several important channels.

With the passing of more than three decades before the *Principles* of McCulloch and Mill appeared, a third stage of industrial development had been reached—a new social attitude, the product, in large part, of utopianism, Owenism, and the revolutions of 1848.

McCulloch is frequently held to be a narrow "follower of Ricardo." If this is intended to convey the impression that he was unaware of or unsympathetic with the economic problems calling for the Government to extend its hand in the guiding of competitive forces that had resulted in many maladjustments—if this is the impression, it is not founded on an examination of McCulloch's *Principles.* His maxim of *pas trop gouverner* was clearly limited by pointing out the numerous cases in which the government *must,* and the many more cases in which it *should,* interfere with unrestrained competition.

To Mill, who approached economic reasoning regarding the laws of distribution (in contrast with the laws of production) from the point of view that such laws depend on human will, it naturally followed that the arrangement of our present economic order rests upon grounds of expediency. He clearly states that the *assuming* of competition was necessary to draw up principles; in actual life it does not exercise unlimited sway. Custom and legal restraint greatly limit competition; and competition is absent in economic orders such as slavery and metayage.

In Mill's economic philosophy is much of Mill's general philosophy. The latter, seen in the reasoning of his *Essay on Liberty* and his observations regarding the desirability of the stationary state and the "Art of Living," reflects the social attitude of dissatisfaction which characterized the third stage of industrial development in which he wrote. While Mill held laissez faire should be the general practice, his suggestion of numerous exceptions (both authoritative and advisory) to this practice might well justify one in contending that he nullified the precept of laissez faire, which his *general* philosophy had caused him to enunciate.

IV

CAIRNES: FREE COMPETITION AS A POSTULATE AND THE LIMITATIONS OF FREE COMPETITION IN PRACTICE

I

IT IS usually said that John Elliot Cairnes was the last of the English classical economists. To the view that he was but a follower of this group of writers, Cairnes himself lent credence by prefacing his most important treatise[1] with the statement:

> Though the following work is an attempt to recast some considerable portion of Political Economy, I should be sorry if it were regarded as in any sense antagonistic in its attitude toward the science built up by the labors of Adam Smith, Malthus, Ricardo, and Mill.

It would seem, therefore, that an examination of Cairnes's use of the concept of competition would add very little to the view we have already obtained from the classical writings with which I dealt in the last chapter. Though in general method and doctrine he was in agreement with Mill and Ricardo, Cairnes's views on free competition, as we shall see, were nevertheless independent and constructive.[2] At least it is unquestionably true, that with that "capacity for disentangling, and exhibiting, the operation of a principle amid an intricate mass of complex facts which constitutes his greatest intellectual gift" (as L. L. Price refers to Cairnes's in the former's *Short History of Political Economy in England*), Cairnes, by clarification and emphasis, gave to the concept of free competition a distinctness that it had not had before in economic reasoning. Indeed, the degree to which he accomplished this justifies the assertion that his writing was not merely that of exposition and elaboration; his treatises mark a new stage in our understanding of the concept of free competition in social and economic philosophy.

Although Cairnes produced no inclusive, systematic

[1] J. E. Cairnes, *Some Leading Principles of Political Economy Newly Expounded* (New York: Harper, 1874).

[2] J. M. Keynes has said, "Cairnes will always be remembered as at once one of Mill's most distinguished disciples, and one of his most vigorous critics." (Palgrave's *Dictionary of Political Economy*, I, 203.) Sidgwick also stated that Cairnes's *Leading Principles of Political Economy* "contributed to impair the unique prestige which Mill's exposition had enjoyed for nearly half a century." (*Principles of Political Economy*, p. 5.)

economic treatise, his writing falls into two rather distinct departments of economic inquiry. These are, first, economic method, and, second, economic doctrine.[3] Section 2 of this chapter will be devoted to the former and Section 3 to the latter.

2

In Cairnes's *The Character and Logical Method of Political Economy*[4] he is concerned with political economy as a science and not with the propounding of maxims of social control. He was probably the first to *sharply* separate the science and the art of economics. He emphatically disagreed with the many people who held the view that a social science is one which deals with social facts, and everything is "Political Economy" which is in anyway connected with the production, distribution, or consumption of wealth. He says:

> Now I am anxious here to insist upon this fundamental point: whatever takes the form of a plan aiming at definite practical ends . . .

[3] It may, indeed, be more accurate to add a third, namely, the application of economic theory to the interpretation of contemporary economic and political phenomena. Cairnes has said, in the preface of his *Essays in Political Economy—Theoretical and Applied*, "The following Essays . . . consist in part of attempts to apply the principles of economic science . . . to the solution of actual problems." Inasmuch, however, as his *Leading Principles* is essentially a commentary on certain existing economic views, it has been necessary, in order to present Cairnes's economic doctrine with more completeness, to draw upon his *Essays* and to regard them as, more or less, a component part of his economic theory.

The foregoing is important to bear in mind because what seem to be inconsistencies in Cairnes's economic theory (when his *Leading Principles* and *Essays* are both taken as expressing his economic theory or doctrine) are in part, at least, explained if one understands that Cairnes did not regard that which dealt with practical ends as economic science (see Sec. 2 of this chapter). While using his *Essays* to present his economic doctrine, one must remember, then, that these essays are primarily intended to express his opinion on political questions in which Cairnes had an active interest and a guiding influence.

[4] 1st ed., 1857; 2nd ed., 1875. All of my references will be to the second edition.

it matters not what the proposal be, whether wide or narrow in its scope, severely judicious or wildly imprudent . . . it has none of the characteristics of a science, and has no just claim to the name.[5]

In treating the logic of political economy, Cairnes employs free competition (or "perfect liberty of action") as a postulate of science; in no sense are his remarks concerning competition (or any of his other assumptions) to be understood as precepts. He proposes to do for Political Economy—that is, for the phenomena of wealth—"what astronomy does for the phenomena of the heavenly bodies." The "constant relations" in economic phenomena and not the pronouncements of judgment "on the worthiness of ends" are those with which political economy as a social science is concerned; it has nothing more to do with laissez faire than it has with communism.[6]

Cairnes, unlike his predecessors, stated clearly the limitations of the assumption of free competition in his economic reasoning. That economic principles, concerned with the phenomena of wealth, did not encompass all phenomena of social life he pointed out by saying that most practical problems present political, moral, educational, artistic aspects as well as economic and the former may be more weighty.[7] It was a "complete mistake" to suppose

[5] *The Character and Logical Method of Political Economy* (2nd ed.; London: Macmillan, 1875), p. 17.

[6] *Ibid.*, pp. 18 ff. Cairnes does say that political economy contributes "*data* toward formation of a sound opinion" regarding ends.

[7] *Ibid.*, p. 21. He emphasizes the same fact again in his essay on "Political Economy and Laissez-Faire." This is found in his *Essays in Political Economy: Theoretical and Applied* (London: Macmillan, 1873). He holds, in this excellent essay, that the maxim of laissez faire "has no scientific basis whatever but is at best a mere handy rule of practice. . . ." The doctrine of laissez faire, he states, involves two assumptions. These are, first, that the interests of human beings are fundamentally the same and that individuals know their interests in the sense that they are coincident with the interest of others, and second, in the absence of coercion they will follow them. Cairnes, while agreeing to the first assumption and granting

"that because Political Economy comprises in its expositions theories of wages, profits, and rent, the science is *therefore* committed to the approval of our present mode of industrial life."

Furthermore Cairnes was explicit that the use of the concept of competition, necessary in determining the laws of economics, was not intended to convey the meaning that competition did in fact govern, equally and everywhere, human relations. He contends that the economist begins with a knowledge of certain principles of social life which are of such dominant character that they may be used as data in determining economic laws. These principles, or data, are: first, "the general desire for physical well-being, and for wealth as the means of obtaining it"; second, the "intellectual power of judging of the efficacy of means to an end, along with the inclination to reach our ends by the easiest and shortest means"; third, the laws of population; and fourth, the physical qualities of the soil. That these were implied assumptions common to the reasoning of the earlier classical economists is well known. In classical writings, however, there is some difference of opinion as to the degree these assumptions express actual conditions and therefore the extent to which economic doctrine needs limitation.[8] It is true that Mill had said:

> In political economy, for instance, empirical laws of human nature are tacitly assumed by English thinkers, which are calculated only for Great Britain and the United States. Among other things, an intensity of competition is constantly supposed, which, as a general mercantile fact, exists in no country in the world except these two.[9]

---

that *human* interests are one, denies—in light of passion, custom, class interest, etc.—that individuals will follow the human interests.

[8] Cf. J. M. Keynes, *Scope and Method of Political Economy*, p. 15 n.

[9] *System of Logic* (New Impression; London: Longmans, 1925), Bk.

It was Cairnes, however, who stated in his lucid manner that there were many subordinate influences which not only would disturb but, in fact, would occasionally *reverse* the operation of the fourfold principles or data which, he said, dominated human relations. His classification of these "subordinate influences" is enlightening as to the extent that "perfect liberty of action," or free competition, is restricted. These subordinate influences are: first, the political and social institutions of a country; second, discoveries in the arts of production; third, motives and principles of action, for example, custom; and fourth, moral and religious considerations.[10]

What proof have we that "perfect liberty of action" does not exist? Cairnes's answer is that profits and wages do not stand according to the actual sacrifices undergone. Not only, he contends, do profits and wages differ in different countries, but inequality "we find also in a less degree in the different departments of productive industry in the same country." Love of country in the former case; ignorance, poverty, and prejudice in the latter are the explanations.[11]

We see then that although Cairnes began with the assertion that an economist possesses the knowledge of the fourfold principles or data which govern economic phenomena, still the knowledge of such "ultimate causes" does not preclude the need of considering the "subordinate influences" which are indicated above. In fact, Cairnes stated that when the latter are sufficiently understood they should be included among the fundamental data or prem-

---

VI, Chap. IX, p. 591. The reader is also reminded of what has been said regarding Mill's reasoning in Sec. 6, Chap. III, above.

[10] *Character and Logical Method of Political Economy*, pp. 43-44.

[11] *Ibid.*, p. 49.

ises. There is constant need of modifying our classifications and definitions with the advance of knowledge of our science "in order to bring them into correspondence with the larger views and more exact ideas which this advance involves."[12] One might say, it seems to me, that free competition, and other terms, are but scaffolding, and as the structure (which the scaffolding has served effectively for some time) expands the scaffolding must be reconstructed.

This gives us Cairnes's view regarding the concept of competition as it applies in the logic of political economy. In the next section we shall consider the use to which this concept is put in his second department of economic inquiry—that of an examination of economic principles.

3

Cairnes did not set before himself the task of writing an exhaustive treatise on the principles of political economy. He attempted rather to criticize and recast "those intermediate principles by means of which the detailed results are connected with the higher causes which produce them."[13] It was in criticizing and in setting forth the limitations and exceptions of the doctrines of preceding writers that Cairnes made his contribution. Inasmuch as his *Leading Principles* is a critical commentary rather than a systematic treatise on economic theory, the organization of Cairnes's book does not take the conventional form of production, exchange, and distribution.[14] Nevertheless,

[12] *Ibid.*, p. 135.

[13] *Leading Principles*, p. 1.

[14] He divides the material of his book about equally into three parts. These are Part I, Value; Part II, Labor and Capital; Part III, International Trade.

organization and completeness of our treatment will be facilitated if the analysis centers about the usual divisions.

As to production:[15] The factor of production with which Cairnes is chiefly concerned is labor. "Of all ideas within the range of economic speculation," he said, "the two most profoundly opposed to each other are cost and the reward of cost. . . ."[16] Continuing, he states the following proposition:

> . . . nor can it be said that they [wages] stand in any constant relation to that which really constitutes cost to him [the laborer]. If they did, wages in all occupations, in all countries, and in all times, would be in proportion to the severity of the toil which they recompensed; whereas the proportion fails not only in different occupations and in different countries, but whenever a general advance or decline takes place in the conditions of productive industry in the *same occupations* and in the *same countries*.[17]

In proof of this proposition Cairnes referred to the advance in money and real wages which had been going on in England for some years, in most of the occupations.

In considering the theory that cost of production governs value he states, as is well known, that wages are in proportion to sacrifices only so far as competition prevails; laborers and capitalists must have effective choice. What did Cairnes's discussion of competition add to this accepted theory?

As I have already pointed out, Mill called attention in his *Logic* to the fact that English economists were prone to suppose an intensity of competition which held only for

[15] Much of what will be stated in this section as being Cairnes's views on production will necessarily include his views on distribution. His discussion, however, lends itself sufficiently to the organization I shall use so as to make it helpful for our purpose.

[16] *Op. cit.*, p. 49.

[17] *Ibid.*, p. 53. Italics mine.

England and the United States. Mill in his *Principles*—as my preceding chapter has shown—frequently discussed the limitation of competition. Now as to the particular question under discussion—the existence of effective choice (free competition) of laborers—he states:

> . . . there is a natural monopoly in favour of skilled labourers against the unskilled, which makes the difference of reward exceed, sometimes in a manifold proportion, what is sufficient merely to equalize their advantages. If unskilled labourers had it in their power to compete with skilled, by merely taking the trouble of learning the trade, the difference of wages might not exceed what would compensate them for that trouble. . . .[18]

Again:

> . . . there are kinds of labour of which the wages are fixed by custom, and not by competition. Such are the fees or charges of professional persons. . . .[19]

And also:

> . . . the difficulty of passing from one class of employment to a class greatly superior, has hitherto caused the wages of all those classes of labourers who are separated from one another by any marked barrier, to depend more than might be supposed upon the increase of the population of each class considered separately.[20]

Mill further points out the lack of competition in labor and capital in different countries. Although capital is becoming "more cosmopolitan" and there is "much greater similarity of manner and institutions than formerly," with the result that population and capital move more freely, still there are extraordinary differences of wages and profits between different parts of the world.[21]

[18] *Principles* (Ashley edition), pp. 391-392.
[19] *Ibid.*, pp. 403-404.
[20] *Ibid.*, pp. 460-461.
[21] *Ibid.*, p. 575.

Such, briefly, was Mill's views on the subject of competition among laborers. It is given to indicate more clearly the contribution of Cairnes's. His contribution to the concept of competition—as to other aspects of economics—was one of emphasis and explanation which, with his unusual lucidity, became more than a change of emphasis and rather a change of prevailing opinion regarding the subject in hand.

To return to Cairnes's discussion. Does the "indispensable condition to the action of cost of production as the regulator of normal values" (that is, effective choice in selecting occupations) exist? In England, he holds, competition is "active and widely prevalent"; in trade it is universal and unlimited. But still *more,* he insists, is necessary for choice to be effective—for competition to be free. This is:

> Not only must there be for dealers the right and power of selling the commodities where they please, and for the workmen the legal right of admission to whatever occupation each prefers, but there must be for laborers and capitalists respectively, the *practical power* of employing their labor and capital in whatever direction each may please. . . . It matters not what the obstacle may be to the effectiveness of choice, whether *law, ignorance,* or *poverty* . . . competition is defeated.[22]

Here we find a clear recognition of that prerequisite to mobility of the factors of production in order that competition may exist which I have termed, in a foregoing chapter,[23] neutralizing of certain social institutions. Cairnes again emphasizes this type of restriction to competition in his discussion of international trade.[24] The nature of the impediments to free movement of labor (and capital) he

[22] *Leading Principles,* p. 60. Italics mine.
[23] Chap. 2, Sec. 4.
[24] *Op. cit.,* pp. 304 ff.

says is threefold: geographical distance; difference in political institutions; and differences in language, religion, and social custom. It is his opinion that the social and political causes are probably "in the present state of the world, more powerful than the physical," especially when the former is connected with race. He cites sugar cultivation in Queensland as a striking illustration in point. The Chinese and Polynesian laborers do not lower wages generally because of the inability of these races to go to higher types of work, increasing competition there, and thereby lowering and equalizing wages generally. "In Australia," he says, "the obstacle to free competition lies in difference of race. In Great Britain the impediments are of a social and material kind; but the economic effects are identical."

Still one must not overstate the case. To those who contend that the difficulty of transferring labor, in view of the time necessary to acquire industrial skill, defeats effective competition, Cairnes's answer is that every laborer need not at all times be capable of being turned to any selected occupation. In order that remuneration may be in proportion to cost only a small diversion of labor—small "in comparison with the aggregate embarked in any important industry"—will suffice. There is labor in "disposable form" as well as capital. A new generation is coming on which bears the same relation to the general labor force as capital in the form of "purchasing power" bears to general capital.[25]

Despite the fact that there is "disposable labor," as there is disposable capital, an important difference exists, and on this difference Cairnes bases the explanation of his well-known fourfold classification or groups of labor. This difference was that "of capital in disposable form

[25] *Ibid.*, pp. 61-65.

any portion may be applied to any industrial purpose," whereas disposable labor—that is, each individual laborer —"can choose his employment only within well-defined limits"; the choice, for labor, is never coextensive with the whole field of industry. Within certain limits there is *complete* freedom of choice, but beyond that a certain range of *practical* exclusion. Within each of the industrial layers superimposed on one another there is effective competition, but as between them there is practical isolation. Hence we have the phenomenon of non-competing groups. Such was Cairnes's view regarding competition in the field of labor.

It seems to me that Cairnes in developing the doctrine of non-competing groups and emphasizing, as he did, the "practical isolation" of such groups, would find it difficult to harmonize with this view the concept of "general" or "average" wages. He states, in explanation of the latter:

> Though labourers in certain departments of industry are practically cut off from competition with labourers in other departments, the competition of capitalists . . . is effective over the whole field. The communication between the different sections of industrial life, which is not kept open by movements of labor, is effectually maintained by the action of capital. . . . In this way our entire industrial organization becomes a connected system. . . . Not only, therefore, are we justified in generalizing the various facts of wages into a single conception, and in discussing "general" or "average" wages, but we have ground for regarding this general or average rate as constituted of elements bound together by a common connection, and forming parts of an integral whole.[26]

This, in my opinion, is not adequate explanation why one may speak of the existence of non-competing groups and still use the concept of a general wage. It suggests, at least, the need of a fuller explanation of the rigidity of

[26] *Ibid.*, p. 156.

the "practical isolation" of which Cairnes speaks. As will be seen in my next chapter, Marshall's views on the existence of non-competing groups were much more flexible (if he believed that such groups existed), and he held that a general rate of wages does not exist.[27]

What Cairnes has said, it may be contended, merely amounts to his accepting and restating the thought contained in Mill's discussion and epitomized in the passages quoted above. This is true so far as the fundamentals upon which his explanation is based; it is not true so far as elucidating the idea of free competition and its limitations are concerned. The constructive part of Cairnes's discussion was not merely to emphasize that between producers —laborers or capitalists—frequently effective competition did not exist. For producers in different countries Mill had already fully developed this in his treatment "Of International Trade" and "Of International Values"[28]— with its important consequence that rewards were not brought into correspondence with cost. But Mill did not extend that reasoning as it also applies where effective competition does not exist between producers "in the same occupations and in the same countries" (to use Cairnes's words). It is true that Mill had indicated[29] the ineffectiveness of such competition, but he did not develop the point. This restriction of competition Cairnes fully discussed and expounded in his doctrine of non-competing groups. Upon

[27] I do not imply that the concept of an "average" or "general" rate or level of wages is not a useful and valid one in economic reasoning. Considering a longer (rather than shorter) period of time and for certain *general* purposes the concept of the average wages may well be used if one remembers its limitations.

[28] *Principles*, Book 3, Chaps. 17 and 18.

[29] In his *Principles*, Bk. 2, Chap. 14, "Of the Differences of Wages in Different Employments," and Bk. 3, Chap. 4, "The Ultimate Analysis of Cost of Production." We have quoted above (see pp. 92-95) from these chapters the passages pertinent to the discussion of competition.

this reasoning he (Cairnes) applied the principle governing international values—which Mill had formulated and called "the Equation of International Demand"—to exchanges between non-competing groups as Mill had applied to exchanges between nations.

While Cairnes stated the limitations of competition with its consequence of reward disproportionate to cost, he did not see in trade unionism a means by which the competitive relationship could be affected to more than a limited extent. His reasoning regarding the inability of trade unions to increase the competitive strength of the laborers followed necessarily from his views regarding the Wages Fund theory. In brief, this was that wages were paid out of capital and, given the state of industry, the total amount paid in wages necessarily bears a fixed relation to total capital. He also stressed Mill's doctrine of the tendency of profits to a minimum and held that profits were constantly near that minimum. Wages, therefore, were affected not by anything that laborers could do, but upon the forces bringing about the accumulation of capital. Increase of competitive strength of the laborers to be exercised against the employers "would inevitably result in a fall in profits," which, already at a "handbreadth of the minimum," would rebound to the laborers' disadvantage in unemployment.

The conclusion Cairnes arrives at, namely, "the permanent elevation of the rate of wages . . . is . . . a feat beyond its [the trade union's] power," had three clear-cut reservations. These were: first, that it applied only to the "*average* rate of wages"; second, to "the *permanent* state of things"; and third, to a country where the condition was *normal*, as, for example, in Great Britain where the rate of profits was near the minimum.[80] That unions can exercise competitive strength to the advantage of certain trades and in new countries where the profits are above the minimum is granted. In hastening the advance of wages, before competition brings about such advance, is the "perfectly legitimate field for Trades-Union action."

As to the indirect action of trade unions toward restricting the supply of labor, Cairnes held that this action is sound if one means by that the promulgating of public opinion concerning the restriction of population, and unsound as applied to particular trades.

In refuting the indirect action of trade unions based upon the "make work" policy it is interesting to notice that the short-time competitive mechanism is not distinguished, by Cairnes, from the long-time forces. Thornton had said:

> Nothing could be more proper than to insist that no workman should accept a lower wage than would suffice for a man's decent maintenance, if the so sufficing wage could thereby be secured to every one requiring it. But at a *given* time the whole quantity of work to be done is a fixed quantity. . . . Something of this kind frequently occurs under the operation of the rule in question. Trade grows slack, so that the employers can no longer afford to pay the prescribed rate except to the best workmen. . . .[81]

Taking issue with this statement, Cairnes held it led to pernicious results such as opposition to machinery, to division of labor, and to free trade. He asserted that the quantity of work to be done at any given time is *not* a fixed quantity, since the amount of work is limited only by the wants of the people. Taking society as a whole Cairnes is of course right, but this was not what Thornton had in

[80] *Leading Principles*, pp. 218 ff.

[81] W. T. Thornton, *On Labor* (2nd ed.; London: Macmillan, 1870), pp. 334-335. Italics mine.

mind. The latter was referring to the position of individual employers and the competitive conditions which they would have to meet in a contracting market.

Such was Cairnes's use of the concept of competition in his reasoning regarding labor. The clarity with which he discussed the limitations of competition among laborers and the causes for such limitation justifies the contention that economic reasoning of the time was not wholly of an abstract character, unappreciative of the actualities of the economic world.

Much, if not all, of what Cairnes said regarding competition with reference to labor he applied to capital as well. In the social process of production, labor and capital are, of course, interdependent. In the analysis of production the mobility or competitiveness of one cannot be discussed as separate from the other. As Bagehot has said:

> This description of the process by which capital is transferred . . . presupposes the existence of transferable labour. . . . Complete freedom of capital presupposes complete freedom of labour, and can only be attained when and where this exists.[82]

There is, however, in Cairnes's use of the concept of competition, with respect to capital, only a difference in emphasis, but where he employs competition in the sense of a maxim there is also a difference in opinion from that of the preceding economic thought.

The basis upon which he grounds his views is expressed in the proposition which Cairnes held in common with Mill:

> That the amount of wealth in a country being given, the proportion of this wealth which shall be invested in industrial operations with a view to profits will depend, first, upon the strength of those qualities

[82] Walter Bagehot, *Economic Studies* (London: Longmans, 1880), pp. 54-55.

in the average character of its inhabitants which lead to productive investment—what Mr. Mill calls "the effective desire of accumulation"; and, secondly, on the opportunities of industrial investment open to the community offering a rate of profit sufficient to call this principle into activity—in a word, on "the extent of the field for investment."[33]

To the foregoing must be added the stress which Cairnes gives to Mill's doctrine of the tendency of profits to a minimum and the latter's view that in a country of economic development such as England the accumulation of capital is constantly in excess of the amount which can be invested in the country at the minimum rate of profit.[34]

The explanation of the "active and widely prevalent" competition of capital in England is presumably found in the strength of the effective desire of accumulation and the institutions of legal freedom, intelligence, and competence. The proof of the competitiveness of capital in the various industries is seen, he says, in the constant movement of capital abroad for foreign investment—"a destination it would scarcely receive while there was a prospect of reaping exceptionally high returns from investment within the country."[35]

In denying the contention of the "school of reasoners" who hold that since building, plant, and material required for one kind of manufacture can be altered only at great expense for use in another, that therefore competition has no real existence, he quotes Bagehot's views as expressed in the latter's *Lombard Street.* Bagehot asserts here that "English capital runs as surely and instantly where it is most wanted, and where there is most to be made of it, as water runs to find its level"; a phenomenon made pos-

[33] Cairnes, *Leading Principles,* p. 169.
[34] *Ibid.,* pp. 217-218.
[35] *Ibid.,* p. 64.

sible by means of the credit mechanism with its brokerage houses and banks. As with labor, so with capital, the "disposable" portion is sufficient to give effect to this competitiveness of capital, is Cairnes's view. Uncommitted capital—money or other purchasing power—seeks the best investments rapidly.[36] Unlike laborers in certain departments of industry who are deprived from competing with laborers in other departments, the competition of capitalists is effective over the whole field.[37]

In view of his stress on the mobility or competitiveness of capital it is somewhat strange that he offers no explanation for the two exceptions he calls to the reader's attention. "The sluggish action of competition" is due, he states, to "the excessive amount of capital which from one cause or another, has found its way into the business of mere distribution."[38] And the other instance where a difference in the degree of competition is suggested is in his statement to the effect that in newly settled communities industrial competition is more general. This is manifested by the range of price in a new country being less than in an old.[39]

In the foregoing, Cairnes's use of the concept of competition has been primarily that of a necessary tool of analysis; in the discussion of capital giving rise to international trade the analysis of the competitive process is employed to draw conclusions as to the desirability of social action. Calling attention to Mill's approval of the infant industry argument in support of protection Cairnes dissents—even considering the limitations which the for-

[36] *Ibid.*, p. 63.
[37] *Ibid.*, p. 156.
[38] *Ibid.*, p. 115. One might say, parenthetically, that the study of marketing practice in recent years has revealed very clearly the explanation.
[39] *Ibid.*, p. 118.

mer makes. Since, says Cairnes, protection does not develop the necessary industrial virtues making for independence "it is not easy to see how its adoption could under any circumstances forward the object in view."[40] The conclusion he reaches is that protection does not call into existence a single branch of production which would not equally have existed under free trade; it merely alters the proportions in which such industries are carried on.

It is surprising that before stating this conclusion Cairnes does not consider the length of time to which his reasoning applies, or again, the existence of possible protectionist policies on the part of other nations as being factors of importance. Furthermore, he himself has asserted (as I have shown in Section 2 of this chapter) that on the relative importance of the conflicting considerations—political, moral, educational, artistic, and economic—"political economy offers no opinion." Cairnes does not heed his own dictum. Here his economic reasoning is used as a basis to infer, if not to express, the impropriety of social control without recognizing the need of modification to which the other social sciences might point. The soundness of the economic reasoning may be unquestioned regarding free international trade and still the *practical policy* of freedom may conceivably be unsound.[41]

We now turn to the third factor of production—land—and the place that the concept of competition plays in the economic reasoning of Cairnes, concerning it.[42] He calls

[40] *Ibid.*, pp. 402 ff.

[41] Cf. Bernard Moses, "Certain Tendencies in Political Economy," *Quarterly Journal of Economics*, XI (1897), 372-387. The article is an interesting discussion of the fact that economic laws are always applied conditional to political and ethical principles.

[42] What he has to say on the subject appeared as an article entitled "Political Economy and Land" in the *Fortnightly Review* for January, 1870, reprinted in his *Essays in Political Economy: Theoretical and Applied* (London: Macmillan, 1873). My references will be to the latter.

attention to the fact that Political Economy has been identified with no intervention—a view added to by the free-trade controversy. Regarding land, Cairnes makes this interesting assertion:

> . . . not merely does economic science, as expounded by its ablest teachers, dispose of a priori objections to a policy of intervention with regard to land, it even furnishes principles fitted to inform and guide such a policy in a positive sense.[43]

Movable property, which can be produced in indefinite quantities, differs from land, which no man has made and which exists in limited quantities. The right of private property does not apply equally to both. The property right has been granted because it results in a greater quantity of wealth being produced, and while this applies to all products of human industry it does not apply to a commodity which "no man has made."[44] Cairnes adds, however, that where qualities have been given to the land by man, this value rests economically on the same property basis as corn or houses. This reasoning, he holds, refutes the objection to legislative action concerning land.

To what extent then shall the play of competitive forces be permitted to act? Only to the extent that cultivators pay to landlords no more than economic rent. The influence said to bring this about is the competition with agriculture of other modes of investing capital. But, says Cairnes, "this argument supposes a state of things which exists in but *few* countries in the world, if indeed it exists, or *ever can exist in any*."[45] For this assumes, he contends, a variety of occupations to which farmers can turn their capital.

[43] *Essays in Political Economy*, p. 189.
[44] *Ibid.*, pp. 190-191.
[45] *Ibid.*, p. 199. Italics mine.

Such a condition does not hold even for England and Scotland.

Cairnes emphatically denies that "free competition" in the use of land can be economically sound.[46] What has happened in Asia, Ireland, and Flanders is the inevitable result where land "is given up to be dealt with on commercial principles unqualified by public opinion, custom, or law." He states that it is the obligation of the government to say what is a "fair rent." The methods to be used may include compulsory leases, recognition and extension of tenant-right, simple fixity of tenure, arbitration courts, the opinion of official experts, etc. His conclusion is unqualified: "The regulation of rent is thus of the very essence of the case; it is felt to be so by all who have really grasped the problem. . . ."[47]

As to exchange: In this department of economic reasoning Cairnes's discussion again added clarity to the nature and limitations of competition. In the play of competition, he indicates that the wholesale markets present an important contrast to the retail markets. His statement regarding the former reads:

> Buyers and sellers in the same town or district, having mostly the same opportunities of information, will not in general differ very widely in their estimates of demand and supply.[48]

In contrast to this:

> In retail dealing it is otherwise. In each place of sale there is but one seller; and though it is possible to compare his terms with the prices demanded elsewhere by others, this cannot always be done on the moment, and may involve much inconvenience and delay. . . .

[46] *Ibid.*, pp. 201 ff.
[47] *Ibid.*, p. 203.
[48] *Leading Principles*, pp. 106-107.

This shows that competition is not inoperative in retail trade, but it shows also the sort of friction under which it works.[49]

Mill had, of course, alluded to this contrast but only with passing comment. For he said:

I must give warning, once for all, that the cases I contemplate are those in which values and prices are determined by competition alone. . . . The values and prices, therefore, to which our conclusions apply, are mercantile values and prices; such prices as are quoted in price-currents; prices in the wholesale markets, in which buying as well as selling is a matter of business. . . .[50]

Mill observed that ignorance, carelessness, indolence, and other causes make retail prices less regular, but his interest was in exchanges where competition was assumed to be free ("supposing all parties to take care of their own interest"—as he puts it) for here only can there be assignable law.

Cairnes's discussion of the difference between competition in retail and wholesale markets adds further explanation to Mill's observation. Retail dealing, says Cairnes, "rests upon a *moral* basis rather than upon an *economic* basis." The lack of competition resulting in the variations in prices in different localities "is not a satisfactory state of things." That "fluctuations" in price—as contrasted to "variety"—are less in the retail market than in the wholesale he calls attention to, and asserts that "moral" factors account for this.[51]

As to distribution: What Cairnes has to say regarding this phase of economic reasoning is confined to wages and rent. The effect of competition in determining each of these brings about different results. As concerns wages,

[49] *Ibid.*, pp. 112-113.
[50] *Principles*, p. 440.
[51] *Leading Principles*, p. 114.

where competition is really free, then remuneration would be according to work done and also to sacrifice endured. That competition cannot be free, Cairnes—as we have seen—proved in his doctrine of non-competing groups of laborers.

Since competition cannot bring about a just distribution, and also since the laborers' lot is growing relatively poorer, Cairnes's solution was that the laborer should be "in one way or another lifted out of the groove in which he at present works, and placed in a position compatible with his becoming a sharer in equal proportion with others in the general advantages arising from industrial progress."[52] This conclusion he arrived at through the view that in the constant growth of national capital there is "a nearly constant decline in the proportion of this capital which goes to support productive labor."[53]

To what degree should the competitive process be controlled? Emphatically denying socialistic control, Cairnes would have, first, habits of saving created and, next, intelligence and moral qualities developed. The end to which this may lead—it is the "sole path" by which laborers may emerge—is coöperation, a means by which they may share in profits as well as wages.[54] The faith of Cairnes (and Mill) in coöperation clearly indicated a lack of ap-

[52] *Ibid.*, p. 285.

[53] *Ibid.*, p. 176.

[54] *Ibid.*, pp. 287 ff. Emphasized in his essays "Coöperation in the State Quarries of North Wales," *Essays in Political Economy*, Essay V. It was not, however, in coöperation as such that Cairnes found the cause for improvement. "The explanation," he says, ". . . is to be found in the slower movements of population in the Welsh districts" (p. 177).

Malthusianism again was sufficient explanation of the deplorable condition of Ireland, regardless of Mill's opinion that the country had suffered from misgovernment. "Education and intercourse are in the last resort the only effectual safeguards against the evil of excessive numbers." (J. E. Cairnes, *Political Essays* [London: Macmillan, 1873], p. 136.)

preciation of the function of the entrepreneur in production.

Concerning rent, free competition in the use of land was unsound, and regulatory action by the state was necessary. Cairnes's reasons for holding these views have been stated in connection with my analysis of his use of the concept of competition in production.

4

To sum up: The writing of Cairnes falls into two fields of economic inquiry—that of method and of doctrine.

In regard to the former, he was probably the first to separate sharply the science of economics from that of its application. Whatever validity there might be, before Cairnes's writing, in the charge that Political Economy and the doctrine of laissez faire were one, certainly this ceased with his writings. Free competition as a postulate was not in any sense to be understood that it was used as a maxim nor even that it expressed what was necessarily and fully true of economic actualities.

The dominant principles of social life, tacitly or expressly used by Cairnes's predecessors, were clarified by him in his emphasis upon the fact that subordinate influences might, indeed, become dominant. Free competition, therefore, was never unrestricted; against "perfect liberty of action" must be reckoned such forces as institutions, discoveries, and motives.

With respect to the use of the concept of free competition in economic doctrine, Cairnes's contribution was that of enunciating the limitations of the concept as used by his predecessors. In the field of production he set forth clearly the lack of competition in the relations of laborers. This doctrine of non-competing groups was an extension of the suggestions given by Mill, but for the purpose of my analysis of competition Cairnes's discussion was also interesting in his recognition of the need of neutralizing certain social institutions if competition is to prevail.

In his discussion of capital, he emphasized that the disposable portion—purchasing power—gave to capital its competitiveness. Although capital—unlike labor—is competitive over the whole field he offers no explanation of the restricted competition in the field of distribution (marketing) nor in newly settled countries.

In the analysis of international trade, the discussion of the competitive process is used to draw conclusions in favor of free trade without recognizing the need of considering non-economic forces, which Cairnes himself has regarded as important.

As to the use of land, "commercial principles" (competition) cannot apply.

The limitations of competition in the field of exchange were more clearly stated in Cairnes's contrast of wholesale and retail markets. In the latter the dealings were to be explained on moral rather than economic grounds.

As to distribution, wages and rent are considered by Cairnes. The impossibility of free competition leads, in the former, to the suggestion of coöperation as a corrective. Regarding rent, political economy pointed definitely to state regulation.

It is sometimes contended that the optimism associated with the philosophy of natural order, or natural liberty, of Smith led necessarily to an attitude of social fatalism or individual liberty in economic relations. This my analysis of the earlier classical writers has disproved. As for

Cairnes, he was explicit in his statement that free competition used as a postulate did not fit actual conditions. Nor was free competition to be used as a maxim, which his discussion of land and rent, for example, fully emphasized.

V

MARSHALL: ECONOMIC FREEDOM AND THE PRINCIPLE OF SUBSTITUTION

I

IN TURNING to the examination of the concept of competition in Marshall's reasoning it is significant to note that we pass from economics as the science of wealth—as Mill and Cairnes put it—to economics as "a study of mankind in the ordinary business of life." The latter is, indeed, a broadened scope of inquiry.[1] It is, says Marshall, "on the one side a study of wealth; and on the other, and *more important* side, a part of the study of man."

The play of competitive forces more directly concerned with economic phenomena is not to be separated from the whole social life of which the economic phenomena are but a part. Marshall has expressed this in his statement that

> There is thus no hard and sharp line of division between those social laws which are, and those which are not, to be regarded also as economic laws. For there is a *continuous* gradation from social laws con-

[1] Veblen has put it, "The science [Economics] comes to be characterized not by the delimitation of a range of facts, as in Cairnes, but as an inquiry into the bearing which *all* have upon men's economic activity." (*The Place of Science in Modern Civilisation*, New York: Huebsch, 1919, p. 172).

cerned almost exclusively with motives that can be measured by price, to social laws in which such motives have little place. . . .[2]

This view of interdependence of social relations and unity of economic phenomena is more specifically expressed in two of his principles. These principles, in my opinion, furnish not only the thread to Marshall's economic reasoning in general, but also to his discussion of the nature and operation of competition in particular.

The first of these two principles is the Principle of Continuity.[3] This important principle carries with it the following significant propositions. First, there is no sharp line of division between conduct and motives which are normal and economic from those that are ethical and altruistic. Second, there is no sharp line dividing long-time economic problems from short-time economic problems. The element of time, "which is the centre of the chief difficulty of almost every economic problem, is itself absolutely continuous . . . and what is a short period for one problem, is a long period for another."[4] And, third, there is no sharp line dividing production, exchange, and distribution. "The theories of the values of labour, and of the things made by it, cannot be separated."[5] Differences, such as they are, are of degree, not of kind.

Continuity, equilibrium—of demand and supply—"is a Fundamental Idea running through the frames of all the various parts of the central problem of Distribution and Exchange." And the counterpart of this principle or idea is found in Marshall's principle of substitution. This is the second principle, to which reference was made as furnish-

[2] *Principles of Economics* (8th ed.; London: Macmillan, 1920), p. 33. Italics mine. All references are to this edition.

[3] *Ibid.*, Preface, pp. vi ff.

[4] *Ibid.*, Preface, p. vii.

[5] *Ibid.*, Preface, p. viii.

ing the thread of economic reasoning in general, and of his discussion of competition in particular.

The principle of substitution provides the explanation of the process by which equilibrium is brought about. And, for the purpose of elucidating Marshall's use of the concept of competition it is particularly important to remember that the form which competition takes is the process of substitution. Furthermore, competition, or the process of substitution, is all-pervasive, applying to alternative objects of consumption and also to alternative factors of production.[6] Marshall observes:

> The production of everything, whether an agent of *production* or a commodity ready for immediate *consumption*, is carried forward up to that limit or margin at which there is equilibrium between the forces of demand and supply. The amount of the thing and its price, the amounts of the several factors or agents of production used in making it, and their prices—all these elements mutually govern one another. . . .[7]

And again he states:

> . . . we may call to mind the *double* relation in which the *various* agents of production stand to one another. On the one hand they are often *rivals* for employment; any one that is more efficient than another in proportion to its cost tending to be substituted for it, and thus limiting the demand for the other. And on the other hand they all constitute the *field* of employment for each other. . . .[8]

This chapter purposes to examine the operation, the limitations, the desirability of this process of competition or substitution, as Marshall sees it. But first as to what he

[6] Cf. *Memorials of Alfred Marshall*, p. 42.

[7] *Principles*, p. 526. Italics mine.

[8] *Ibid.*, p. 665. Italics mine. Cf. also, for example, pp. 341, 355, and 404. This, of course, makes the laws of value, supply, and demand the focus—the guiding and controlling element—equally in production and in distribution.

regards the general nature of this competitive process to be.

2

"The strict meaning of competition," says Marshall, "seems to be the racing of one person against another, with special reference to bidding for the sale or purchase of anything."[9] Although such racing is undoubtedly more intense than it was formerly, it is not the fundamental characteristic of modern industrial life. Not only is such racing secondary but, in fact, "an accidental consequence from the fundamental characteristics of modern industrial life." Rather, the characteristics of present-day life are self-reliance, independence, deliberate choice, and forethought. These are the connotations of terms like Economic Freedom and Free Enterprise.[10]

But it is to be understood that in characterizing the present order as Marshall does and designating it as Economic Freedom, he does not wish the terms to imply any moral or desirable qualities. Competition—substitution—"tends to make those methods of organization prevail which are best fitted to *thrive in* their environment; but not necessarily those best fitted to *benefit* their environment."[11] The organization which offers the lowest price and hence displaces others need not give those desirable indirect and ultimate services which many businesses could give if they could only have obtained a fair start.

From this point of view, in Marshall's opinion, cer-

[9] *Ibid.*, p. 5.

[10] *Ibid.*, p. 10. The reader's attention is called to the fact that although Marshall stresses the distinctions he makes between "competition" and "economic freedom" he uses the terms "competition," "economic freedom," "free enterprise," and "substitution" as synonymous.

[11] *Ibid.*, pp. 596-597. Italics his.

tainly more desirable is a coöperative order rather than one of economic freedom or competition, for he says,

> If competition is contrasted with energetic coöperation in unselfish work for the public good, then even the *best* forms of competition are relatively evil; while its harsher and meaner forms are hateful. And in a world in which all men were *perfectly virtuous*, competition would be out of place. . . .[12]

The competitive order is not, therefore, the ideal order. It is because human qualities are what they *now* are that there is good in the results of competition. In a letter to Bishop Auckland, Marshall makes clear that the Christian Socialists, failing to see this, have done harm in their attacks upon the competitive order. He said:

> . . . I would submit that very much more harm is being done in the present age by uncertainties as to the meaning of "competition." It has base forms. . . . But what you say with reference to some kinds of competition which are unwholesome is apt, I think, to be exploited for selfish purposes with reference to other kinds of competition. When a man exerts himself to arrest or diminish competition, his motive may be the public good: but as a matter of fact it very seldom is. In at least nineteen cases out of twenty his motive is to prevent his being at a disadvantage in spite of his being less energetic as a worker, less ready to throw away obsolete machinery, etc., as a capitalist, than those whose competition he finds disagreeable.[13]

Nor is the competitive régime necessarily to be regarded as the most effective organization of production. Speaking of the process of substitution brought about by the competition of entrepreneurs, Marshall says,

> . . . it works blindly, or rather wastefully; it forces many to succumb who might have done excellent work if they had been favoured at first: and, in conjunction with the tendency to increasing return it

[12] *Ibid.*, pp. 8-9. Italics mine.
[13] *Memorials*, p. 392.

strengthens those who are strong, and hands over the business of the weak to those who have already obtained a partial monopoly.[14]

Coming to a point upon which many present-day writers are confused, Marshall states that the nature of our order of "economic freedom," with its characteristics of deliberateness and self-reliance, does not preclude elements of both coöperation and government control. In Marshall's view, the extension of these is in entire accord with an order of "economic freedom." He did not believe that "competition" and "monopoly" are classifications which cover the whole field of industry and trade. The joint performance of special tasks, such as are performed by trade and manufacturers' associations, and, indeed, the "constructive part of the work of German cartels" (for that can be separated from efforts directed toward monopolistic ends)—such "associated efforts need not encroach on the freedom of each business to manage its own affairs in its own way."[15] Marshall grants that coöperation of this kind cannot be harmonized with that "aggressive competition" of the first half of the last century.[16] He says,

> And some prominent writers have disparaged the spirit of economic freedom by the assumption that it involves that old bitter contentiousness. But, in fact, there is no necessary connection between the two.[17]

As to the place of government in a competitive order another point of distinction exists between the usual interpretation given to the term "free competition" and Mar-

[14] *Principles*, p. 663.

[15] *Industry and Trade* (3rd ed.; London: Macmillan, 1920), pp. 178-179.

[16] This he would not need to grant, for elsewhere in speaking of the contrast between monopolistic and competitive conditions he holds that such a contrast "is open to misconception. For . . . the fiercest and cruelest forms of competition are found in markets which are no longer quite free, but have been already brought in some measure under monopolistic control." (*Ibid.*, p. 394.)

[17] *Ibid.*, p. 179.

shall's "economic freedom" or "free enterprise." The latter provides for an ever widening range of governmental activities. Increased honesty and integrity of government administration

> . . . have coöperated with technical progress to enlarge the scope for the beneficial intervention of government since Mill's death even more than during his long life. Government has now many new, large, and subtle resources for finding out where it can do more harm than good. . . . Thus we can now safely venture on many public undertakings which a little while ago would have been technically unworkable, or which would have probably been perverted to the selfish and corrupt purposes of those who had the ear of Government. But on the other hand, this very enlargement opens out so many and so arduous new public duties that no Government, not even the German, can nearly catch up the work that is specially its own. Thus a new emphasis is given to the watchword, Laissez faire:—Let everyone work with all his might; and most of all let the Government arouse itself to do that work which is vital, and which none but Government can do efficiently.[18]

Government intervention is, therefore, in accord with, not,

[18] Alfred Marshall, "The Social Possibilities of Economic Chivalry," *Economic Journal*, XVII (1907), p. 19.

While this is an interesting and significant discussion of the soundness of extended government activity, and a discussion that one might readily agree to, Marshall omits what to me seems to be the important issue. What are the *criteria* in determining when "beneficial interference of government" may occur and also "for finding out where it can do more harm than good"? It would seem that many activities, which, in the *past*, if they were to be accomplished, had to be performed by the government, can *today* be undertaken by individual enterprise through the aid of the legal entity with perpetual existence, that is, the corporation. I have in mind, for example, reforestation and reclamation. Because of the great length of time before remuneration can occur it is contended by some economists that private enterprise is inadequate. While this may be true, it seems to me that *if the economic need* exists for (say) reclamation, the flexible, perpetual device, which the corporation increasingly provides should be adequate. The government is no more endowed with vision as to the economic needs of the future (which do not exist now) than individual owners of a corporation.

The criteria for determining when "beneficial interference of government" may occur should, *first*, be determined.

as many writers have held, contrary to the order of economic freedom.

One point remains to be considered in our examination of Marshall's view as to the general nature of present-day competition. To what extent, and by what forces, is the order of economic freedom—as manifested by the operation of the principle of substitution—mitigated? The process of substitution, Marshall emphasizes, does not assume that competition is perfect, for the latter requires a complete knowledge of the state of the market.[19] While this may apply to business in Lombard Street, it does not hold for labor and capital in general. When he uses the concept of competition, free enterprise, or substitution, he attributes to people the ability, forethought, and motives which well-informed persons, considering the general conditions of time and place, may be expected to have. "Wayward and impulsive action, sordid and noble motives mingle their threads together."

Numerous as are the counteracting influences, competition, substitution, economic freedom, remain the dominant forces. Speaking of substitution, Marshall points out:

> It may be restricted by custom or law, by professional etiquette or trade-union regulation: it may be weakened by want of enterprise, or it may be softened by a generous unwillingness to part with old associates. But it *never* ceases to act, and it *permeates all* the economic adjustments of the modern world.[20]

[19] *Principles*, pp. 540-541.

[20] *Ibid.*, p. 405. Italics mine.

It is well to emphasize that although competition is *a* dominant force it is not the *only* dominant force, a fact to which Marshall's discussion clearly points. He specifically warns against understanding "normal" as that which the undisturbed play of competition would bring about. This is "undeniable from an abstract as well as from a practical point of view" because the term normal "has often to be applied to conditions in which perfectly free competition does *not* exist, and can hardly even be *supposed* to exist; and even where free competition is most dominant, the normal

This, then, is the nature of Marshall's concept of competition, or rather, of economic freedom. Self-reliance, independence, deliberate choice, forethought in everyday life; growing expansion of associative and governmental activities; economic freedom and substitution counteracted by numerous and diverse non-economic forces—these are the component elements of present-day competition.

3

We now turn our attention to the place which the concept of competition—or economic freedom—takes in Marshall's reasoning regarding the factors of production. In what sense and to what degree does competition influence each of these factors? In other words, does each factor lend itself in the same manner to what Marshall has termed the "Fundamental Idea," that is, the equilibrium of demand and supply?

The general answer to this question—and the central thesis of Marshall's reasoning—is to be found in his statement:

> . . . the incomes which are being earned by *all* agents of production, *human* as well as *material*, and those which appear likely to be earned by them in the future, exercise a ceaseless influence on those persons by whose action the future supplies of these agents are determined. There is a *constant tendency* toward a position of normal equilibrium, in which the supply of each of three agents shall stand in such a relation to the demand for its services, as to give to those who have provided the supply a sufficient reward for their efforts and sacrifices.[21]

As to labor: For the problem in hand—the competitive-

conditions of every fact and tendency will include *vital* elements that are not a part of competition nor even akin to it." (*Principles*, p. 35. Cf. a letter by Marshall to Clark, *Memorials*, p. 414.)

[21] *Ibid.*, pp. 576-577. Italics mine.

ness of labor, the degree of rapidity and constancy in the response of labor to differences in income in different occupations and places, is the important question. Does the "ceaseless influence" of changes of income, referred to by Marshall in the foregoing passage, operate *quickly*, *regularly*, and *effectively* or slowly and sluggishly? If the former—a quick and effective response of labor to the "ceaseless influence" of income—is true then labor may be said to be competitive, free, and mobile. To this, Marshall gives an uncertain answer.

Of fundamental importance to this discussion are certain peculiarities of labor which "affect not merely the form, but also the substance of the action of the forces of demand and supply; and to *some* extent they limit and hamper the free action of those forces."[22] The particular significance of these peculiarities, with regard to the problem of the mobility or competitiveness of labor, is the fact that the influences of some of these peculiarities are *cumulative* in their effect, and the longer they persist the greater they retard mobility.

It is important to note that two of these peculiarities are held to have consequences the evil (that is, the hindering of the adjustment of supply to demand, or in other words, obstructing free action of competition) of which is non-cumulative;[23] one has consequences which are cumulative;[24] of another the results are either non-cumulative or cumulative according to whether one has in mind higher or lower ranks of society;[25] and, finally, the consequences

[22] *Ibid.*, p. 559. Italics mine.

[23] That the seller of labor must deliver it (the product—labor) himself and, the other, that labor power is perishable, that is, the time lost cannot be recovered.

[24] That the laborer is at a disadvantage in bargaining, which, however, does not apply to certain classes of labor.

[25] That the worker sells his work but retains property in himself, the

of the fifth peculiarity manifest themselves primarily through accentuating or ameliorating the other peculiarities.[26]

What the *net* effect of these peculiarities of labor is upon its mobility Marshall does not indicate. He reaches no general conclusion as to the competitiveness of labor and the "constant tendency towards a position of normal equilibrium," of which he speaks. These obviously apply with varying degree to different types of labor.

Mobility or competitiveness of labor is of a twofold nature, namely, "vertical" and "horizontal." By the former I mean a competition of those laborers in lower grades with those in higher grades of work; by the latter is meant, of course, competition of workers in one trade with those of another trade within the same general field. Regarding vertical competition, Marshall's discussion, it would seem to me, can only be understood in light of his important Principle of Continuity, discussed in the first section of this chapter. A significant proposition of this principle is that there is no sharp dividing line between long- and short-time economic problems "and what is a short period for one problem is a long period for another." This applies to the point in hand. One cannot generalize regarding the rate of vertical mobility. Marshall's view, in my opinion, is that vertical competition varies according to the circumstances, place, and time under consideration. As to the first, for example the broadened vision of parents —the consequence of general, public education—would be an important factor in increasing upward mobility due to

important consequence of which is that those who bear the expense of producing this product (labor) receive very little of the selling price this product commands.

[26] The length of time needed for training. (For Marshall's discussion of the above-mentioned peculiarities see his *Principles*, pp. 558-576.)

training given to children of such parents; as to the second (that of place), a new community with relative scarcity of labor presents an environment conducive to vertical mobility; and, as to the third (time), "an event," says Marshall, "as the American war, will raise from the lower ranks of labour many men who bear themselves well in difficult and responsible posts." It is clear that where circumstances, place, and time are all favorable, the vertical mobility must be rapid and constant; where one of these important factors counteracts another such mobility may be slow to the point of bringing about the existence of separated strata of society—non-competing groups.

This, it would seem, is the tenor of Marshall's view regarding vertical mobility. Changes in demand for labor in the higher grades, *given time* mobility occurs. He says,

> There is then on the *whole* a broad movement from below upward. Perhaps not so many as formerly rise at once from the position of working men to that of employers: but there are *more* who get on sufficiently far to give their sons a good chance of attaining to the highest posts. The complete rise is not so very often accomplished in one generation; it is more often spread over two; but the total volume of the movement upward is probably *greater* than it has ever been.[27]

Rather than non-competing groups of laborers, occupations are arranged, as it were, on a long flight of steps, with, it is true, some steps broad enough "to act as landing stages."[28] But in spite of these "landing stages," Marshall no doubt believed vertical competition to be increasing, for in his last writing—and many years after the statement quoted above—he was emphatic concerning

> . . . the incessant rise of members of the lower strata to a position of effective direct competition for employment in higher grade work.

[27] *Principles*, p. 310. Cf., especially, p. 217. Italics mine.
[28] *Principles*, p. 218. Cf. pp. 308-309, 312, 313.

. . . It tends with marvellous power so to assort employees among various industries, and among various businesses in each country, that every man is employed on that work in which his personal efficiency is most appropriate.[29]

As to horizontal mobility, Marshall *did* reach a general conclusion with no uncertainty of expression. Manual skill which is so specialized that it cannot be transferred from one occupation to another is becoming less and less important in present-day production.[30] *General* ability "is every year rising in importance relatively to that manual skill and technical knowledge which are specialized to one branch of industry."[31]

Not only does the ever increasing general, transferable ability increase competition of employee with employee but it *also* increases competition of *employer* with *employer* for the services of labor. Because general efficiency has been developed, Marshall points out,

Alert employers in industries, that are apparently wide apart, are simultaneously considering enlargements of old processes or introductions of new processes that will draw directly or indirectly on kindred supplies of labourers. . . . Thus, the various strata of the employed class are continually competing with one another for employment over a great part, though not over the whole, of the field of industry. They do not compete for the same tasks as a rule: but they do habitually compete for employment in making the same product by different processes; or in making products which subserve practically the same purpose.[32]

[29] Alfred Marshall, *Money, Credit, and Commerce* (London: Macmillan, 1923), p. 241.

[30] *Op. cit.*, p. 206.

[31] *Principles*, p. 573. Again, however, Marshall with his exactitude of expression brings into consideration, at another place, the ever important element of time. Speaking of the influence of machinery increasing the demand for general intelligence he states that although a workman today can pass without great loss of efficiency to other work, yet he does *not* do so until he has tried to get employment in his old lines; "and therefore the barriers are as effective as stronger ones would be so far as the minor fluctuations of trade from week to week are concerned." (*Ibid.*, p. 260.)

[32] *Money, Credit and Commerce*, pp. 240-241.

Hence horizontal competition is active, constant, and widespread. The passage quoted above states with remarkable clarity the nature of this increasing competition—an increasing competition which socialists and many economists have been equally remarkable in their failure to comprehend.

As to capital: In accord with Marshall's principle of continuity (which was discussed in the first section of this chapter as being a basic idea in his use of the concept of competition) he says,

> . . . there is no sharp line of division between *floating* capital and that which has been "sunk" for a special branch of production, nor between new and old investments of capital; each group shades into the other gradually.[83]

While that which I say in the following analysis regarding the competitiveness of capital refers to that portion of capital which is "free,"[84] it applies to a *degree*, or at least it cannot be sharply separated from, fixed capital.

And in accord with Marshall's principle of substitution, the competitiveness of capital manifests itself by the twofold process of substituting more or less of one factor of production for more or less of *another* factor, as well as the competition of component elements of each factor.[85] Many kinds of labor, raw material, machinery, and organization are essential to the production of any product. The constant competition which is occurring between the multitudinous forms of capital—and other agents of production as well—is evidenced by the continuous process

[83] *Principles*, Preface, p. viii.

[84] Marshall also uses the terms "floating," "fluid," and "general purchasing power."

[85] As an example of the first—more labor and less machinery; of the latter—more machinery of the same kind (say, to expand the output of the main product) as against diversified equipment to produce several "lines."

of substitution. Every producer must be constantly attempting to determine the relative efficiency of the various agents of production he employs as well as that of those he *might* employ. Such relative efficiency can be determined with at least some approximation by every producer through the simple method of recording changes in net addition to the value of his total product. Refinement of cost accounting methods, alone, has added tremendously to the process of substitution or competition by enabling the producer with far greater accuracy to determine, separately, the relative efficiency of his "input" elements.[26] Simultaneously, of course, the producer drives the employment of each of the forms of capital (and other agents of production) to the margin at which the net product from such capital is equal to the price the producer pays for that capital.

In this competing-substituting mechanism the productive process tends toward equilibrium, or equality of net returns, due to continuous alternative uses that different forms of capital—and other agents of production—are put. As Marshall has phrased it:

> The advantages of economic freedom are never more strikingly manifest than when a business man endowed with genius is trying experi-

[26] Besides cost accounting one might add scientific management in all its phases, for example, time and motion study, routing and scheduling of work, timing of production programs, traffic management, laboratory experimental work, associative bureaus and institutes, etc.

The extent to which the process of substitution is carried by the producer in his effort in securing the largest *net* addition to the value of his product is interestingly seen in the production of a product enjoying great elasticity of demand, as for example, motor cars. Small reduction in cost and selling price greatly increases output. What seems to be almost *insignificantly* small substitutions of certain contrivances for others, in a particular make of an automobile, can only be understood by estimating the addition which that substitution makes to the net value of the total yearly output. The small addition to the net value of the individual car becomes a tremendous yearly value when multiplied by over a million times which a company secures by producing more than a million cars a year.

ments, at his own risk, to see whether some new method, or combination of old methods, will be more efficient than the old.[37]

Such then is the cycle of competition of capital: capital in the form of general purchasing power is turned by the producer into the various forms of fixed capital (in combination with other agents of production), the emergence of a salable product, the replenishing of the free capital (general purchasing power), and its reinvestment again bringing about automatically the competition of capital.[38] What does Marshall perceive to be the extent, the trend, the limitations of this competition?

In the tremendous growth of the competitiveness of capital three conditions are fundamental according to Marshall. The first of these is what he refers to as "the marvellous growth in recent times of a spirit of honesty and uprightness in commercial matters."[39] This alone explains the practicality of the joint-stock companies. The faith engendered by business morality has induced people with little or no special knowledge of trade "to give their capital into the hands of others employed by them." Decreased size of shares, increased number of investors, increased intelligence of those who supply capital are all elements increasing the competition of capital.[40]

The second fundamental condition in explaining the growth of the competitiveness of capital is seen in the fact that while

It is true that in almost every business there is a constant increase in the amount of capital required to make a fair start; but there is a much

[37] *Principles*, p. 406.
[38] Cf. Marshall, *Principles*, pp. 341 and 411.
[39] *Ibid.*, p. 303.
[40] Marshall, *Industry and Trade*, pp. 320 ff.

more rapid increase in the amount of capital which is owned by people who do not want to use it themselves.[41]

Expansion in the volume of the loan fund due to man's growing mastery over nature and rise above a subsistence level, together with a faith in the integrity of others, has made possible increased competition in the use of capital, of which the growth in the corporation is an important manifestation.

The third basic condition which is accentuating the competitiveness of capital is that "rigidity has been succeeded by plasticity: the methods of industry which were . . . stereotyped, now change with bewildering quickness."[42] This phenomenon is, of course, but one of the results of all those economic and non-economic institutions which have caused, in social life generally, rationalism and liberalism to increasingly supplant custom and intolerance.

But may not this order of broadening economic freedom eventually lead to the dominance of industry by few enterprises and the destruction of competition? The steady tendency toward specialization of work and of plant, the ever growing volume and fluidity of capital, and the "almost unlimited capitalistic resources" necessary to carry on marketing efficiently over a wide area have all been conducive to enlarging the size of the representative business unit.[43] Has the result been a decrease of competition? Regarding this point Marshall observes,

. . . though monopoly and free competition are ideally wide apart, yet in practice they shade into one another by imperceptible degrees: that there is an element of monopoly in nearly all competitive business: and that nearly *all* monopolies that are of any practical importance in the present age, hold much of their power by an uncertain tenure; so

[41] *Principles*, p. 308. Italics mine.
[42] *Ibid.*, p. 245.
[43] Marshall, *Industry and Trade*, pp. 508-511.

that they would lose it ere long, if they ignored the possibilities of competition, *direct* and *indirect*.[44]

In fact, he contends, the fiercest and cruelest forms of competition are found in markets which are no longer quite free, but have been already brought in some measure under monopolistic control.[45]

This contention, in my view, is open to two criticisms. The nature of the competition referred to here has nothing in common with the qualities inherent in his "economic freedom," and Marshall has frequently used "competition" and "economic freedom" interchangeably. In the second place, intensity and duration of competition are not distinguished. It is, of course, the latter which is most important, and there is no necessary relation between intensity and duration.

Marshall's general views regarding competition as it applies to capital are difficult to determine. The extended analysis presented by his *Industry and Trade* gives one no certain views regarding the nature of the changes which are taking place in our present order of economic freedom. It seems, according to Marshall, that a phase of most monopolistic arrangements can be more aptly referred to as "constructive association."[46] These associations are in accord with an order of economic freedom. But are the "constructive associations," generally speaking, outnumbered by the "destructive" type, that is, is the displacing of competition by monopoly the dominant and necessary tendency? Marshall's view would depend greatly upon the interpretation placed upon his significant but undeveloped statement:

[44] *Ibid.*, p. 397.
[45] *Ibid.*, pp. 395-396. Cf. p. 512.
[46] *Ibid.*, p. 654.

It [German opinion] has not yet learned that though monopolistic powers in certain directions are necessary results of modern conditions, they are apt to cause grave evils unless controlled. . . .[47]

One finds no answer to what the "certain directions" are, what the *relative* importance of other powers is, in what sense such monopolistic powers are "*necessary*" results, what the scope included within the term "modern conditions" (social, or only economic) is, and what the direct or indirect results of these "grave evils" are.

Nevertheless the important place the concept of competition plays in Marshall's descriptive as well as analytical writing concerning industry and trade gives the drift to his view that the dominant feature of economic relations is that of increasing competition. That it continue so would require, it is true, control such as is exercised by our Federal Trade Commission—work which Marshall heartily endorsed—in order that combinations may be limited to the type of "constructive associations." But other social forces productive of growing competitiveness of capital play a more important rôle. As indicative of these forces, he asserts:

There is every reason to hope that the progress of trade morality will continue, aided in the future as it has been in the past, by a diminution of trade secrecy and by increased publicity in every form; and thus collective and democratic forms of business management may be able to extend themselves in many directions in which they have hitherto failed. . . .[48]

As to management and organization: The extent and nature of competition in management depends largely upon the relation which the supply of those who have the qualities necessary for management stands to the demand

[47] *Ibid.*, p. 576.
[48] *Principles*, pp. 303-304.

for such services. With the increase in the size and complexity of the representative firm is there an increasingly larger number of those who can perform managerial work? If so, competition in this realm of economic activity increases. On the other hand, if the rate of growth in the number of those who can render such services is not keeping pace with the increasing demand of society for such managers, it reflects a lack of mobility and competition in this field. If various causes combine to retard movement into the managerial group a non-competing group emerges.

The basic proposition which Marshall states regarding competition in management is found in his assertion that the

> . . . share of the normal expenses of production of any commodity which is commonly classed as profits, is so *controlled on every side by the action of substitution,* that it cannot long diverge from the normal supply . . . price of the ability and energy required for managing the business, and . . . the normal supply price of that organization. . . .
>
> The supply of business power is large and elastic, since the area from which it is drawn is wide. Everyone has the business of his own life to conduct; and in this he can gain some training for business management. . . .[49]

It is his opinion then that not only is the supply of managing ability drawn from a wide area but also *general* faculties rather than specialized knowledge "*increase* in importance as the scale of business increases." In fact such faculties count for *more* than does skill in lower grades of work. For our analysis of the concept of competition in Marshall's reasoning concerning management, the following contention is his main thesis:

> Since then business ability in command of capital moves with *great ease horizontally* from a trade which is over-crowded to one which

[49] *Ibid.*, pp. 605-606. Italics mine.

offers good openings for it: and since it moves with *great ease vertically*, the abler man rising to the higher posts in their own trade, we see . . . the supply of business ability in command of capital accommodates itself, as a general rule, to the demand for it. . . .[50]

Competition, then, manifests itself in the field of management by vertical and horizontal mobility, by the process of substitution, and the existence of a supply price for business ability just as there is a supply price for other goods or elements. Consequently business managers not only do not constitute a caste but, quite the contrary, the whole wage-earning class "without going out of their way are all consciously or unconsciously competitors for posts of business command."[51]

It is to be doubted whether Marshall substantiates his argument concerning the free play of competition in management—the great ease of both vertical and horizontal movement by which supply of business management adjusts itself to demand. It seems to me that Marshall's view reflects in part the established and diversified productive organization of an older country. Such an environment presents more numerous gradations in openings for different types of abilities, and the process of substitution would operate both horizontally and vertically to place managers in work in which they were effective. Again, Marshall's discussion tacitly refers to conditions where no technical innovations occur sharply, which, of course, was more true of his English environment than it would be of a newer country. In such an environment *administrative* management counts for more and *creative* management for less.

It is significant that the general qualities which Mar-

[50] *Ibid.*, p. 313. Italics mine.
[51] *Ibid.*, p. 309. Cf. p. 299.

shall regards as essential for management ("judgment, promptness, carefulness and steadfastness") are the *general* characteristics of people who have long enjoyed an order of economic freedom. These characteristics suffice for administrative management. *Creative* management—so important in a newer country with its marked innovations of technique and organization—calls for other qualities, such, for example, as imagination, judgment, and courage. The supply of this type of management is not "large and elastic." Creative leadership, in my opinion, demands attributes which, although developed by a favorable environment, are of an *inborn* nature.[52] Differences in native endowment Marshall does not adequately consider in his discussion of management and organization. It is, indeed, these differences which count for most in creative leadership, and to management or business ability of this sort Marshall's phrases of horizontal and vertical movement of "great ease" are inapplicable.

But at least within certain ranges of management and organization Marshall's contention that increased competition or mobility has occurred is well taken. The growth of public education, which has brought about at least some of the necessary qualities of management, and the growth of joint stock companies, which has provided very large and diversified opportunities to men without capital or connections, have been of paramount importance in bringing about mobility.[53] Since Marshall's early writing the extension of the former (that of education) is particularly notable in its increasing the supply and mobility—or adaptability—of management. Rather than the educational

[52] Cf. F. W. Taussig, *Principles of Economics* (3rd ed.; New York: Macmillan, 1921), II, Chap. 49, Sec. 4.

[53] *Ibid.*, p. 302.

influence of coöperative societies—concerning which Marshall's optimism again reflected the environment of an older country—I have in mind that phase of public education which is reducing much of business management from an art to a science.

As to land: In Marshall's reasoning concerning land as an agent of production the concept of competition plays essentially the same rôle. Marshall's view in general is:

> Each crop strives against others for the possession of the land; and if any one crop shows signs of being more remunerative than before relatively to others, the cultivators will devote more of their land and resources to it. The change may be retarded by habit, or diffidence, or obstinacy, or limitations of the cultivator's knowledge; or by the terms of his lease. But it will still be true in the main that each cultivator—to recall once more the dominant principle of substitution—"taking account of his own means, will push the investment of capital in his business in each several directions until what appears in his judgment to be the margin of profitableness is reached. . . ."[54]

The foregoing statement, while asserting that competition working through the process of substitution is operative for land as for the other agents of production, allows for the influence of counteracting non-economic forces. "The economic theory of rent, the Ricardian theory as it is sometimes called," says Marshall, "does not apply to modern English land tenure without many corrections and limitations both as regards substance and form."[55] While the English system of land tenure is competitive in its essence, "the conditions of agriculture even in England offer a strong resistance to the full action of free competition."[56]

[54] *Ibid.*, p. 435.
[55] *Ibid.*, pp. 639-640.
[56] *Ibid.*, p. 656. Hence the failures of the English land tenure system in

The non-economic forces mentioned by Marshall as counteracting competition are but part of the explanation. Cairnes's discussion of this particular point, as stated in the preceding chapter, is more conclusive. Competitiveness of land assumes a variety of occupations to which owners or tenants of land can turn their capital and labor. Can such a condition exist in the utilization of land, or is Marshall's implication true that the conditions of agriculture, generally, offer "strong resistance to the full action of free competition"?

As to the influence of competitive forces in agriculture, Marshall's discussion is inadequate. Where land is utilized as it is by our completely diversified midwestern farms we have mobility and competitiveness of the agents of production comparable to that found in industry. Let us examine this briefly.

Changes in the value of the products of land, frequently anticipated by the intelligent landowner through governmental services as agricultural outlooks and market reports, are followed—with increasing promptness—by the altering of the proportions which labor and capital bear to land. In this sense substitution and competition occur and, in this sense, land can be said to be competitive. To a notable degree such large, diversified farming is akin to manufacturing. The intelligent landowner with far more informational and educational (private, coöperative, and governmental) agencies at his disposal than the small manufacturer, and with command over credit to give effect to his decisions, increases or decreases the *proportion* of land which he uses relatively to his other cost-input fac-

Ireland where competitive business habits are not so strong as in England and, therefore, could not so fully offset the conditions resisting the action of competition.

tors. Land to such an individual farmer is but one of the forms of capital to be varied according to the fluctuations in the selling price of his various products and also according to the purchase price of his diverse input factors. If a fall occurs in the price of small grains (as has been experienced in the last few years) he decreases his grain output and increases his investment in various forms of capital (other than land) and thereby increases his dairy and other outputs. In so doing he decreases the proportion of land in his production process in a very real sense. In this, and in no other sense, land is mobile and competitive.

It is obvious that in Marshall's English environment the non-economic factors, of which he spoke, would make the land system, although "competitive in its essence," non-competitive in practice.

In this section I have considered the concept of competition in Marshall's reasoning as it concerns the field of production. His view of the nature and limitations of competition of labor, capital, management, and land, as he has expounded it in his various writings, has been examined. We now give our attention to the concept of competition as it applies in the field of exchange.

4

It is doubtful whether any discussion can furnish better illustration of the development of a concept than is provided by the use of competition in Marshall's discussion of value and exchange as compared to the "free competition" of earlier economic writing.

To begin with, it is to be remembered that the great diversity of circumstances concerning markets and exchange makes generalizations concerning competition in this field impossible. As Marshall observes,

> Thus at one extreme are world markets in which competition acts directly from all parts of the globe; and at the other those secluded markets in which all direct competition from afar is shut out, though indirect and transmitted competition may make itself felt even in these; and about midway between these extremes lie the great majority of the markets which the economist and business man have to study.[57]

Putting aside a very brief discussion of those temporary equilibria of demand and supply in which supply is merely the immediately available supply unaffected by conditions of production, we come to the nature of competitive forces which bring equilibrium to "normal" demand and supply. Here, says Marshall,

> . . . we *assume* that the forces of demand and supply have free play; that there is no close combination among dealers on either side, but each acts for himself, and there is much free competition. . . . But though everyone acts for himself, his knowledge of what others are doing is supposed to be generally sufficient to prevent him from taking a lower or paying a higher price than others are doing.[58]

With particular reference to the demand side it must be further assumed that the general circumstances of the market remain unchanged. The diversity on the supply side also calls for the assumption of the "representative firm."

It is clear that Marshall's use of competition here is not in the sense of "free" or "perfect" competition. On the contrary, he says,

> Of course Normal does *not* mean Competitive. Market prices and Normal prices are alike brought about by a *multitude* of influences, of

[57] *Ibid.*, p. 329.
[58] *Ibid.*, p. 341. Italics mine.

which some rest on a *moral* basis and some on a *physical*; of which *some* are competitive and some are not.[59]

Having now the general nature of competition, as Marshall conceives that it operates in the market, we may examine the operation of competition more closely. Concerning the demand side little need be said. The process of substitution operates to the end that purchasers will distribute their purchasing power in such a way that the things purchased will have the same marginal utility to them.

When we turn to the supply side, however, competition and substitution become exceedingly involved and complex.[60] Two factors, it seems to me, are outstanding in this complexity. These are, first, the increasing degree of technical and of economic "jointness" of supply and/or demand. In the second place, the development of transportation, communication, and marketing technique has, of course, brought into each market a larger number of those who supply and, also, a far greater diversity of circumstances under which the supply is produced.

Regarding the first of these two, it is important to recall that jointness of an economic nature, rather than that of a natural or technical sort, is, by far, the greater in importance. Concerning joint demand, "The tyranny," says Marshall, "which one factor of production of a commodity might in some cases exercise . . . is tempered by the principle of substitution." Technical development has obviously increased rivalry or competition of products through widening the scope of substitutes.

Of greater interest to us is the increasing degree of

[59] *Ibid.*, pp. 347-348. Italics mine.

[60] ". . . the doctrine of the distribution of means between different uses has less important and less interesting applications in the science of demand than in that of supply," says Marshall. (*Principles*, p. 118 n.)

economic jointness of supply. Unused productive capacity of any sort has resulted in increasing the number of products any producer supplies. Since the producer is interested in augmenting his total income, and furthermore since it is impossible to determine the proportions in which the total costs should be distributed among the several products, the competitive strength he presents is stronger and more flexible.[61]

Increased competitiveness has also occurred in the market from another type of jointness which technical development and advertising have extended. More demands have a composite supply. As Marshall says,

> A demand can often be satisfied by any one of several routes, according to the principle of substitution. These routes are rivals or competitors with one another; and the corresponding supplies of commodities are rival or *competitive* supplies relatively to one another.[62]

Regarding the second factor of which I spoke above—development of transportation, communication, and marketing—it is clear that consumers are brought in touch with an ever greater number of producers. Producing under conditions of joint cost, distant producers by means of allocating costs of production in favor of their products supplying distant markets may enter these markets and compete.[63] It is true, of course, that marketing practices of this sort may be destructive of competition when the production of a commodity conforms sharply to the law of increasing returns.

Such then is the increased competitiveness of the present-day market. On the demand side: growing purchasing power; heightened intelligence of purchasers resulting

[61] Marshall, *Principles*, p. 390.
[62] *Ibid.*, p. 390. Italics mine.
[63] Cf. *Ibid.*, p. 396.

not only from education, in general, but also from informational activities of producers (such as advertising) induced by the rivalry for patronage—these widen the scope of the consumers' choice and strengthen their competitive position.[64] On the supply side: increased economic jointness of supply, the development of substitutes for materials needed in the production process, and the ever widening scope of the market are aspects of intensified competition.

To come to another aspect of the nature of competition in the field of exchange: Marshall does not hold that the play of competitive forces and the emergence of a competitive price is conducive to the maximum amount of satisfaction. To suppose this, he asserts, is to assume "that all differences in wealth may be neglected" and it is also to ignore the fact that with commodities responding to increasing return "the direct expense of a bounty sufficient to call forth a greatly increased supply at a much lower price, would be much less than the consequent increase of consumers' surplus."[65] Hence, in this field of competition,

[64] Interesting and what seems to me to be quite significant is the recent development of consumers' bureaus or associations, of various kinds, to render information as to qualities and prices of various products. Possibly the largest of these is the Better Business Bureau, one of which may be found in every large city of the United States. These are financed voluntarily by business men. They have done a tremendous amount of work in stamping out misleading and false advertising. It is doubtful whether the value of their service (although largely unknown to the public, as it is) can be overestimated.

The emergence of consumers' associations—membership to which may be had at a nominal fee—possibly marks a significant move. It is stated that information which they give to members is based upon most careful examination even to chemical and mechanical analyses.

Also the establishment of a state consumers' bureau, within recent years by one or two of our western states—although open as such a project would be to maladministration—points to a program of potential importance.

[65] *Principles*, pp. 470 ff. Cf. *Memorials*, p. 162.

as in others, economic freedom is neither ideal nor inevitable.

Conscious not only of the great practical importance of weaknesses of human motives and qualities but also of the inadequacy of theory in measuring the actual consequences of the social control to which theoretical reasoning pointed (it is interesting to speculate as to which—so far as the two are not the same—loomed the larger in Marshall's mind), he did not believe there was valid ground, on this score, for government interference. The control of exchange and value, however, which the shortcoming of the doctrine of maximum satisfaction suggests is not to be overlooked; for, says Marshall,

> . . . they show that *much* remains to be done, by a careful collection of the statistics of demand and supply, and a scientific interpretation of their results, in order to discover what are the limits of the work that society can with advantage do toward those channels in which they will add the *most* to the sum of happiness.[66]

5

As I have pointed out, a proposition which Marshall draws from his principle of continuity is that there is no sharp line dividing production and distribution. Since production and distribution are but counterparts of the same process, in a "coöperative-exchange" order, much of what I have said of Marshall's discussion of competition as related to production is necessarily pertinent to his views on competition as related to distribution. There remains, however, the examination of the nature and limitations of competition in the determination of the shares of the national dividend. With this we are now concerned.

Concerning wages: Marshall points out that competi-

[66] *Principles*, p. 475.

tive forces of demand and supply in a commodity market and in a labor market have this in common, namely, that keenest competition will not cause price to be alike for two things which are like in name but not in quality or, again, which are really alike but differ in the conditions of sale.[67] This has been overlooked by Cliffe Leslie and others who have referred to local variations of wages as tending to prove that mobility of laborers did not exist and competition is ineffective. On the contrary, if variations in wages to which they refer correspond with efficiency it proves the effectiveness of competition. But this makes no claim as to the actual existence of such effective competition even in the same neighborhood. The tendency of competition to equalize efficiency-earning in the same district would be stronger, according to Marshall, under certain conditions. He clarifies this by saying:

> . . . the greater is the mobility of labour, the less strictly specialized it is, the more keenly parents are on the lookout for the most advantageous occupations for their children the more rapidly they are able to adapt themselves to changes in economic conditions, and lastly the slower and less violent these changes are.[68]

Only to the extent that there is complete mobility of labor are wages in accord with efficiency and effort. I have indicated in Section 2 of this chapter that regarding the *net* effect of the peculiarities of labor upon mobility Marshall was not definite. That competition is the dominant force in the determination of wages is necessarily included in Marshall's view that there is a constant tendency toward a position of normal equilibrium in which the supply of each of the agents of production (including labor)

[67] *Ibid.*, pp. 546-547.
[68] *Ibid.*, p. 549.

would receive "a sufficient reward for their efforts and sacrifices."[69]

Although wages are "sufficient" to call forth a *supply* of labor, this equilibrium, again, was not to be regarded as a *desirable* end. Elsewhere, in pointing out that the chief remedy for low wages is better education, he continues,

> The aim of social endeavour must be to increase the numbers of those who are capable of the more difficult work of the world, and to diminish the number of those who can do only unintelligent work, or who perhaps cannot even do that.[70]

Concerning interest: Just as competition does not equalize remuneration to labor where elements other than effort and efficiency are involved to a varying degree, so likewise competition does not equalize the earnings of capital when elements other than waiting are involved. The elements other than simply waiting which make up the earnings of capital are, of course, different degrees of risk and of management. Not only is the tendency of competition not to equalize *gross* interest but "on the contrary, the more thoroughly lenders and borrowers understand their business, the more certainly will some classes of borrowers obtain loans at a lower rate than others."[71]

As to *net* interest, due to "the marvelously efficient organization of the modern money market by which capital is transferred," a very small difference between rates to be had "in two different modes of investment in the same Western country will cause capital to flow . . . from one to another."

Concerning profit: Competition did not operate to

[69] *Ibid.*, p. 577.
[70] *Money, Credit, and Commerce*, p. 263.
[71] *Principles*, p. 591.

bring profits to equality. Rather, Marshall held, the present order offers a great variety of managerial tasks, and competition operates to bring about a correspondence between ability and the managing work.[72] In this diversity of tasks and gradations of efficiency there emerge different normal rates of profit in accord with the type of organization, risk, and character of ability required. At least this is the result of competition on profits to those undertakers "who follow beaten tracks." Those, however, "who open out new and improved methods of business" seldom get the full reward that competitive forces should award them considering the indirect services they perform for society.[73]

That competition could not cause a tendency of profits to reach a common level necessarily followed from Marshall's view as to what constitutes profits. He says,

> Profits, in my opinion, are not an economic entity. They include some interest on capital, some earnings of ability and work, and often some insurance against risk. . . . The elements of which profits are composed obey different laws, and they enter in different proportions (whatever definition of "profits" be taken) in different industries, in the same industry in different places, and in large and small businesses even in the same industry and in the same place.[74]

Concerning rent: I have pointed out that Marshall held that while the English system of land tenure was *com-*

[72] *Ibid.*, Bk. IV, Chap. XII.

[73] *Ibid.*, p. 597.

[74] *Official Papers by Alfred Marshall* (Edited by J. M. Keynes; London: Macmillan, 1926), p. 356. Cf. *Money, Credit, and Commerce*, p. 291.

Marshall's statement quoted here (to the effect that profits are not an economic entity, the elements of which obey different laws) disposes, it seems to me, of the charge made by Lionel Robbins that the weakness of the concept of the Representative Firm leads into difficulties in Marshall's reasoning on profits. Robbins says, "If in the long-period adjustment all firms were representative, then clearly in any industry all profits would be equal." ("The Representative Firm," *Economic Journal*, XXXVIII [1928], 403.)

petitive in essence, the conditions of agriculture offered resistance to the action of free competition. At this point it remains to be noted that competition for the use of land as an agent of production is not the only source of rent, for Marshall says:

> . . . the rent of land is no unique fact, but simply the chief species of a large genus of economic phenomena; and . . . but merely one of the chief applications of a particular corollary from the general theory of demand and supply. . . .[75]

And while pure rent was scarcely ever the whole income from land, so also elements of true rent are found in wages and interest.[76] The return on fixed capital and from unusual abilities is more properly treated as a rent.

Marshall's exceedingly useful concept of quasi-rent is but a way of stating that the income from any agent of production for a given length of time—short in some cases and long in others—bears no necessary relation to cost of producing such an agent. Particular forms of fixed capital or unusual ability do not stand in a competitive relation to the demand for such agents, for competition assumes mobility and this, for a time, is precluded in such forms of capital and ability. Marshall's doctrine of quasi-rent directs attention to the fact that here the leveling effect of competition is slow. As time passes, mobility—increased supply—occurs and what has been, for a time, non-competitive income, or quasi-rent, becomes a competitive income of interest on capital or wages to labor.

6

To sum up: The broadened scope of economic inquiry, the interdependence of social relations, and the unity of

[75] *Principles*, p. 629.
[76] *Ibid.*, p. 421.

economic phenomena are the striking characteristics of Marshall's economic philosophy. His reasoning concerning competition is based upon, or is in accord with, the principles of continuity. Equilibrium is the "Fundamental Idea"; substitution is the process which gives it effect.

In understanding Marshall's view as to the general nature of present-day competition it is to be pointed out that the connotations of such terms as "Economic Freedom" and "Free Enterprise" are more apt than that of "Competition." Marshall nevertheless uses these terms interchangeably. Our present order of economic freedom is not ideal but, considering present human qualities, most workable.

A point upon which socialistic writers are frequently amiss is in their insistence that "free competition" precludes coöperative action and government control. This is not only contrary to Marshall's view but furthermore he shows that an order of economic freedom calls for a widening scope of both in general, and the latter in particular.

The process of substitution, by which competition is given effect, does not assume that competition, or substitution, is perfect. Counteracted as it is by numerous forces, competition remains the dominant force.

Marshall's view as to the nature and extent of the competitiveness of the agents of production is, in part, unexpressed or uncertain. It seems to me, however, that Marshall's principle of continuity, an important proposition of which is that the element of time is the center of difficulties in economic conclusions, clarifies partly Marshall's views. The net effect of the peculiarities of labor upon its vertical and horizontal mobility and competitiveness is an example of the element of time being an important factor.

The period necessary to bring about mobility—adjustment to changed environment—is short under certain conditions of life but long under other conditions.

Although Marshall's discussion may suggest the existence of factors hindering vertical mobility to the point of bringing about the existence of non-competing groups of labor, his last writing upon the subject emphasized the "incessant rise" from lower to higher grades of work. It is his view that the increase in the relative importance of "general qualities" is unquestionably causing greater horizontal mobility.

Competitiveness of capital is given effect by means of the substitution process, made possible by the existence of free capital. Substitution, in its various forms, is tremendously increased by the development of such agencies, for example, as cost accounting, various forms of scientific management, and the money market in all of its departments and activities. Indeed, as Marshall says, nowhere are the advantages of economic freedom more strikingly manifest than these forces of competition in the hands of an enterprising man. He rightly insists that in this increased competitiveness of capital the growth of business morality, increase in the volume of the loan fund, and the growing plasticity of social life are fundamental prerequisites.

Marshall's view on the possibility of the supersession of competition by monopoly, or the degree to which this has now occurred, is not clearly stated. The relative importance of certain factors and the relation they bear to an order of economic freedom is not developed. These, as we find them in his *Industry and Trade*, are *constructive* associations, certain marketing practices, government control, and the progress of trade morality. The trend of

Marshall's argument, it would seem, is that competition in the use of capital is playing a larger part although the form which such competition is taking is essentially different. The change is what I have referred to in an earlier chapter as the development of personal and corporative competition into that of associative competition.

Marshall held, emphatically, that management as an agent of production was exceedingly mobile and competitive. Horizontal and vertical movements occur with great ease. This view, in my opinion, is not only in accord with the environment in which Marshall wrote but also reflects that he was speaking, tacitly, of *administrative* rather than creative management. His views, therefore, as to the nature of competition regarding this agent of production are inadequate.

Although competition in the use of land is manifested by the constant process of substitution, the non-economic forces counteracting competition, says Marshall, are strong. He did not consider the operation of competitive forces in the use of land, which are so strikingly manifest in the operation of our diversified midwestern farms.

In Marshall's reasoning concerning competition in the field of exchange the complexity and extent of present-day competition are more fully seen than elsewhere.

On the demand side, Marshall points out that the process of substitution operates to the end that purchases yield equal marginal utilities. He does not emphasize—as it well may be—that increased purchasing power and, far more, improved intelligence from manifold sources have widened the scope of consumers' choice and strengthened their competitive position, as may be seen in the multiplying number of demands which have composite supplies.

On the supply side, increased competition is manifested in the growth of economic jointness of supply, the development of substitutes for materials needed in the production process, and the ever widening scope of the market. But errors in the doctrine of maximum satisfaction prove that unrestricted competitive exchange is not to be regarded as conducive to greatest satisfaction.

In distribution, competition equalizes *efficiency* wages. Whether in reality there exists mobility sufficient for this cannot be determined in light of Marshall's discussion of the peculiarities of labor. His view that the constant tendency is toward a position of normal equilibrium in which laborers receive "a sufficient reward for their efforts and sacrifices" is ambiguous.

Competition equalizes net interest, and the money market is increasingly making free capital more mobile.

"Profits" not being an economic entity, the constituent elements obey different laws and competition does not cause profits to come to a common level. Rather for each gradation of efficiency a normal rate of profit emerges in accord with the type of organization, risk, and ability required.

Rent to land, said Marshall, though determined by a competitive process was greatly influenced by other factors. And elements of rent are found in other distributive shares. To point to the slowness with which the forces of competition affected these elements, Marshall's quasi-rent doctrine was particularly designed.

VI

PIGOU: THE LIMITATIONS OF COMPETITION—THE THEORETIC ANALYSIS

I

IT IS a notable fact that in the views of the economists we have examined thus far the concept of competition was tacitly or expressly used as the basis of economic reasoning, and the limitations of the competitive order, per se, were not considered.[1] This, of course, does not mean that economists, even back to Adam Smith and his immediate followers, were unaware or indifferent to social maladjustments that may have been greatly aggravated by the play of competitive forces. On the contrary, they frequently pointed to the need of government interference with such forces, as the foregoing chapters have made clear. And, again, as I have indicated, when free competition was used as a concept the competition which they had in mind was not "free" in the sense of "unregulated" competition but, rather, "free" in the sense of "frictionless" competition. The latter (or economic competition as developed in Chapter II), to be sure, requires regulation of competitive forces in all departments of economic activity varying in degree according to the circumstances of the time and place under consideration.

Nevertheless desirable government intervention in the

[1] Relative to this, Adolf Wagner said in his review of Marshall's *Principles of Economics*: "Like most English economists, Marshall treats private industry, and that organization of industry which rests on private property, as matters of course, given by "nature," so to speak; treating the institution of property as something absolute or purely economic, and not as something which has developed by historic growth. . . . Too little attention is paid to the historic development of industry, and to those developments, already foreshadowed for the future, beyond the system of simple free exchange and private industry—changes not toward socialism, but something which resembles socialism more closely than it does the present régime." (*Quarterly Journal of Economics*, V [1891], p. 333.)

competitive order and the degree to which such order was frictionless was not primarily discussed. This was most nearly approached in the broadened scope and complexity of competition as found in Marshall's discussion. Implications as to the desirability of far-reaching control of competitive forces are clearly seen in his discussion of the "Theory of Changes of Normal Demand and Supply in Relation to the Doctrine of Maximum Satisfaction,"[2] but as to the practical importance of these implications he was quite uncertain.

In the present chapter, and the two chapters which follow, we shall give our attention to an examination of writings where the primary concern is elucidating desirable restrictions or regulations of competition with the view toward social betterment. Recent English economic writing presents two different, thoroughgoing approaches to this aspect of competition: the theoretic, in the writings of Pigou; and the pragmatic, in the writings of the Fabians, or earlier English socialists, and also in the later, and present English critics of the competitive order. The plane and temper of the scientific inquiry of the former (the theoretic) has been matched by the sincerity and intellectual leadership of the latter (the pragmatic). The present chapter will examine the nature and limitations of competition as expressed by Pigou. The following chapter will treat with the Fabians' approach.

2

The general nature of Pigou's problem and his approach[3] may be seen in his view regarding the purpose of economic study. He says,

[2] *Principles*, Book V, Chap. 13.

[3] A brief statement, at least, of this is necessary although it might not

> . . . the type of science that the economist will endeavour to develop must be one adapted to form the basis of an art. It will not, indeed, itself be an art, to directly enunciate precepts of government. It is a positive science of what is and tends to be, not a normative science of what ought to be. Nor will it limit itself to those fields of positive scientific inquiry which have an obvious relevance to immediate practical problems. This course would hamper thorough investigation and shut out inquiries that might ultimately bear fruit.[4]

And the goal sought in economic inquiry—that of making "more easy practical measures to promote welfare"—is an altogether attainable one, since

> The conception of the National Dividend is not an academic toy but a *practical instrument of great power* designed for service in the concrete solution of social problems. . . . The dividend constitutes the kernel of economic theory because . . . it is the centre of sound philanthropic endeavour.[5]

This has brought us to Pigou's approach to the problem: welfare is to be promoted through the instrument of the national dividend. This "instrument of great power" may be consciously controlled toward the increasing of welfare rather than be subject to the spontaneous direction of competitive influences. And concerning the relation which welfare bears to the national dividend, Pigou sets forth certain propositions which are basic to his whole analysis. These we shall now note.

In the first place, the elements of welfare are states of consciousness, and secondly, that welfare can be brought

---

seem to be directly related to the present study of Pigou's views on competition. As we shall see in this section, however, the basis and extent of Pigou's criticism of the competitive order is found in certain of his views and propositions which precede his analysis. Upon these he builds his case.

[4] *The Economics of Welfare* (2nd ed.; London: Macmillan, 1924), p. 5. All references will be to this edition unless otherwise stated.

[5] Pigou's review of Marshall's *Principles of Economics*, 5th Edition, *Economic Journal*, XVII (1907), 532-535. Italics mine.

under the category of greater or less.[6] Regarding the second proposition, the validity of Pigou's approach necessitates that welfare be susceptible to quantitative measurement. This requires that his analysis be restricted to only "that part of social welfare that can be brought directly or indirectly into relation with the measuring-rod of money." Thirdly, unless specific evidence exists to the contrary a change in economic welfare is "probably equivalent in direction, though not in magnitude, to the effect on total welfare."[7] Fourthly, a more equal distribution of the national dividend increases economic welfare (provided such distribution does react to decrease the dividend).[8] And, finally, that production guided by self-interest (competition) will not tend to bring about equality between the values of the marginal *social* net products of investment in different industries but, rather, competition brings equality *only* in the values of marginal *private* products.[9] In this

[6] Pigou, *op. cit.*, p. 10.

[7] *Ibid.*, p. 20. Italics his.

[8] *Ibid.*, p. 78. A point raised by Pigou—while it has no direct bearing upon his general analysis—is of interest to us in our understanding of his views upon the limitations of the competitive order. The point in question concerns the relation of desires and satisfactions. (Cf. Pigou, *op. cit.*, Chap. 2, Part 1.) The discrepancy or divergence of desire and satisfaction, he holds, has economic significance in our "irrational preference" of present desires for future desires. "This reveals a far-reaching economic disharmony" with the important consequence that "the aggregate amount of economic satisfaction which people in fact enjoy is much less than it would be if their telescopic faculty were not *perverted*," p. 26. Pigou does not believe that competition will correct this "perversion" or "irrationality," and the duty of the state is to counteract "*in some degree*" this evil.

This discussion of the relation of present to future desires, it seems to me, is but a particular case of the general question whether commercial values are social values. It is my opinion that not only does Pigou not substantiate his contention but also that his reasoning is erroneous. Granting that our desires are perverted, as Pigou claims, the conclusion we are led to is not "*some* artificial encouragement to investment," as he asserts, but rather, in my judgment, to the need of broad, public education by means of which wants may assume proper perspective.

[9] *Ibid.*, p. 161.

discrepancy lies the limitation of competition as a means of maximizing welfare, for by the "*social* net product" Pigou means the "aggregate contribution to the *national dividend*"; by "private net product" he means "the contribution (which may be greater or less than the above) that is capable of being sold and the proceeds added to the *earnings* of the person responsible for the unit of investment."[10] Equality in marginal social net products is the significant equality, for in maximizing the contribution to the national dividend it maximizes economic welfare, since the two concepts, national dividend and economic welfare, are coördinate.[11]

These are the propositions upon which Pigou founds his explanation of the limitations of competition. Social intervention in the competitive process is necessary to the end that welfare be increased.

3

In the last section we considered the nature of Pigou's problem and the approach which he proposes to make in his treatment. We now turn to a closely related phase of my examination of the nature and limitations of competition as seen in Pigou's writing. This phase is the *scope* of his treatment of competition or, in other words, the extent to which his discussion of desirable social control *is* a treatment of the actual limitations of competition. It seems to me that it is highly important to bear this consideration in mind, for in Pigou's tenuous discussion proportion and reality may easily be lost sight of.

There are four outstanding characteristics regarding Pigou's treatment as to the desirable social control over

[10] *Loc. cit.*
[11] *Ibid.*, p. 31.

competition to which one might point in defining the scope of his treatment. First, he *restricts* his inquiry to that part of social welfare which is susceptible to measurement in money, calls this economic welfare, and holds that we may, unless "there is specific evidence to the contrary" regard the effect on economic welfare as "*probably* equivalent in direction, though not in magnitude, to the effect on total welfare."[12]

This presumption regarding the direct relation between economic welfare and welfare in general (total welfare), is, of course, open to criticism. The "content" of welfare is too broad to fall within the scope of materialism. Hawtrey, in writing on this point, states the issue emphatically:

> In identifying welfare with satisfactions, Professor Pigou is implicitly assuming in the individual a disposition to prefer the greater good, just as the hedonist assumed a disposition to prefer the greater pleasure. The former assumption is no closer approximation to the truth than the latter, and *we cannot adopt it*. We must reserve our freedom to say whether and to what extent any *particular* kind of satisfaction is to be regarded as welfare.[13]

Although Hawtrey's observation is valid and points to a significant limitation in Pigou's analysis, it seems to me that the criticism may readily be answered. In economic analysis any given (one) philosophy of life is inadequate. This is even true for economic reasoning where, as in western Europe and in America, some degree of mutuality in social institutions prevails. Nevertheless, it can be held that, given the western world with its *present* social organization and the point of view which *predominates*, economic goods and services play an enormously important

[12] It was noted in the preceding section that Pigou makes this a basic proposition in his analysis. We are now concerned with the question as to the manner and degree in which this affects the scope of his inquiry.

[13] *The Economic Problem*, pp. 184-185. Italics mine.

rôle in the satisfactions of everyone and of the masses in particular, living as they do in relative poverty. From this point of view Pigou's approach is valid and its importance is far from being restricted to an inconsequential detail.

A second characteristic of Pigou's reasoning as to desirable social control over competition is that such control is to be exercised largely in the field of production.[14] This is due, possibly, to what seems to me is a third noteworthy characteristic of Pigou's analysis, namely, that the competitive order, as a whole, is to be accepted, and such social control as is desirable shall be applied within and *through* competitive influences. This has been most aptly stated by F. H. Knight, who says,

> In successive parts and chapters of the book [*Economics of Welfare*], he [Pigou] examines, one would say, practically every conceivable influence which may affect the size, distribution, and regularity of flow of the national dividend. He does not *answer*, or *raise*, any of the large general questions as to the effectiveness or ineffectiveness of the *existing* social system relative to some *other* system which might conceivably *replace* it. It is frankly a "piecemeal" treatment that he gives . . .[15]

And fourthly, the degree to which control of competition, which can be demonstrated to be valid in theory, may be effective in practice is difficult, if not impossible, to determine from Pigou's exposition. As I have pointed out, he declared confidently that "the National Dividend is not an academic toy but a *practical* instrument of great power." Seventeen years later he wrote,

[14] Commenting on this, in his brief review of Pigou's *Economics of Welfare*, Cannan wrote, "Thirty years ago a common saying was that enough had been done about production—it was time to turn to distribution. Now a certain reaction against that rather foolish cry is in full swing. . . . Professor Pigou, like others, is subject to the influence . . . and this book is more reactionary (in quite a good sense of the word) than *Wealth and Welfare*." (*Economic Journal*, XXXI [1921], 213.)

[15] "Some Books on Fundamentals," *Journal of Political Economy*, XXXI (1923), 351. Italics mine.

> It is not pretended that, at the present stage of its development, economic science is able to provide an organon even remotely approaching to what it requires for its ideal. Full guidance for practice requires, to borrow Dr. Marshall's phrase, capacity to carry out quantitative, not merely qualitative, analysis . . . this . . . Economic Science at present almost entirely lacks. Before the application of general laws to particular problems can yield quantitative results, these laws must be susceptible of quantitative statement. . . . And, unfortunately, the task of setting out economic laws in precise form has scarcely been begun.[16]

The reasons for lack of preciseness Pigou attributes to the numerousness of the relations involved, the impossibility of direct experimentation under controlled conditions, and —even more serious—that "constants" are different at different times. Still, economic analyses, he holds, "are not mere gymnastic" but rather "instruments for bettering of human life."[17]

Explanation such as the foregoing would be adequate if made concerning a book of general nature like one on "principles" or "foundations." But Pigou's writing is not of this sort; it purports to deal with control which specific weaknesses of competitive forces have made desirable. Pigou's view on competition, or at least on the desirability of actual regulation of it, depends upon the interpretation one chooses to give to the direct answer which he himself made to Clapham when the latter characterized Pigou's analysis as "Empty Economic Boxes."[18] Pigou's answer was,

> Practical usefulness, not necessarily, of course, immediate and direct, but still practical usefulness of *some sort,* is what I look for from this particular department of knowledge.[19]

[16] *Economics of Welfare,* p. 8.
[17] *Ibid.,* 3rd (last) edition, Preface, p. vii.
[18] *Economic Journal,* XXXII (1922), 305-314.
[19] "Empty Economic Boxes: A Reply," *Ibid.,* p. 461. Italics mine.

4

The purpose of this section is twofold: first, we shall examine Pigou's treatment of competition in the field of production; and secondly, we shall consider the government intervention of competitive production which he evaluates in light of the failure of competition to be productive of greatest welfare.

The central thesis of Pigou's view of competition in the field of production is set forth in his statement that

> . . . private enterprise left to itself, even when it operates under conditions of simple competition, often leads to a distribution of resources less favourable to the national dividend than some other possible distributions. In some occupations the value of the marginal private net product of the resources employed is less than the value of the marginal social net product, with the result too little is invested; in other industries the value of the marginal private net product is the larger, and too much is invested; in yet others the exercise of monopoly power contracts output, and investment falls much below what the public interest requires.[20]

In Pigou's explanation of the limitations of competition in failing to bring about such a distribution in productive resources as to create the largest social net product—and, therefore, welfare—he calls attention to the fact that self-interest may act along different "routes." These routes are what Pigou terms "simple competition," and various sorts of monopolistic action.[21]

[20] *Economics of Welfare*, p. 347.

[21] Pigou distinguishes "monopolistic competition," "simple monopoly," "discriminating monopoly" (*Ibid.*, pp. 237-258). For the purpose of our analysis—the relation of the operation of competition to welfare—these distinctions are not precisely relevant although they are obviously important for other purposes such as, for example, price determination.

In this chapter I shall consider first, the limitations of competition under

"Simple competition" exists when "the supply of each seller constitutes so small a part of the aggregate supply that his advantage is best consulted if he 'accepts market prices without trying, of set purpose, to modify them.' "[22] It is, of course, true that free play of self-interest is conducive to equalizing of marginal net products (although *not* marginal *social* net products). Hindrances or immobility counteract this equalization. On this score Pigou limits his discussion to but three types of obstacle, namely, ignorance, cost of movement, and imperfect divisibility.[23] The reduction of these is occurring to the end that quicker and greater equalization of marginal returns is made possible. The consequence is an increase in the national dividend and economic welfare.

Nevertheless, production under "simple competition," Pigou holds, cannot result in maximum social net product inasmuch as,

> in some occupations, a part of the product of a unit of resources consists of something, which, instead of being sold by the investor, is transferred, *without gain or loss to him*, for the benefit or damage of other people.[24]

This, one might say, raises an issue of a different order than that involved in "hindrances" mentioned above. Marginal private net product and marginal social net product *cannot* in the absence of regulation be harmonized.

Who are the "other people" referred to by Pigou as receiving uncompensated transfers (positive or negative)? They fall into three "principal groups":

---

simple competition, and secondly, under the general conditions of monopolization.

[22] *Ibid.*, p. 222 (Quoted from Pareto, *Cours d'économie politique*, i, p. 20).

[23] *Ibid.*, Part 2, Chaps. 5-7.

[24] *Ibid.*, p. 152.

(1) The owners of durable instruments of production of which the investor is a tenant; (2) members of the public other than those persons who purchase what the investor has to sell; (3) those persons who purchase what the investor has to sell.[25]

In regard to the first group: It seems to me that Pigou's discussion of the tenancy contract or relation as being an instance of simple competition is misleading. Although consistent with his definition of simple competition, we have here an instance of where the concept of "economic competition" states the issue more directly. It was developed in Section 4, Chapter II, of this book that the essence of economic competition is mobility of the factors of production.[26] As I pointed out in that connection, mobility requires, as one prerequisite, neutralizing or eliminating those social institutions which retard the unrestricted movement of the factors of production to places and activities where return is greatest.[27] Pigou's discussion of this tenancy relation as "one of three principal groups" is misleading for the reason that what the tenancy relation illustrates is but a particular instance of the general case of social institutions causing immobility. It furnishes no basis for generalization regarding the nature of competition per se, as one might infer from Pigou's treatment.

To turn to his second principal group, noted above, where competition fails to equalize private and social net products. Here the production and sale of a product by (say) A to B *necessarily* causes services or disservices to be rendered to other persons (C, D, and E) for which, in the nature of the case, payment or penalties cannot be enforced.[28] Where C, D, and E receive services (the case of

[25] *Loc. cit.*
[26] Cf. *supra*, p. 30.
[27] Cf. *supra*, pp. 35 ff. (Also cf. footnote No. 44.)
[28] *Economics of Welfare*, p. 161.

a well-placed lighthouse and scientific research leading to inventions) the *social* net product is larger than the private net product; the case of disservices (the owner of a site building for a factory in a residential section) causes the *social* net product to be smaller than the private net product. Here by intervention, says Pigou, it is "possible for the State, if it so chooses, to remove the divergence in any field by 'extraordinary encouragements' or 'extraordinary restraints.' "

In connection with this second principal group and Pigou's reasoning relative to it, it is my opinion that it illustrates the limitations of Pigou's analysis and the erroneous inferences that may be drawn from it. He has (for purposes of commensurability) limited the range of "welfare" to the economic, and the scope of "private net product" to that which is capable of being sold. Consistent with this limitation we reach, with Pigou, the possibility (the desirability is another question) of "extraordinary encouragements" as a means of increasing production of one sort, and by "extraordinary restraints" decreasing production of another sort, to the end that the national dividend and welfare is augmented. May not the conclusion differ, at least in degree—and to an important degree—if the "private net product" is broadened to include as it does, returns to the investor other than the economic? In other words, the investor A in his sale of a product to B which renders beneficial services to C, D, and E frequently is motivated by the numerous non-economic motives the satisfaction of which calls for non-economic returns to a degree as important as the economic.

Production in which the social product is much larger than the "private net product" (in Pigou's sense) is ever expanding as a result of increasing social consciousness.

Welfare work within the factory and community betterment outside the factory are noteworthy manifestations of this.

It is true, Pigou does consider the "duty to take account of certain indirect consequences which our action produces upon other people," but this is done elsewhere[29] and such considerations do not play a sufficient part in his *Economics of Welfare.* The inferences to be drawn from his discussion on welfare may be vitiated, to an appreciable extent, if we check them by non-economic factors in social life—checking which is difficult and not always suggested in the tenuous discussion of *Economics of Welfare.*

What I have said applies to the point in hand. Interference (which Pigou suggests in the competitive productive process, where a divergence of social and private net products occurs) by means of "extraordinary encouragements or restraints" through the direct mechanism of bounties and taxes may be brought about by the indirect process of public enlightenment and the feeling of social responsibility on the part of producers. To such responsibility the "generals" of industry are increasingly responding; competition, in its associative forms, aided by education in its manifold agencies, is causing the "captains" to fall in line. The indirect method may not only be more effective, in the long run, but also less costly.

Pigou's third group—as we have noted above—are composed of those who purchase what the investor has to sell, and this investor or producer transfers in the process of production and sale gain to others for which he (the producer) is not compensated. This involves the consid-

[29] *Essays in Applied Economics* (London: P. S. King, 1923), "Employers and Economic Chivalry," pp. 12-23.

eration of production under constant and varying cost—increasing, and decreasing.

In the case of constant cost, competitive production equalizes the values of marginal private net products and marginal social net product. Competition is therefore conducive to maximizing the national dividend and economic welfare. The same can be said (approximately) of increasing cost production.[30] With decreasing cost industries, the case differs. Here the gains accruing from the economies which bring about increasing returns cannot stay with the producers, due to the fact that exceptional profits increase output and drive prices down. Hence social net product exceeds private net product. Here, again, competition may be improved upon, it is Pigou's opinion, by the state granting a bounty to industries of increasing returns.

Against the criticism that this conclusion is impotent inasmuch as it is quite impossible to allocate the industries to the proper cost category,[31] Pigou avers that the reason-

[30] *Economics of Welfare*, p. 194. This view Pigou arrived at after the criticism by the late Allyn A. Young when the former first held that in such production the social net product was less than the private net product. This is erroneous since industries of diminishing returns merely involve a *transfer* of income between different parts of the community. It is, therefore, unlike industries of increasing returns where enlarged output means a *net* change of income (*Quarterly Journal of Economics*, XXVII [1913], 673-685).

[31] Stated forcefully by Clapham in his article "Empty Economic Boxes" (cf. *supra*, p. 177). One might add, of course, other criticisms, as for example, the difficulty of measuring elasticity of supply relative to elasticity of demand for the various products in which one might be interested; the effect of cyclical influences varying—as they do—according to the nature of the industry, of the place, and of the time; the uncertainties of administration in giving "extraordinary" encouragement to selected industries; and all of this in an environment in which industrial technique, in particular, and economic and social relations, in general, are rapidly changing!

F. H. Knight attacks, on grounds differing from that of Clapham's, the usefulness of Pigou's conclusion as to the disharmony between individual and social interest due to the phenomena of increasing and decreasing cost. Knight contends the theory "involves some error and much displaced emphasis. Most of the disharmony discussed by Pigou is better accounted for

ing involved has value. One finds he rests his case upon two points, namely, that it exposes "sophistical dogmatism" and that "rough probable judgments" should be possible.[32] To me the indirect value of the former is greater than the direct value of the latter.

This, then, is Pigou's substantiation of his thesis that private enterprise left to itself, even when it operates under conditions of "simple competition" is less conducive to welfare than when organization of production is given government control.

Now as to private enterprise operating not under "simple" competition but under various sorts and degrees of monopolistic action. The limitations of competition (that is, the failure to maximize social welfare) which are due to the monopolistic character into which the competitive order may develop—such limitations are indeterminate to a considerable degree. Approaching this question by analyzing the simplest form, Pigou begins with the case of duopoly where the two monopolists are not carrying on warfare in which the present is sacrificed against future gain.[33] The quantity of productive resources employed, under such circumstances, Pigou believes to be indeterminate, either individually or jointly considered.[34] It suffices to say that the quantity invested by the two monopolists "is likely to be less" than under simple competitive condition and consequently production is probably considerably less than "ideal."[35] Introducing "cut-throat competition"

---

in connection with *pioneering* than with any properties of cost curves" (cf. "The General Theory of Price," *Journal of Political Economy*, XXXVI [1928], 353-370).

[32] *Economics of Welfare*, p. 199.

[33] *Ibid.*, p. 237.

[34] In this conclusion he agrees with Edgeworth rather than Cournot.

[35] Pigou, *op. cit.*, p. 239. "Ideal" investment or production exists when the amount of investment in any given industry is carried exactly to the

does not alter the conclusion except that temporarily production *need* not be less than the ideal amount.[86] Nor does the further complication of simple monopoly or that of discriminating monopoly change the case except in degree.[87] The national dividend—social welfare—tends to suffer when productive organization is determined under purely competitive conditions, or when greater or less degree of monopolistic action is present; the competitive system must be qualified and guarded, social control *must* be exercised if the productive employment of resources is to attain its best. But although this is the conclusion of Pigou's reasoning, his position must not be misunderstood. This he states as follows:

> In any industry, where there is reason to believe that the free play of self-interest will cause an amount of resources to be invested different from the amount that is required in the best interest of the national dividend, there is a *primâ facie* case for governmental intervention. This case cannot become more than a *primâ facie* one, until we have considered the qualifications, which governmental agencies may be expected to possess for intervening advantageously. It is not sufficient to contrast the imperfect adjustments of unfettered private enterprise with the best adjustments that economists in their studies can imagine.[88]

We shall now examine Pigou's views as to the forms or methods of state intervention in the competitive system.

My consideration of Pigou's views on state intervention

---

point at which the value of the marginal social net product in that industry is equal to the marginal social net product of resources in general. (Cf. *Ibid.*, p. 196.)

[86] Although "cut-throat" competition may push the output of the monopolists up to the ideal amount this does not mean that such a condition is conducive to maximizing the national dividend if for no other reason than the range of possible industrial fluctuation is enlarged as a consequence of such competition. (Cf. Pigou, *Industrial Fluctuations*, London: Macmillan, 1927, p. 74.)

[87] Pigou, *Economics of Welfare*, Part 2, Chaps. 15-16.

[88] *Ibid.*, pp. 300-301.

will be treated according to the following order: first, increasing mobility of the agents of production; secondly, regulation of competitive prices; thirdly, public control; and fourthly, public operation.

As to the first: The three causes of immobility which Pigou considers, namely, ignorance, cost of movement, and imperfect divisibility are, indeed, weighty ones and may—if interpreted broadly enough—encompass most obstacles to movement. On the removal of ignorance at state expense Pigou's opinion is, strangely enough, that

> A cheapening of knowledge . . . brought about by the transference of a part of the cost . . . to the State, is quite a different thing and works quite differently from a cheapening brought about by a real fall in cost . . . when the cheapening is due to transference, the resultant increase of equality is an increase beyond what *relatively to existing conditions*, is most advantageous.[39]

In my view, his reasoning with the emphasis on "existing conditions" is open to serious misunderstanding. A program of intervention by the state in the competitive order is never concerned entirely, or primarily, with the "existing conditions." Such conditions may have obtained fairly—indeed, absolutely—satisfactory balance of competitive forces, and still by proper interjection of an impetus or a control agent a more desirable balance of forces may eventuate.[40]

As a consequence of the increasing number of professional financiers, ignorance with reference to financial matters and comparative prospects of different occupations,

[39] *Ibid.*, p. 132. Italics his. This, however, should be compared with the discussion in Section 5 of this chapter (cf. *post.*, pp. 198 ff.). There a somewhat different conclusion of Pigou's is indicated.

[40] It is true that Pigou's footnote (*loc. cit.*) meets the objection to which I have called attention. But his note does *not* remove the erroneous emphasis in his conclusion that state expenditure on education increases equality beyond that which "is most advantageous."

Pigou believes, "is probably much less important than it appears to be among those persons by whose agency the flow of resources into different occupations is in the main directed."[41] It is interesting to note here that Pigou regards the German practice of forbidding small-sized shares in the flotation of new companies and the intimate control by banks of industrial companies as "a more fundamental remedy" of evils arising from financial ignorance than that which he terms our American attitude of public regulation of prospectuses and stock exchange practices.

Immobility caused by cost of movement is accentuated, says Pigou, by the fact that

> Those persons who have to direct their children's choice of a career are not rendered efficient by the selective influence of competition. Fathers who invest their sons' activities unremuneratively are not expelled by bankruptcy from the profession of fatherhood.[42]

If the national dividend is to be maximized it is necessary to provide "a rational sorting of children of different intellectual qualities" and to give them the guidance which competition does not give. Labor exchanges working in coöperation with the educational system, Pigou believes to be necessary.[43]

Error in distribution of labor also occurs from a type of cost to movement which Pigou calls "artificial restrictions upon movement imposed from without."[44] Trade union restrictions and custom are important here. The latter particularly affects the mobility of people of different race and color, and also women workers. This discussion of Pigou's to the American reader impresses him with that element which is common to much of the English eco-

[41] *Op. cit.*, pp. 135 ff.
[42] *Ibid.*, p. 461.
[43] *Ibid.*, pp. 463 ff.
[44] *Ibid.*, p. 477.

nomic reasoning, namely, the effect which the older environment with its greater degree of fixity has upon economic reasoning.

Now as to Pigou's position of the nature of that governmental interference in the competitive régime which seems desirable. In brief,

> . . . up to a point, it is probable that the expenditure of public money in promoting mobility would improve the national dividend. It is necessary, however, for the State to watch this expenditure carefully; for, if it is carried too far, the cost of it will exceed the gain.[45]

This, one can say, is obviously true, and leaves of course unanswered the really important questions, as, for example, what criteria should determine the time, the place, the occupations, the duration, the extent, and the administration of such public expenditure.

Mobility may also be advanced by greater divisibility of the agents of production. Pigou holds:

> It follows that largeness and complexity in the units in terms of which transactions are made act in the same way as costs of movement. In general they obstruct the tendency of self-interest to make the returns obtainable by each of the several factors of production equal in all uses.[46]

The increasing divisibility of capital is very well discussed. Pigou points to saving banks and division of risk and ownership through multiple forms of securities as giving divisibility and mobility to capital.

It is noteworthy that in connection with the obstacle to mobility presented by imperfect divisibility, Pigou's treatment should again be strikingly incomplete. It seems to me that imperfect divisibility applies particularly to land and, to an appreciable degree, to management. In regard

[45] *Ibid.*, p. 481.
[46] *Ibid.*, p. 143.

to the former, the economic friction caused by the large landholdings of England is of great significance. It is true that while the problem presented by imperfect divisibility of land is not discussed in the *Economics of Welfare* it is treated briefly elsewhere.[47] The conclusion he arrives at is,

> . . . if the play of self-interest is left free of interference, it is not likely to lead to so full a development of allotments and small holdings as is socially advantageous. It follows that State action designed to counteract this failure is *primâ facie* desirable.[48]

Such are Pigou's views on state interference with competition which is directed toward increasing the mobility of agents of production. Now as to the second type of interference, namely, regulation of competitive prices. The examination of government regulation of prices leads him to the conclusion that the abnormal circumstances of the War give no grounds for doubting that a permanent policy of price fixing would injure the national dividend.[49] When, in competitive industries, prices are artificially kept down, the necessary counterpart of price fixing is "state regulation of supplies." The criterion presented during the War, by virtue of the comparative urgency among competing uses, is not present, says Pigou, in peace activities. The fixed, relatively simple end in view during war is replaced by a multiplicity of ends, or satisfactions, and high degree of changeableness in time of peace. Hence the impossibility of this kind of social control of competition.[50]

The two types of intervention in the foregoing discussion are those applicable "where self-interest, acting through simple competition, failed to make the national dividend as large as it might be made." When monopolis-

[47] *Essays in Applied Economics*, pp. 92-102.
[48] *Ibid.*, p. 98. Cf. *Economics of Welfare*, Part 2, Chap. 9.
[49] *Economics of Welfare*, p. 214.
[50] *Ibid.*, Part 2, Chap. 12. Cf. Part 2, Chap. 19.

tic conditions have emerged, the third and fourth type of intervention mentioned above, namely, public control and public operation, are those to be considered.

Regarding public control or public operation, this, according to Pigou, can be said *in general*: for any given piece of interference, we now possess greater likelihood of success. Increased intelligence on the part of the electorate and improvement in the working of public authority are the explanations in point.[51] But *against* this he calls attention to four significant "disadvantages of municipal and national representative assemblies, as organs for control or the operation of business." They are: first, these bodies are primarily chosen for other purposes; secondly, their personnel is fluctuating; thirdly, the areas to which public authorities are allocated are determined by non-commercial considerations; and fourthly, regular governmental bodies—especially elective—are liable to electoral pressure.

Serious as these disadvantages are, Pigou's opinion on the possibilities, in general, of improvement of the competitive order by means of state intervention is significantly unequivocal:

> The first, second, and fourth are practically done away with under a system of municipal government such as prevails in Germany. . . . All four disadvantages can be overcome perhaps even more effectively, by the recently developed invention of "Commissions," that is to say, bodies of men appointed by governmental authorities for the express purpose of industrial operation or control.[52]

Having considered state intervention, in general, we turn to such intervention which takes the form of programs of public control. In what manner may such control

[51] *Ibid.*, pp. 302 ff.
[52] *Ibid.*, p. 303.

be applied? In the first place, the state may attempt the policy of preventing monopoly power from arising, or, if it has arisen, destroy it. Pigou regards this policy as ineffective due to the difficulty of enforcement, also that dissolution of combinations "is much more likely to lead to monopolistic than to simple competition," and finally, combinations are not productive of monopoly only but also of benefits.

A second policy of control, which he considers as open to the state, is that of "conserving *potential* rather than actual competition." This policy is expressed by penalizing "clubbing" devices of various types used by the strong firms to kill the weaker.[53] Pigou rightly observes that although evasion occurs, the designating of practices as "unfair" reacts favorably to create the strong force of respectability.

His third possible policy of control is that of direct methods.[54] This amounts to controlling prices or making general provisions against "unreasonable" charges, as illustrated by our Interstate Commerce Commission's supervision over rates. With this type of control, Pigou regards the crux of the problem to be that of determining what

[53] What seems to me as the most recent and interesting form of such "clubbing" devices is illustrated by the practices of American grocery chain stores. They had until recent years almost unlimited power in their strategic use of "leaders" (goods sold at or below invoice cost) during industrial depression when the price appeal is the strongest. This has led to certain reorganizations in both the wholesale and retail field which are exceedingly good illustrations of what I have occasionally referred to in this book as "associative competition." Independent retailers' buying associations, advertising associations, and many other organizations and practices have grown with remarkable rapidity. They now balance, to a large extent, the competitive strength of the chain organization. Although wholesalers threatened to appeal for Federal Trade Commission action against the use of "leaders" by chain stores, such appeal—to my knowledge—was not made. A balancing of competitive forces has, at least to an appreciable extent, occurred without governmental action.

[54] *Op. cit.*, pp. 325 ff.

profits, in the various enterprises regulated, are considered normal. The differences in the degree of risk and qualities of management involved in different enterprises cannot be determined. Furthermore, introduction of control, in recognition of vested rights, should be introduced only "after an interval of notice, and then by gradual steps."[55] Nor is the expense involved in the duplication of expenditure and energy necessitated by government control to be ignored.

We have noted that the fourth form of government intervention in the competitive order is that of public operation. Considerations supporting the conclusion Pigou arrives at that "public operation is likely . . . as a general rule to be inferior from the standpoint of the [national] dividend to public control" are particularly well taken.[56] A publicly operated enterprise is apt to be maintained by artificial support; although less efficient than its rivals,[57] "a public body engaged in industrial operations is *likely* to restrict unduly" the willingness to make ventures necessary for industrial enterprise; and too it is highly impossible that the areas of control most economical for industrial administration will also be the political areas.

From the foregoing examination of Pigou's reasoning concerning competition as the means of allocating productive resources we have seen that the ideal organization, in which the national dividend and welfare would be maximum, is impossible. This establishes a *primâ facie* case for government intervention in the competitive order. On

[55] *Ibid.*, p. 345.
[56] *Ibid.*, pp. 357 ff.
[57] Pigou mentions here the practice of shifting expenses of one governmental department to another, and also obstructing introduction of improvements in order to maintain revenue.

continuing one's examination of the nature and extent of desirable intervention it is noteworthy that such intervention, to Pigou, does not involve far-reaching changes in any part of the competitive order. We find that it is indeed true (as indicated in Section 3 above) that the scope of his consideration does not include the effectiveness of other systems of productive organization that might actually replace it. Finally, although Pigou believes that the disadvantages which adhere to the governmental structure as an economic organization are being reduced decidedly, nevertheless, when one examines the fourfold forms of government intervention to which he directs attention, the employment of none of them seems to offer advantage.

In the following section my analysis will be concerned with Pigou's reasoning relative to the limitations of competition in the field of distribution.

5

In dealing with the scope of Pigou's treatment of competition, in Section 3 of this chapter, attention was called to the fact that he limited his discussion very largely to production. When one turns to distribution one sees that he is convinced that the limitations of competition are to be found largely, if not entirely, in the manner in which the competitive order determines wages, rather than the other distributive shares. As the late Allyn A. Young put it, "In his discussion of the distribution of the National Dividend, Pigou deals almost exclusively with labor problems."[58] The only explanation which Pigou makes for confining his reasoning to the share of the national dividend which goes to labor is found in his statement,

[58] "Pigou's *Wealth and Welfare*," *Quarterly Journal of Economics*, XXVII (1913), 685.

> It is not, of course, pretended that *all* the influences that are relevant have been brought under review. On the contrary, many of the more remote causae causarum, such as those that determine the general attitude of people toward work and saving, as well as many less remote causes that affect the development of mechanical inventions and improved methods . . . have been *deliberately* left on one side. This *deficiency* I do not propose to remedy.[59]

In this we have, of course, no explanation as to why the effectiveness of competition in its determination of the distributive shares which goes to land and to management is to be neglected. Pigou's treatment, however, can be rationalized on the basis of the proposition that a more equal distribution increases economic welfare.[60] In the field of distribution he proposes to examine,

> . . . in what circumstances it is possible for the absolute share of the dividend accruing to the poor to be increased by causes which at the same time diminish the volume of the dividend as a whole; and the relation of disharmonies of this character, when they occur, to economic welfare.[61]

Inasmuch as the poor fall largely in the wage-earning class, an analysis of wages becomes, one might say, equivalent to an analysis of social welfare.

The possibility of control of competitive forces, with the end in view of increasing welfare by the means of decreasing inequality in distribution of wealth, raises the question of the validity of Pareto's law. Pareto's thesis was "that it is impossible for the absolute share of the poor to be increased by any cause which does not at the same time increase the national dividend as a whole."[62] It is, of course,

[59] *Economics of Welfare*, p. 603. Italics mine. Cf. Chap. 10, Part 1.
[60] Cf. *supra*, Sec. 2 (this chapter).
[61] *Economics of Welfare*, 3rd ed., Preface, p. vi. Cf. *Ibid.*, 2nd ed., pp. 614-615.
[62] *Ibid.*, p. 606.

clear—as Pigou points out—that distribution of income is greatly influenced by change in legal, monetary, and social institutions.[63]

Regardless, however, of the refutation that can be made of Pareto's law, interference with the competitive forces of distribution plays a remarkably small part in Pigou's reasoning. On the general question of manipulation of wages, he holds,

> . . . manipulation of wage rates cannot benefit labour in the *aggregate* without causing the reward offered to saving to be diminished. . . . In this way an indirect influence is set in play tending to make the remuneration of labour in future years decrease.[64]

Elsewhere he asserts that evil consequences resulted from forcing wage rates too high in the post-war period. He says:

> . . . partly through State action, and partly through added strength given to work-people's organizations engaged in wage bargaining by the development of unemployment insurance, wage rates have, over a wide area, been set at a level which is too high. . . . The very large percentage of unemployment during the whole of the last six years is due in considerable measure to this new factor in our economic life.[65]

Even had no industrial fluctuation occurred, Pigou holds that a large number of employable would have been unemployed. Wage subsidies, feasible in principle as a remedy, would be bungled in practice. In concerning himself with "wage rates" and "labour in the aggregate," it seems to me that Pigou misses the issue. The pertinent issue is really a twofold one: first, that of creating a greater *di-*

[63] The effects of changes in these institutions are strikingly illustrated by curbing property rights, e.g., inheritance, by inflation, and by breakdown of the forces of custom.

[64] *Op. cit.*, pp. 648-649.

[65] "Wage Policy and Unemployment," *Economic Journal*, XXXVII (1927), 355-368.

versity of industrial activities in order that by matching the requirements of the task and the capacity of the laborer we may secure the highest efficiency from all workers regardless of mental or physical qualification; and secondly, that of facilitating movement from occupations and places where wages are low to occupations (including managerial activities) and places where wages are high. The former is necessarily increased by the growth of division of labor and free trade; the latter requires governmental and private programs, the most important of which is the educational. The resulting mobility—economic competition—would bring about *equalizing* of wages, and the phenomenon of inordinately high wage rates would largely disappear.

To come to "what is in practice by far the most important field of possible disharmony," namely, direct transferences from the relatively rich to the relatively poor. Such transferences may be, first, voluntary, and secondly, coercive. Transference, says Pigou, *primâ facie must* increase, "and it can certainly be so arranged that it *shall* increase, the real income available for the poor."[66] The method by which transferences occur, he holds, is the determining factor whether the effect will be an increased national dividend.

Voluntary transference (in contrast to that which may be said of coercive transference), Pigou states, necessarily increases the national dividend and welfare. He notes that the most obvious form such transferences take "is that of generous conduct toward workpeople" by employers. And it is possible to increase the amount of such transferences from the rich to the poor, as Pigou humorously but significantly observes:

[66] *Economics of Welfare,* p. 657.

Thus, the transference of resources from the rich can be purchased, in a delicately veiled manner, by honours and decorations that cost nobody anything. . . . To confer the Order of Merit broadcast among excellent bricklayers would annihilate its attractive power for the class in whose behoof it was originally designed. This difficulty can, however, be overcome to a great extent by the creation of new orders, instead of the extension of old.[67]

It seems strange to me that Pigou does not consider whether the voluntary transferences to the poor might not be productive of greater social welfare if instead of being made as transferences the resources took the form of expansion of plant and equipment. The growth in social welfare flowing from increased output, lower prices, higher real wages, are to be set against the increase of welfare that comes from "benevolent voluntary transferences." This comparison is not difficult to make: The former takes the shape of goods which market price—and potential profit—indicates as being wanted, the latter takes the shape of welfare work, public parks, etc. Inasmuch as the masses constitute the largest market and their demand is the source of largest profits it might well be argued that growth of social welfare, flowing from the products of increased plant and equipment, is much greater than the welfare which results from voluntary transferences in the form of "welfare work" since the masses have no way of registering either the *kind* or the *intensity* of the desires for various sorts of welfare work. In the rendering of satisfaction through increased productive plant, the wealthy (or their agents, the investment banks) are guided in their judgment by the masses—the poor; in rendering satisfac-

[67] *Ibid.*, pp. 664-665. (One might say, incidentally, that this ingenuity the German government did not seem to possess during the War. After economic resources decreased and rations were exceedingly poor, "Iron Crosses" became notoriously common, even among soldiers in the trenches.)

tion by voluntary transferences, the wealthy have no guide other than their own personal likes and dislikes, which, due to their environment, have little in common with the likes or dislikes of the poor. Furthermore, the social psychology of dependence and paternalism which arises from stressing voluntary transferences is certain to be destructive of increased welfare in the future.

To turn to coercive transferences which, of course, take the form of taxes graduated against the rich. Although "lines of reaction" to such taxes may be distinguished, Pigou reaches the conclusion that

> The general result . . . is, unfortunately, very nebulous. It is probable on the whole that, unlike the expectation of voluntary transferences from the rich, the expectation of coercive transferences from them by taxation will do harm to the dividend, particularly if the taxation imposed is heavy or steeply graduated. But we cannot determine the size of the adverse influence, even when the quantity of revenue to be raised and the scheme of taxation to be enforced are exactly set out.[68]

When we approach this sort of intervention in the competitive order from the angle of the poor, Pigou holds that in the reaction upon the national dividend we must distinguish transferences—brought about by taxes—which differentiate against idleness, transferences which are neutral, and transferences which differentiate in favor of idleness.[69] Transferences of the first sort—illustrated by the Danish old-age pensions which require a minimum amount of work and saving by the recipient in order to qualify—increase the national dividend. Whether transferences are neutral depends, says Pigou, on the form they take. Money grants will usually cause a diminution of the national dividend, whereas if the form is that of "things"

[68] *Ibid.*, p. 676.
[69] *Ibid.*, pp. 677 ff.

(public parks, general sanitary measures, etc.) the result is to increase the national dividend. Transferences of the third sort (in favor of idleness) are involved in all Poor Law systems and must damage the national dividend. This fact calls for stringent administration of Poor Laws.

Having then restricted the field of transferences that may economically be made, Pigou arrives at "certain principal sorts of transferences."[70] Industrial training, medical attendance, training and nurture to the normal children of the poor, when properly managed, are certain to benefit the national dividend.

In this, of course, we can readily agree with Pigou. And one arrives at Pigou's conclusion:

> There is . . . reason to believe that the ordinary play of economic forces tends unduly to contract investment in the persons of the normal poor, with the result that the marginal return to resources invested in the poor and their children is higher than the marginal return to resources invested in machines.[71]

But in our attempt to understand the limitations of competition and the extent to which intervention should occur, Pigou's discussion helps us but very little. Here, as elsewhere, it is most disconcerting to find that the scope of his discussion is restricted, and from the cases brought within that discussion it is quite impossible to determine in what manner and degree they can serve as bases of generalization. He is examining, as he puts it, "separately the effects of *certain* principal sorts of transference."[72] Is this to be understood that there are *many* other sorts of transferences—interventions in the play of competition—and if so are they all valid or are some to be regarded as invalid? Concerning the former, what of their relative importance?

[70] *Ibid.*, pp. 703 ff.
[71] *Ibid.*, p. 702.
[72] *Ibid.*, p. 703. Italics mine.

In concluding this examination of Pigou's treatment of competition in the field of distribution, there is one aspect of his treatment which is stated clearly and effectively. This aspect of competition has not received sufficient attention. He rightly asserts:

> It is the duty of a civilized State to lay down certain minimum conditions in every department of life, below which it refuses to allow any of its free citizens to fall. . . . The exact level at which the several standards should be set is naturally different in different countries. It should be higher in those that are rich than in those that are poor. But everywhere *some* system of standards should be set up, and lapse below any one of them should be made the occasion of intervention by the public authorities.[73]

This is in accord with my view, frequently expressed in this book, namely, that economic competition calls for "standard setting"; it does *not* call for a negative policy on the part of the government.[74] For the enforcement of such standards, as Pigou states, we may need international labor legislation, and, if one country advances ahead of the others—or especially if it establishes an effective minimum alone—immigration restrictions must be established.

6

To recapitulate: Pigou's approach to the analysis of the problem of welfare is through the national dividend. The national dividend, it is his opinion, is an instrument of great power to be consciously controlled. In his analysis five propositions are fundamental. These are: first, that the elements of welfare are states of consciousness; secondly, that welfare can be brought under the category of greater or less; thirdly, increase in economic welfare—un-

[73] *Essays in Applied Economics*, pp. 112-113. Cf. *Economics of Welfare*, Part 4, Chap. 12.

[74] Cf. *supra*, Chap. II, Sec. 4, pp. 28-45.

less there is specific evidence to the contrary—increases total welfare; fourthly, a more equal distribution of the national dividend increases economic welfare; and fifthly, that production guided by self-interest (competition) will not tend to equalize marginal social net products of the different industries: competition brings equality in the values of marginal *private* net products.

As to the *scope* of Pigou's analysis of the limitations of competition, it is important to bear in mind, in a critical examination of his tenuous discussion, that four characteristics of his treatment narrow not only the field of his inquiry but also its usefulness. First, he deals only with that part of welfare which is measurable in money; secondly, his consideration of desirable social control over competition is almost exclusively in the field of production; thirdly, social control shall be applied essentially within and through competitive influences rather than directing such control toward the displacement of the competitive order; and fourthly, the degree to which control of competition, that may be demonstrated to be valid in theory, may also be effective in practice, is quite impossible to determine from Pigou's analysis.

Pigou's discussion of competition in production may be examined, first, with reference to the nature of the limitations of competition, and secondly, his evaluation of governmental intervention. Regarding the former he demonstrates that competition, whether simple or monopolistic, tends not to maximize the national dividend and welfare. This holds even if obstacles to mobility are removed. Thus a *primâ facie* case for governmental intervention is established.

The intervention he evaluates is of fourfold nature:

First, increasing mobility of the agents of production; secondly, regulation of competitive prices; thirdly, public control; and fourthly, public operation. Although Pigou calls attention to serious disadvantages of the political structure serving as an economic organization, nevertheless he unequivocally concludes that these disadvantages can be, and are, practically removed. When one examines, however, the fourfold forms of intervention Pigou considers, the inferences one may clearly draw are that intervention cannot at best greatly maximize the national dividend and that the practicality of intervention is even more questionable.

Pigou's investigation of competition in distribution makes only an extended examination of wages. No explanation is made for confining his reasoning to this distributive share alone excepting his statement that other "influences . . . have been deliberately left on one side." One may rationalize Pigou's analysis on the basis of his proposition that greater equality of distribution of income increases welfare. Since the poor fall largely in the wage-earning class, the distributive share of wages suffices in considerable part for his purpose.

In the discussion of wages, Pigou does not give attention to what, in my view, is the important problem, namely, the increase of economic competition to the end of *balancing* wages. His analysis of "manipulation of wage rates" is not relevant to the main issue.

The "most important field of possible disharmony," Pigou holds, is that of transferences from the rich to the poor. Voluntary transferences he rightly asserts increase the national dividend and welfare. He does not consider what would seem to be the equally, or more, important question whether resources transferred in this manner could not be productive of *greater* welfare through increased productivity of effectively invested capital.

Compulsory transferences may have favorable, neutral, or unfavorable consequences. The examination which follows concerning "certain principal sorts of transferences" leaves unanswered the number of *other* sorts of transferences Pigou might well have analyzed, not only as to their validity but also their relative importance.

His discussion of national minimum standards, which undoubtedly call for international labor legislation and immigration restrictions, is well taken. The standards of which Pigou speaks, in my opinion, are but one of the phases of economic competition which calls for a positive rather than negative policy of government in all departments of economic activity.

VII

THE ENGLISH FABIAN SOCIALISTS: THE LIMITATIONS OF COMPETITION—THE PRAGMATIC ANALYSIS

I

POSSIBLY nowhere has such varied and searching criticism been directed at the operation of competition as that given it in the writings of English critics of the present competitive or "capitalistic" order. Not only has this criticism been characterized, on the whole, by intellectual honesty and motivated by genuine public interest, but also it has been undertaken by those who are well versed in social and economic philosophy. Again, what stands out as a dominant feature of this English criticism of competition is a tolerance for conflicting views that has resulted in an interesting eclecticism and fusion of George's "idealism," Marx's revolutionary class struggle, Fabian intellectual "permeation," Liberal rationalism, and Guild socialists' "functional" democracy. And whatever this variegated social philosophy may lack in consistency, the leadership of that forceful triad of Sidney Webb the scholar, Bernard Shaw the spokesman, and Ramsay MacDonald the politician, has, in part, offset.

This English criticism (which for the sake of convenience I shall term "socialism," as the adherents would emphatically and proudly uphold it to be) undoubtedly has shaped, and is shaping, economic thinking of critically minded people in general, and the English electorate with Liberal and Labour Party affiliation in particular. This is evidenced by the increased discussion of such subjects as nationalization, municipalization, socialization, and rationalization of industry.

Aside from the interest in English socialism as an intellectual movement, it is important in this book—concerned, as it is, with a critical examination of "free competition"—to take into account the criticisms of the English socialists of the competitive order and their views concerning the limitations of competition. These views are unequivocal. The socialistic indictment of competition contains such counts as: first, much poverty prevails; second, inequality in wealth accentuates this; third, there is inequality of personal freedom; fourth, capitalism is unsound both as to production and distribution of wealth.[1] Or again,

> We may say at once that, in our opinion, this dictatorship of the capitalist did, on the balance, in spite of the atrocious debit account for which Ruskin coined the word "illth," more good than evil; at any rate, from the latter part of the eighteenth to about the middle of the nineteenth century. During the latter part of the nineteenth century its success, on balance, was *doubtful*; and in the twentieth century, even in respect of the increase in national figures (we purposely, like Ruskin, hesitate to use the word "wealth"), *its drawbacks outweigh* its advantages.[2]

Together with this view, it is (or was) confidently held that the World War has brought—whether by sheer Marxian "inevitableness" or through conscious regulation,

[1] Cf., e.g., Sidney and Beatrice Webb, *The Decay of Capitalist Civilisation*, p. 5. Also an exceedingly well-written résumé containing a wide variety of indictments is found in O. D. Skelton, *Socialism: A Critical Analysis* (Boston: Houghton Mifflin, 1911), Chap. 2.

[2] *Ibid.*, p. 78. Italics mine.

it is not always clear—the breakdown of the competitive or capitalistic order nearer.[8]

Upon what reasoning concerning competition do such views as cited above rest? Too frequently socialists' views, merely because they are those of socialists, are disposed of summarily as fulminations based on the usual fallacies of the labor theory of value and an exploitation theory of distribution. Because of the intellectual leadership of English socialism, its eclecticism and constitutional methods, and its influence on both the Liberal and Labour Parties, it seems well to examine with some care and completeness the views of English socialists on competition. In so doing, this chapter and the one which follows will be limited in their scope in two general ways, namely, to the writings of those who may be said to have been the leaders of thought and whose work falls in the field of economic doctrine rather than that *purely* of propaganda, and secondly, to the writings concerned with principles and fundamentals rather than the detailed applications.

In one's consideration of the English socialists' attack upon the limitations of competition a separation of what might be termed "early English socialism" should be made from "later and present-day English socialism." The former is Fabianism; the latter is a doctrine that in important respects is *essentially* different from the Fabian creed.

In making this separation and treating in this chapter the English Fabian socialists, as separate from later and present-day socialism (discussed in the chapter to follow), it is important to remember that the latter is not to be

[8] Cf. Sidney Webb, *Toward Social Democracy?* (London: Fabian Society, 1916), p. 3. Also, e.g., H. G. Wells, *What Is Coming* (London: Cassell and Co., 1916), Chap. 3.

thought of as a supersession of the former. To a peculiar degree the socialistic criticism of competition which I refer to as English, in contrast to Utopianism or Marxianism, is a moving current into which have converged many streams. Nevertheless, with the emergence of Guild Socialism and what may be termed as later and present-day English socialism, the nature and direction of the main current of thought is sufficiently different so as to be misleading if not dealt with separately. It has seemed necessary, therefore, to treat later and present-day English socialism in Chapter VIII, rather than merely as a part of the present chapter on the Fabian doctrine.

And now we turn to a brief consideration of Fabian socialism: the development of its ideas and influence, its basic propositions, and its method.

2

The socialism of a country is very largely the product of the social and political philosophy which that nation's institutional life has developed. The early industrialization of England; the individualism and liberalism resulting from the work of such men as Mill and Gladstone; the political institutions permitting freedom of speech, writing, and association; the insular pride in perpetuating traditions, as, for example, the peerage—these are some of the factors that make English socialism "Fabian" rather than Marxian. The severity and rigidity of the latter can only be understood against the Continental background which produced, quite naturally and at the same time, both the revolutions of 1848 and the "Communist Manifesto." True, the Marxian "religion" had in England—as elsewhere—its devout followers who furnished a strong undertone, but the thinking and action which is called

"Fabian" furnish the dominant overtone in English criticism of the competitive order. In my examination of the limitation of competition as seen from the pragmatic—the socialist's—point of view, we go, therefore, directly to the Fabian doctrine.

The development of Fabian organization[4] represents a synthesis of a variety of intellectual forces of which Marx was but one and Owen, Ruskin, and Davidson were others. Undoubtedly the strongest force and the one which gave to modern English socialism its original organized impetus was that of Henry George. This is stated by Mr. E. R. Pease, one of the few who were at the first meeting of the group that was later to form the Fabian Society, and who has been the chief officer of that Society since 1890, as follows:

> To George belongs the extraordinary merit of recognizing the right way of social salvation. The Socialists of earlier days had proposed segregated communities; the Co-operators had tried voluntary associations; the Positivists advocated moral suasion; the Chartists favoured force, physical or political; the Marxists talked revolution and remembered the Paris Commune. . . . George recognized that in the Western States political institutions could be moulded to suit the will of the

[4] The following brief sketch of the development of Fabian ideas and influence is intended to give the necessary background for the sections of this chapter in which I shall make a critical examination of the attack of the Fabians upon competition. It is not intended as a history of the growth of Fabian Socialism, nor would this serve much purpose in an analysis such as the present one. For one who is interested in going further into this historical phase of the subject I would commend four works that are exceedingly useful, for the general reader, on various phases of the subject. These are E. R. Pease, *History of the Fabian Society*; Max Beer, *History of British Socialism*; Joseph Clayton, *Rise and Decline of Socialism in Great Britain*; and Thomas Kirkup, *A History of Socialism.* These secondary sources are, however, entirely inadequate, and a large amount of scattered primary material in the form of tracts, reports, leaflets, and journal articles is indispensable. My documentation indicates those which have been most useful for my purpose.

electorate. . . . From Henry George I think it may be taken that the early Fabians learned to associate the new gospel with the old political method.[5]

To which both of the leaders of Fabian Socialism, Bernard Shaw and Sidney Webb, emphatically agree; the former stating that George gave "direction" to English socialism[6] and the latter asserting that Henry George "provided the motive force for the use of an organized socialist party in the United Kingdom."[7]

This is significant not because the Fabians stopped with what George conceived to be "The True Remedy"[8] but rather because they unquestionably accepted George's means to the end, that is, working through and not in opposition to existing democratic political institutions. Consequently with the formation of the Fabian Society in 1884 socialism was given a hearing by influential, liberal-minded people who were not receptive to socialism of other organizations such as the Social Democratic Federation, with their Marxian revolutionary doctrine in its dogmatic form.[9] Accepting the reasoning of George, the Fabians took as their text that the evils of competition (poverty in particular) are preventable by governmental action, and working through existing governmental bodies has been the dominant characteristic of effective English socialism.

[5] *The History of the Fabian Society* (London: A. C. Fifield, 1916), pp. 20-21.

[6] *Ibid.*, Appendix I, p. 260.

[7] *The Cambridge Modern History* (Ed. by Ward, Prothero, and Leathes; London: Macmillan, 1910), XII, 759.

[8] "We must make land common property." Cf. *Progress and Poverty* (25th anniversary ed.; New York: Doubleday, Page, 1925), Book 6, Chap. 2.

[9] It is interesting to note that in the same year (1884) the Social Democratic Federation, the Socialist League, and the Fabian Society were established. Marx died in 1883 and the S. D. F. was the product of the efforts of Marx's English disciple, H. M. Hyndman.

A notable fact in the development of Fabian Socialism has been the aversion (or at least complete indifference) of the adherents of Fabian views to the securing of a large number of followers,[10] to the creation of a political organization to put into effect their program, or even to any affiliation with existing political parties. Sidney Webb, who became a member in 1885, gave definite direction to Fabian efforts by preparing statistical information concerning undesirable conditions in London with suggestions for reform[11] and also an eight-hour-day bill for introduction into Parliament.[12] This clearly demonstrated that not only was socialism not to be a once for all throwing overboard the competitive order but rather a turning over to the hands of the government, from the hands of the individual, this or that activity. This did not mean necessarily the hands of the *central* government nor did it mean *all* economic activities. Effort was directed to secure support in local elections for Progressive representatives who were largely influenced by Fabian views—a plan which was notably successful in shaping the policy of that very important body, the London County Council.[13] The success in local politics was due, no doubt, to the virtual monopoly which the Fabians had developed in producing political pamphlets pointing out the need of a particular reform measure.

The Independent Labour Party founded in 1893 adopted the Fabian policy, and the "permeation" of the

[10] *The Forty-Seventh Annual Report* (1930) *of the Fabian Society* (the last one available to me) gives the membership as 1,985, of which 1,266 are men and 719 are women.

[11] *Fabian Tract No. 8.* (All of the Fabian Tracts have been published by the Fabian Society.)

[12] The Fabian Society, *Fabian Tract No. 9.*

[13] Joseph Clayton, *The Rise and Decline of Socialism in Great Britain 1884-1924* (London: Faber and Gwyer, 1926), p. 45.

Liberals was facilitated by virtue of the fact that the members of the Fabian Society were, for the most part, Liberals.[14] Then came the establishment of the Labour Party itself in 1906 built upon the nucleus of the Labour Representation Committee of 1900 that had been appointed the previous year by the Trade Union Congress. This was a significant event for Fabian influence, for although the Fabian Society had but one member on the Committee as against two from the Independent Labour Party and two from the Social Democratic Federation, nevertheless the leadership of the Party went to Ramsay MacDonald who alone was able to bring a strong Left Wing with Marxian conviction into closer harmony with Fabian ideas and methods. At the same time, moreover, MacDonald brought sufficient unity in the labor ranks to make possible the severance of labor's complete dependence upon the Liberals. And what was probably more important,

> MacDonald was the one man competent to reconcile the middle class to the idea of a Labour Government. The Fabian Society was excellent at proving the unreasonableness of anti-Socialism; it did not undertake a campaign for converting the middle class to the idea of government by Trade Union officials.[15]

[14] Pease, *op. cit.*, pp. 101-120. And as to the Independent Labour Party nearly *all* of its leaders were, or had been, members of the Fabian Society. (*Ibid.*, p. 208.)

[15] Clayton, *op. cit.*, p. 127.

Although accepting the Fabians' program as a guide to his political organizing work, Ramsay MacDonald was not an active member of the Fabian Society. At the inception of the Society, MacDonald had associated himself with those who had formed the "Fellowship of the New Life" rather than with that section of the group who decided to organize the Fabian Society. From the dissolution of the former (in 1898) until 1900 MacDonald was a member of the Fabian Society when he resigned because the Society refused to condemn the South African War. (Pease, *op. cit.*, pp. 28-35, and Clayton, *op. cit.*, p. 47. A very interesting, intimate sketch of MacDonald's rise to power in the labor movement appears on pp. 118-123 of Clayton.)

But one tract (*Fabian Tract No. 64*, 2pp., 1895), "How to Lose and How to Win an Election," bears his name.

With this brief résumé of the development of Fabian ideas and influences we may now turn to a statement of the basic propositions upon which Fabian socialists grounded their reasoning in their attack upon the operation of competition.

The credo of the socialists who come within the fold of the Fabian belief is found in the "Basis" (constitution) of the Society, adopted at its origin, which reads as follows:

> The Fabian Society . . . aims at the reorganization of Society by the emancipation of Land and Industrial Capital from individual and class ownership, and the vesting of them in the community for the general benefit. In this way only can the natural and acquired advantages of the country be equitably shared by the whole people.
>
> The Society accordingly works for the extinction of private property in Land and of the consequent individual appropriation in the form of Rent, and of the price paid for permission to use the earth as well as for the advantages of superior soils and sites.
>
> The Society, further, works for the transfer to the community of the administration of such industrial capital as can conveniently be managed socially. For, owing to the monopoly of the means of production in the past, industrial inventions and the transformation of surplus income into Capital have mainly enriched the proprietary class, the worker being now dependent upon that class for leave to earn a living.
>
> If these measures be carried out, without compensation (though not without such relief to expropriated individuals as may seem fit to the community), Rent and Interest will be added to the reward of labour, the idle class now living on the labour of others will necessarily disappear, and practical equality of opportunity will be maintained by the spontaneous action of economic forces with much less interference with personal liberty than the present system entails.[16]

[16] *Fabian Tract No. 7* (1896) inside back cover page. I shall not, at this point, make a critical examination of the Fabian propositions which this section of the chapter sets forth. Such examination will be made in Secs. 3-5 when we come to the criticism of the tacit or expressed use of these propositions in the Fabian treatises setting forth the limitations of competition and the changes which they (the Fabian Socialists) would advocate in the present economic order.

After considerable dissension raised by such refractory (and transitory) members as, for example, H. G. Wells, significant amendment has been recently made to paragraphs 2, 3, and 4. These three paragraphs have since been replaced by one paragraph—the second—which reads:

> The Society accordingly works for the extinction of private property in land, with equitable consideration of established expectations, and due provision as to the tenure of the home and the homestead; for the transfer to the community, by constitutional methods, of all such industries as can be conducted socially; and for the establishment, as the governing consideration in the regulation of production, distribution, and service, of the common good instead of private profit.[17]

Such is the general starting point. The particular propositions which they draw from this are: (1) Poverty is the inevitable outcome of private ownership of capital and the competitive system.[18] (2) Capital, privately owned, serves as an instrument of exploitation; and land and capital are indistinguishable. Savers of capital are to be rewarded as inventors, that is, only for a period "necessary for the creation and interest of our capital." What society has maintained and fructified should pass to society after a "limited" period.[19] (3) Industries should be socialized to the end that the livelihood of the people is "entirely independent of private Capitalism." Appropriation of economic rent of land and capital should take place by means

[17] Adopted May 23, 1919. Cf. *Fabian Tract No. 192* and occasionally in tracts thereafter. At the same time a paragraph was included affirming that the Society is a constituent part of the Labour Party and of the International Socialist Congress but that this does not preclude its participation in any movement toward its own objects.

[18] The Fabian Society, "Why Are the Many Poor," *Fabian Tract No. 1* (1884), *passim.*

[19] The Fabian Society, "Capital and Land," *Fabian Tract No. 7* (1893), *passim.*

of "the most suitable public authorities"—parochial, municipal, provincial, or central.[20] Fabian Socialism

> . . . does *not* suggest that the state should *monopolize industry* as against private enterprise or individual initiative further than may be necessary to make the livelihood of the people and their access to the sources of production completely independent of both. The freedom of individuals to test the social value of new inventions; to initiate improved methods of production; to anticipate and lead public enterprise in catering for new social wants; to practice all arts, crafts, and professions independently: in short, to complete the social organization by adding the resources of private activity and judgment to those of public routine. . . .[21]

(4) Inequalities in income should be redressed (partially) by the state employing its power to tax. (5) There should be constant elaboration of collective provision for dependents and, more than that, increasing regulation should be inspired by the idea of a national minimum of education,

[20] The special interest of the Fabians in local government as a means of obtaining socialistic progress is seen in the Fabian Society maintaining for many years an informal information bureau on law and practice of local government administration. In 1919 The Local Government Inquiry Bureau was established which answers "many inquiries each year on the various problems of local government, the powers and duties of local authorities, the law of elections, etc., etc. . . . Besides dealing with these numerous day-to-day inquiries, Mr. Robson devoted a good deal of time to the preparation of special memoranda on specific questions of interest in the Local Government world, such as Municipal Banking, the question of the Milk Supply, and Housing and Rent Restriction Acts" (*Fabian Society, 40th Annual Rept.*, 1923, p. 13).

Even greater direction and control of local governments were made possible by the establishment of the new journal, *The Local Government News*, the first issue of which came in Jan. 1924. (*The Fabian Society, 41st Annual Rept.*, 1924, p. 14.)

[21] The Fabian Society, "Report on Fabian Policy," *Fabian Tract No. 70* (1896), pp. 3-6. Italics mine. It has seemed well to quote its own words since according to statements which appear here and there in Fabian literature this particular tract was (and is) the most deliberate and accurate presentation of its views. Cf. the particular program which it then sponsored to give effect to its generalizations, in its resolutions to the Trade Union Congress of 1896. (*Ibid.*, pp. 8-10.)

sanitation, leisure, and subsistence.[22] (6) The important organic changes in the competitive order which socialism necessitates must be democratic and acceptable to the majority, gradual and causing no dislocation, moral, and constitutional.[23] (7) There should be progressive absorption by taxation of unearned incomes of all forms, not only that of rent and interest but also "rent of ability" which the income tax and taxes on real property secure only in part.[24]

The foregoing are the propositions upon which the Fabian socialists base their attack on the limitations of competition and the competitive order. It is obvious that the method by which these propositions are to be put into effect is highly important, and this shall now be considered briefly.

The method by which Fabian socialists attempt to accomplish the desired readjustments in the competitive order is so well known that one need give but little space to this aspect of Fabian Socialism. But this very familiarity with the *means* to the end leads frequently to the misapprehension that the means, or methods of procedure, are the ends desired. The end toward which Fabian Socialism is working is implied or stated in the foregoing propositions, and it will be clearly seen when we come, in the

[22] Propositions (4) and (5) are added by Webb. Cf. *Cambridge Modern History*, Vol. 12, Chap. 23, p. 760. Throughout his various writings a "national minimum" is the dominant criterion for regulation. Webb gave effect to this by working out completely the educational reform program which the Fabian Society sponsored. This according to Pease (*op. cit.*, pp. 142-148) was entirely the work of Sidney Webb and it is substantially the system of administration established by the Act of 1902, under which present-day English education is organized. The transfer of the control of all elementary schools to local authorities made possible a step toward a "national minimum," namely, "the public feeding of school children."

[23] Sidney Webb, "Socialism in England," *American Economic Association Publications*, IV (1889), pp. 11-15.

[24] *Ibid.*, p. 15.

following section of this chapter, to the critical examination of their reasoning in each of the departments (production, exchange, distribution, and consumption) of economic activity.

To the intelligent critic of the competitive order it was apparent that a rigid materialistic conception of history, with its corollary of inevitable class struggle; a labor theory of value with a conception of market and "surplus" value as the mechanism of capitalist exploitation of labor; "laws" of capitalist development with the *inevitable* consequence of breakdown of capitalism due to the *necessary* increase in the "industrial reserve army" and in misery—this was grounded in part on social and governmental conditions of the past and also on false reasoning. The Marxian apparatus was not in accord with English conditions. Although, as we shall see, the fallaciousness of the Marxian theory of value and of Marx's theory of distribution (at least the latter) was not altogether clear to the Fabian socialists, it was obvious to them that in a democratic state the Marxian *method* of fomenting class struggle was both uncertain and unnecessarily costly.

A revolutionary movement of the working classes was not what Webb conceived socialism to be. Rather it was the result of a series of national problems of an economic and social character which a democratic state should solve through the action of existing legislative bodies and the consent of the majority. The historian of British socialism, M. Beer, has aptly put it,

> Socialism had to be adapted to democracy. This adaptation has been performed by Sidney Webb. It represents the transition from Marxism to Fabianism, or from social revolutionary doctrine to social practice.[25]

[25] Cf. M. Beer, *A History of British Socialism* (London: G. Bell and Sons, 1921), II, 277.

Hence the Fabian policy of "permeating" the electorate with an interest to support legislation for the correction of a social problem.

The issuance of *Fabian Essays in Socialism* marked the first important publication.[26] It has been in constant circulation and has also been translated into foreign languages. The most effective part of the Fabian method has been the publication of tracts and the last published is now (April 1935) Number 242. These fall into four rather distinct groups on: first, Fabian policy; secondly, general socialism; thirdly, the application of socialism to particular problems; and fourthly, powers and duties of local governments.

The other important aspect of Fabian method of "permeation" is that of conducting series of lectures.[27] These lectures are given to large audiences and undoubtedly are effective in extending the adherence to the propositions fundamental to Fabian Socialism as well as to build support for whatever governmental activities may at the time be sought.

Such then is English socialism, influenced by the development of Fabian ideas, basic propositions, and methods. Having these closely interrelated aspects of Fabianism before us, we shall now turn to an examination of the limitations of competition, as seen by Fabian socialists, in the field of production.

[26] Edited by Bernard Shaw (London: Fabian Society, 1889). The essays are by Shaw, Webb, Clarke, Oliver, Wallas, and Mrs. Besant. In 1920 another edition of this work was published.

[27] *The Annual Report* for 1924, for example, shows three series—one on "Questions of the Day" (2 lectures), another on "Europe in Revolution" (6 lectures), and a third on "Is Civilisation Decaying?" (6 lectures).

3

This section proposes to treat the socialists' reasoning concerning the limitations of competition as seen in competitive production. I shall consider first their statement of the case; secondly, the causes—as they see it—which give rise to these competitive evils; and thirdly, the remedies which they propose.

According to the leader of Fabian socialist thought, approximately from the middle of the nineteenth century,

> . . . more penetrating observers began to urge that the dictatorship of the capitalist had not only hopeless limitations in wealth production, but was actually producing a great deal that was the very reverse of wealth.[28]

This comes as the well-seasoned opinion of one who has been a constant student of economic organization for almost a half-century and upon whom there had increasingly fallen the obligation to formulate the views of the political organization which assumed leadership in England. To refer to that highly entertaining dramatist, but nevertheless equally irreproachable and irrepressible economist-spokesman, George Bernard Shaw, we find it recorded, in what he terms his "last will and testament to humanity":

> Uncontrolled motion is terrible. Fancy yourself in a car which you do not know how to steer and cannot stop, with an inexhaustible supply of petrol in the tank, rushing along at fifty miles an hour on an island strewn with rocks, and bounded by cliff precipices! That is what living under Capitalism feels like when you come to understand it.[29]

[28] S. and B. Webb, *The Decay of Capitalist Civilisation*, p. 85.

[29] *The Intelligent Woman's Guide to Socialism and Capitalism* (New York: Brentano, 1928), p. 315.

The perfectly remarkable religious fervor with which Bernard Shaw has

In the competitive order—capitalism—"it is impossible to create an interest in production that is not *also* an interest in *decay* and *destruction*." This "destruction" as Webb sees it is precisely this: a damaging and destroying of the instruments of production "by capitalist Profit Makers"; the ruin of natural resources, "not due to malice of man, but the *inevitable* result of profit-making enterprise"; the "worsening of commodities"; the supply of pernicious commodities and services; the "hypertrophy of selling agencies"; "over-production"; growth of monopoly and negation of individual "freedom"; and the false judgments of the "Court of Profit."[80]

Throughout Webb's unequivocal and emphatic denunciation there is implied, and frequently expressed, the view that the *necessary* consequences of competition (coupled, of course, with the institutions—e.g., inheritance—common to the present order) are not only the foregoing evils but also the more general phenomena of dividing society into "castes" of rich and poor, altogether inefficient consumption, parasitic idleness, irresponsible authority by

---

served his "Social-Democracy" can hardly be appreciated. A persistent lecturer for the Fabian Society, he spoke every Sunday "on some subject which I wanted to teach myself; and it was not until I had come to the point of being able to deliver separate lectures, without notes, on Rent, Interest, Profits, Wages, Toryism, Liberalism, Socialism, Communism, Anarchism, Trade-Unionism, Co-operation, Democracy, the Division of Society into Classes, and the Suitability of Human Nature to Systems of Just Distribution, that I was able to handle Social-Democracy as it must be handled before it can be preached in such a way as to present it to every sort of man from his particular point of view." (G. Bernard Shaw, "The Fabian Society," *Fabian Tract No. 41*, 1892, p. 17.) Cf. also Pease, *op. cit.*, *passim.*

And his activity as a lecturer has never waned! He has appeared on countless programs as speaker or chairman from the very inception of the Fabian Society to the present date, and his influence, although not in terms of concrete party organization, must have been tremendous.

[80] S. and B. Webb, *op. cit.*, pp. 88-140. Italics mine.

those whose selection is not based upon capacity to exercise authority, and in fact,

> The whole range of the present competitive Individualism manifestly tends, indeed, to the glorification not of honest personal service, but of the pursuit of personal gain—not the production of wealth, but the obtaining of riches.[81]

This, needless to say, is the most complete, unequivocal, damning criticism of competition of anyone whose writings have been as widely read, whose work at least in the historical phases of economics so readily acknowledged, whose agitation has been so effective (on a national scope, in educational organization and poor-law administration, and even more widely on a municipal scope), and whose thinking so directive of those into whose hands the government of England is entrusted, as that of Sidney Webb.[82] And strangely enough in the various discussions and comments, in English journals, of socialism in general, and Webb's writing in particular, no critical examination has been made of the economic philosophy upon which present-day English socialism rests. To this economic philosophy we now give our attention.

Throughout Webb's reasoning (as well as in most of the modern criticisms of the competitive order) there is the implied assumption that market values are *not* measures of the social significance of various commodities and services and hence are false directors of productive activity. To deny *or* to affirm this contention, in my view, raises

[81] *Ibid.*, p. 15.

[82] Although not measurable, the influence of the hundreds of thousands of copies of the 242 tracts published by the Fabian socialists up to the present time must have been very great. Of one tract alone, for example (it happens to be No. 82 on the Workmen's Compensation Act of 1897), 120,000 copies were sold the first year! Another publication, "Fabian Essays in Socialism," has passed its 50th thousand. To *all* of these Webb has contributed, and 48 of the 242 tracts he himself has written.

unanswerable questions, or, at all events, necessitates assumptions upon which to base one's reasoning that would obtain very little common agreement. In reasoning upon this question one rapidly gets into subjective and incommensurable elements as, for example, utilitarianism and materialism as a philosophy of life, and representation as a philosophy of government. But upon this much one can safely assert that there is agreement: Market price is the *only* measurement of valuation by the largest number of people—the social group.[38] Valuation in any other manner, whether by a benevolent, omniscient despot or by the specially selected civil service board of a socialist government, is valuation based upon a criterion other than general consumers' choice. That to remove valuation and guidance of production from the "Court of Profit" (to use Webb's expression) to the court of a government board is to replace the court of the many by the court of the few, it seems to me, is clear.

[38] There are those who insist that since inequality in wealth and income means "weighted" purchasing power in favor of the wealthy that, therefore, market prices reflect chiefly the valuation of the wealthy. For luxuries *at any one time* this, it seems to me, is true, but due to elasticity of demand which luxuries, as a class, enjoy as well as production under increasing returns, prices eventuate even for these commodities which tend to reflect the valuation of the many. There are, of course, numerous interesting illustrations of this.

As to the general class of things falling into the category of "the conventional" or "the necessary," the large purchasing power of the wealthy means *potential* rather than *actual* weighting of market prices. This is true inasmuch as wants of this nature are soon satisfied (especially in a country where, generally speaking, the desire to display wealth gives way to what Professor Carver terms a "workbench philosophy of life"). The balance of the income of the wealthy therefore goes, by way of the specialized middlemen (the investment banks), into those investments offering the largest financial return and that means (due to the phenomenon of decreasing cost with increasing output) into manufacturing commodities which have a large present and potential market—the *masses*. It is an interesting fact that the fortunes based upon manufacturing activities have been made more and more in the production of commodities for the millions of consumers and *not* for the relatively few with their "weighted" purchasing power.

The assertion might well be made by the socialists that consumers' choices (market values), although the valuation of the many, are nevertheless not measures of the social significance of various commodities, and therefore exchange and consumption upon the basis of market values should not be left uncontrolled. This is the stand which they would logically have to take to be consistent; it is *not*, however, the stand the Fabian socialists (as well as socialists in general) take, as we shall clearly see in Sections 3 and 5 of this chapter.

It goes without saying that an economist who accepts the utility theory of value as an explanation of the price phenomenon is not precluded from holding that market values *in light of desired ends* (economic, ethical, political, aesthetic, which do not enter at all into the explanation of price per se) are not productive of welfare—economic or other. This is but another way of saying that there are certain kinds of utilities which our competitive productive organization is not economically suitable to produce and which the group, that is, the Government, is peculiarly adapted to provide. Public education is merely one of an increasing number of such "products." This is not only in accord with the teachings of classical political economy but, moreover, it is the very essence of laissez faire, true individualism, and *economic* competition (which Chapter II of this book has developed). Apropos of this, Sidgwick has aptly said, "The argument for laissez faire dealt only with the tendency to promote the most economic and effective production of wealth."[84]

To revert to Webb's statement of the case and the limitations of competition in the field of production. Although

[84] H. Sidgwick, "Economic Socialism," *Contemporary Review*, L (1886), 623.

vaguely implied and indirectly used, a labor theory of value is a necessary element in the Fabian socialists' reasoning (as it prominently and frankly is in Marxian and other socialistic doctrine).[85]

But what has been more openly, or rather more consciously, adopted of the Marxian doctrine by the Fabians is Marx's theory of capital, that is, in the competitive order capital is the mechanism of exploitation. It is clearly seen in the quotations given above and especially in such assertions as that individualism "manifestly" tends to the "pursuit of personal gain" at the expense of production of wealth.

Here as elsewhere the English socialists fail to distinguish the permanent, basic, necessary elements of competition from those that are *not an essential part* of the competitive order. In the absence of both intellectual dishonesty and naïveté, it is singular that the Fabian socialists who strongly profess to throw Marx overboard, can nevertheless fail to make this distinction! The fact is, this distinction is not made and in their statement of the case as well as throughout their reasoning there is clearly the implication that competition as it now operates is *necessarily* the competition upon which to generalize. Of course, the question remains as to what are the essential elements of the competitive order. These, from my point of view, are set forth in Chapter II above.

[85] This has escaped the notice of such a careful student as Ernest Barker, *Political Thought in England: From Spencer to the Present Day* (London: William and Norgate, 1919?). He says, "As Bentham threw aside the old conception of natural rights for that of utility, so, if less drastically, the Fabians threw aside the older theory of value as based entirely on labour . . . for a theory of marginal values based on utility . . ." (p. 215).

Such an analysis I would hold to be inexact, as can be seen not only from the general drift of the Fabian argument but also in Sidney Webb, "Socialism: True and False," *Fabian Tract No. 51* (1894), p. 17. Cf. also S. and B. Webb, *Decay of Capitalist Civilisation*, p. 15.

It is because the Fabian methods of "permeation" or those common to state socialism (ineptly referred to as "opportunism") are utterly different from the Marxian that the elements common to their economic philosophy is overlooked. Because the Fabians contend, and it is generally believed, that "English socialism is wholly different from Marxism,"[86] it has seemed well to present in Section 1 of this chapter the synthesis which Fabian Socialism represents before undertaking a critical examination of its economic reasoning. While, it is true, Fabian Socialism is wholly different from the Marxian in background, development, and method, it has, we have seen, certain basic errors in economic reasoning common to most socialistic economic philosophy and to that of Marx in particular.

We have examined the Fabian statement of the case concerning the limitations of competition in production. Now as to the causes to which the English socialists attribute these limitations. The cause which stands first and foremost in the socialists' opinion is, of course, private ownership in land and capital. Webb, for example, says:

> The political economist now knows that [even] with free competition and private property in land and capital, no individual can possibly obtain the full results of his own labour.[87]

This statement, which is representative of the same idea expressed in various forms,[88] is based upon a fundamental confusion regarding the marginal analysis. Throughout Webb's and Shaw's writing there is a clear-cut failure to understand the distinction of the marginal *producer* and

[86] William Clarke, "Socialism in English Politics," *Political Science Quarterly*, III (1888), 570. Clarke was a co-author of *Fabian Essays* and one of the original leaders.

[87] *Fabian Essays in Socialism*, p. 59.

[88] Cf. *supra*, Chap. II, Sec. 5, pp. 45-50.

the marginal *output*. To them the marginal *producer* determines the price of the product and of the factors of production employed. It is their opinion that the intramarginal producer, securing the price in the market of the highest-cost producer and paying for his input-cost factors only that paid by the least efficient firm, secures thereby a rent to land, a rent to capital used, a rent to management, and a rent on the laborers employed.

To dispose of this erroneous exaggeration of the rent concept one need but say that it is the marginal *output* of *any* producer that is price determining. Marshall's concept of the representative firm is of aid in setting this in clear relief. It is true, of course, that the possession of non-reproducible elements of production yields the possessor a "rent," and the possession of other input-cost factors whose respective supplies possess varying degrees of inelasticity will yield quasi-rents varying to a corresponding degree. The freer the economic competition the more quickly will prices of the product produced and of the agents of production employed absorb the so-called "rents" of the producer which he is enjoying on reproducible elements of his production process.

In production there are unearned rewards accruing from possession of natural resources, of partial or complete monopoly, and of unusual inborn qualities. That such rewards could be appropriated by society without affecting the supply is clear. The time and degree of society's appropriating such rents depend on, first, the development of economic (and psychological) technique for the ascertaining and measuring of such "rents" and then, secondly, the expedience of applying through a political organization the measures which the social appropriation of rents would necessitate. The latter raises the question of the *net* balance between cost and gain. Does it cost (in the broad sense of the word) society more than it is worth?

The significant fact of scarcity and inelasticity of supply —the causes which underlie this phenomenon and back to which all economic problems go (in so far as social problems *are* economic)—the socialists fail to see. And more particularly they fail to recognize that private ownership is merely a method of decentralizing administration of productive activities and thereby harnessing and utilizing that powerful, complex economic force one calls by that sadly misunderstood term "self-interest," and by means of which alone (it seems) self-competence and responsibility can be developed. If a part or all of the reward obtained by individuals through the right of private ownership is unearned, that part or all, as the case may be, obviously can be taken by society without infringing upon that in which society is interested, namely, the supply of goods or services. It seems impossible that socialists cannot see that through the instrumentality of taxes in their manifold forms the competitive order is constantly striving to put to the social uses of all the *unearned* incomes of individuals, rather than using taxation merely for revenue purposes alone.

To be logically consistent in their statement of the causes of the evils of the competitive order, the socialists should frankly accept an out-and-out materialistic interpretation of history and place the present economic motives of man, self-interest (among others), as a *result* (and not a cause) of the economic environment. A change in such environment (removal of private property, for example) would necessarily be creative of other (and better) motives. On this particular score, the Marxian doctrine must at least be credited with logical consistency, or at least more logical consistency than one finds in the Fabian doctrine.

Upon this phase—as upon others—the Fabian socialist economic reasoning is superficial and misleading. There is neither, on the one hand, acceptance or rejection of a materialistic interpretation of history (and that which goes with this doctrine) nor, on the other hand, an examination of the content and source of that which the economist calls "self-interest." There is, by the Fabian, merely the assertion that the "Capitalist System"—private ownership of land and capital—is based on an "immoral and untrue" assumption, namely, that the exercise of an individual's function as a producer rests upon his "morbid passion" for riches.[39] Such an assertion by the socialist reflects, it would seem unnecessary to say, an utterly fallacious conception of the motives which find expression in the competitive régime.[40]

To proceed: Another cause of the limitations of the competitive order (which is really a corollary of private ownership of capital and land) the Fabian socialist asserts is found in the "hopeless and impossible" competition of the small producer with the large to the end that there is an "ever-widening margin of the unemployed class."[41]

[39] S. & B. Webb, *A Constitution for the Socialist Commonwealth of Great Britain* (London: Longmans, 1920), p. 350.

[40] In his Inaugural Lecture at Oxford, D. H. MacGregor stated apropos of this, that: "The pursuit of self-interest is that *whole system* of interests, having a social radius, but maintained by the purposes and activities of an individual. Fame or reputation may be motives more narrowly selfish than the pursuit of wealth." (Cf. "Motives and Standards in Industry," *Economic Journal*, XXXIII [1923], 6. Italics mine.)

[41] *Fabian Essays in Socialism* (Essay by Wm. Clarke), pp. 68-69. Clarke unwittingly furnishes an extreme and amusing instance of the error into which reasoning by analogy may lead one. He holds that the "huge farms of Dakota" with their use of machinery has caused the displacement of human labor and the increase of unemployment! This is so diametrically opposed to fact as to be ludicrous. Farming of any sort in the Dakotas and in Minnesota was (and is) *only* economically possible by *large* producing

Two distinct fallacies, in my judgment, are involved in this contention. In the first place, large-scale *management* is not distinguished from large-scale ownership. The former not only does not necessitate the latter but, on the contrary, with the development of large-scale producing units and management—and hence the need of tapping numerous reservoirs of capital, small as well as large—we have had a tremendous increase of small-scale owners (producers) through the mechanism of securities of small denominations and an increasing *insistence* by large-scale management that customers and employees shall become part owners.

The second fallacy which Clarke's statement (which again is typical of those held by socialists generally) reflects is to tacitly relate competition to a particular *kind* (and size) of competing unit. This leads to the erroneous conclusion that since competition eliminates the small-scale producer whose whole "set-up" is not economical, that therefore competition decreases in scope and intensity. The opposite conclusion (as my analysis has developed elsewhere)[42] is true. That the single proprietorship, partnership, and corporation has each in its turn given way to what is rapidly becoming "associative competition" is, of course, the very means by which competition in an economic (although not in a "biological") sense has increased. This, it seems to me, is perfectly clear if one has worked back into the essence of economic competition.

We now turn to the third phase of this section, namely,

---

units, and instead of causing unemployment it has brought about the phenomenal demand for many thousands of workers in the grain fields in excess of the small farmers it drove out of small-grain farming in the older sections of the country.

[42] Cf. *supra*, Chap. II, Sec. 1 (Competition as to form and as to results), pp. 9-15.

the remedies proposed by Fabian socialists to eliminate the evils of competitive production.

"Socialists," says Sidney Webb, "are only advocating the conscious adoption of a principle of social organization which the world has already found to be the inevitable outcome of Democracy and the Industrial Revolution."[43] This "conscious social organization," one finds, is such that would give effect to the seven basic propositions which Fabian socialists maintain and to which attention has been directed in the preceding section.[44] And not only has that organization been worked out by the Fabian socialists with notable completeness but with that eclecticism which is peculiarly English socialism. We may well agree with the English economist, D. H. Robertson, who writes concerning Webb's "Constitution for the Socialist Commonwealth of Great Britain," that it "must be regarded as in some sense the crown and consummation of all their labours."[45]

Before entering upon a critical examination of what the English socialists submit as a *socialist* program it is important to clarify an issue which has misled not only the socialists in their attack upon the limitations of "free competition" but also has deluded present-day writers who write upon various phases of competition. That to which I refer is the use of collective action and ownership as the criterion of "socialism" in contradistinction to the competitive order. Such a view rests upon the theory that the essence of economic competition is to be found in that which has been termed in Chapter II of this book "com-

[43] *Fabian Essays in Socialism*, p. 32.

[44] Cf. *supra*, pp. 213-216.

[45] *Economic Journal*, XXXI (1921), 62. I would amend this to say that it is the summation of *English* socialism, in general, to quite an important degree.

petition as an institution," in which the analogy of biological struggle and survival is drawn. As a corollary of this it is held that "free competition" (used interchangeably with "individualism" and "laissez faire") exists in the *absence* of a *positive* governmental policy.

As illustrative of this view we see, for example, a statement of a leader of Fabian Socialism:

> The first of the long series of enactments for the protection of labour was passed in 1802: it was the beginning of the end of laissez faire.[46]

And further in speaking of the spread of municipalization in England, Clarke holds that, therefore, no country is "more rapidly and more certainly [going] in the socialist direction." This is diametrically opposed to the conclusion one arrives at if his theory of competition rests upon that which I have maintained is the essence of economic competition.[47] A *positive* governmental policy is a prerequisite of economic competition.

According to my analysis collective action, per se, is merely a method by which certain utilities are created which would not be produced (in desired quantities or quality) by individuals. Public education is but one of an increasing number of such utilities. Collective action is not only consistent with economic competition but an increasing amount of this action is necessary for maintaining and expanding such competition. The Fabians, as well as other socialists, who enthusiastically proclaim the increasing part which the municipality, the state, the coöperative society take in economic activity to be the manifest proof of the establishment of socialism and the "unconscious abandon-

[46] Wm. Clarke, "Socialism in English Politics," *Political Science Quarterly*, III (1888), 553.

[47] Cf. *supra*, Chap. II, Sec. 4, pp. 28-45.

ment of individualism," are merely being misled by their own play of words. Inasmuch as such economic activities are what I have termed "associative competition" (and which to a considerable degree are as naturally displacing corporative competition as corporative competition has displaced the partnership competition)—the socialists should logically have insisted that the widespread establishment of the industrial corporation in the 70's and 80's (with its consequent displacement of individual proprietors) *was* socialism, and the holding company (as well as the "trust" of more recent times) *is* socialism!

It is precisely because the socialists have not seen the essence of economic competition, with the changing form which the competing unit must necessarily take as a result of changing technique of production, that they are led into such quandaries as:

> Paradoxical as it may seem, one of the principal objects of the socialist is greatly to *increase* the amount of "*private property*" but to concentrate it entirely in the forms of wealth for which the institution is fitting.[48]

And an even more striking illustration is their statement (which they italicized throughout!) that in most services undertaken by the government,

> There is every reason to infer that, in comparison with joint stock capitalism, government management of industry means, ultimately, in this way a larger number of independent employers. . . .[49]

Having disposed of this issue, which has misled socialists regarding the nature of the competitive order, in what

[48] S. & B. Webb, *Decay of Capitalist Civilisation*, p. 68 n. Italics mine. And also cf. the absolutely contradictory views in *Ibid.*, *passim*, and S. Webb, *Toward Social Democracy?* (London: Fabian Society, 1916), p. 7.

[49] *New Statesman*, V (No. 109, May 8, 1915), Special Supplement on State and Municipal Enterprise, p. 32.

manner do the Fabian socialists propose to remedy the limitations of competition in production?

As we have seen, the credo of the English socialists as found in the original "Basis" of the Fabian Society was the "reorganisation of Society by the emancipation of *Land* and Industrial *Capital* from individual and class ownership."[50] This was somewhat indefinitely qualified with regard to both land and capital. Extinction of private property in land should be conditioned, according to the original "Basis," upon the granting of "such relief as may seem *fit* to the community," and, in the revised "Basis" of 1919, the condition is upon an "*equitable* consideration of established expectation."[51] As to capital, extinction of private property is limited to "such industries as *can* be conducted socially." And to give effect to this transference of property, it is the present-day thesis of the English socialists that the "application to industry as to political government of a carefully co-ordinate Democracy offers the best expedient."[52]

Inasmuch as individuals have not one will or purpose, four distinct "democracies" are conceived,[53] namely, Democracies of Consumers, of Producers, of Citizens in their political relations, and of Citizens in their social relations. As to the "Political Democracy" (the third of the foregoing) it relates to problems such as national defense, foreign relations, order and justice; the "Social Democracy" (the fourth) is concerned with, for example, the distribution of the national income and the administration of

[50] Cf. *supra*, p. 213.
[51] Cf. *supra*, p. 214.
[52] S. & B. Webb, *A Constitution for the Socialist Commonwealth of Great Britain*, p. 101.
[53] Webb's discussion relates only to the economic life, for he specifically states that "Democracy does not cover the whole of life," e.g., literature, science, art, religion.

national resources. The point which the Fabians desire to make is that the national constitution should provide for a Political Parliament and a Social Parliament. Although each is to be equal, coördinate, and supreme in its own sphere, nevertheless the Social Parliament should be granted power over property and taxation, right of eminent domain and expropriation, public services such as health and education, transportation and communication, provision for non-effectives, "allocation of particular resources to particular needs," and distribution of rent and surplus value.[54]

It is incomprehensible that careful students of social organization, as English socialists have been, can seriously suggest that a division of democracies of the kind set forth can be made in our highly complex and closely interrelated society. It unquestionably reflects the influence of the prolific Guild socialist, G. D. H. Cole.

A notable feature of the more recent English socialistic attack upon competitive production which sharply distinguishes it from early Fabian Socialism as well as from that which is generally thought to be socialism today, is Webb's view regarding forms of "public ownership." Transference of ownership from the individual does *not* mean that it shall necessarily go to the national government. Fewer than "a dozen" should be owned or operated by the national government; a larger number by municipalities; and the "great mass" of commodities prepared directly for consumption fall most appropriately into the "Coöperative Movement."[55]

[54] S. & B. Webb, *op. cit.*, pp. 102-122.

[55] *Ibid.*, pp. 148-149. Elsewhere Webb reduces the "nationally organized" industries to "only a *half* a dozen." Immediate nationalization of railways, canals, and mining (including oil) should take place. Afforestation, insurance, current and deposit banking "is equally pressing." (p. 168.)

Although, in this analysis, we are not interested in the matters of organization which are merely of a factual nature, it is important to note that it is quite impossible to see any provision for a coördination or liaison of the fourfold democracies in the socialist program. This is but another way of saying what I have already indicated, namely, that such divisions are merely artificial.

Again, for example, in regard to the "Democracy of Producers": While it appears that the managers of lower rank are to be chosen directly, the important managers are to be selected by a "Selection Committee or Appointment Board."[56] "Yet," says Webb naïvely, "the door need not be closed on further experiments."[57]

It is remarkable that it should be suggested that the tremendous responsibility of the management of nationalized industries be thrown upon a "Social Parliament" and its National Boards without frankly facing the difficulties involved. With the rapidly changing technique in industry and, indeed, the rapidly changing position which an industry maintains in the whole economic organization of a nation, the problem of determining what may be wanted

---

Webb does not mean the transference of ownership to municipalities as they *now* exist. There is need of reorganizing local governments in order that their areas may be determined with reference to the "functions" entrusted to them. Also there must be reorganization for municipal governments (in accord with that of the national government), that is, democracy of producers, democracy of consumers, and democracy of citizens. (*Ibid.*, pp. 203-212.)

On Webb's view regarding the growing place of consumers' coöperation as "a genuine and practical alternative to the Capitalist System" see S. & B. Webb, "The Coöperative Movement," *New Statesman*, III (No. 60, May 30, 1914), Special Supplement, pp. 1-34.

[56] This is fully discussed in S. & B. Webb, "Can the Organisation of Industry be Based exclusively on Associations of Producers?" *New Statesman*, II (No. 45, Feb. 14, 1914), Special Supplement, pp. 1-31. The article is an exceptionally interesting and valuable survey of associations of producers.

[57] *Ibid.*, p. 163.

in management (to say nothing of the more immediate difficulties) seems quite impossible on a scale that is social in scope and on a basis that is governmental in approach. For a thoroughly standardized as well as relatively stabilized industry, such as mining, civil service recruitment may be adequate. This, it is true, certainly is the tenor of Lord Haldane's testimony before the Royal Commission on the Coal Mines, which furnished, to an important degree, the basis of the Majority Report of the Sankey Commission in favor of nationalization.[58] It is quite incredible, however, that anyone can hold that the almost complete line and staff organization of the army, which is obviously required for discipline and directness of action, can throw any light upon the administration of industrial work where the organization must be almost purely of the functional type—a type differing not only in the problems of the mechanics of organization but also in the problems of objective, of motivation, of *esprit de corps.*

At any rate, the important point in Webb's discussion of organization is to separate current administration and questions of policy. The latter is concerned with quality and quantity, how, when, and where to produce, and should be directed, the Webbs hold, by the Social Parliament. This Parliament, in turn, would be guided by representatives of consumers and representatives of producers.[59]

So much for a brief statement as to what the English socialists conceive the organization of production to be if the limitations of competition are to be corrected. This

[58] Lord Haldane's testimony is reprinted in *The Problem of Nationalization* (London: Allen and Unwin, 1921).

[59] *Ibid.*, p. 179.

brief survey makes no pretense of doing justice to the matured program of the Fabian socialists, a program which represents many years of intensive research and practically undivided thought of such sincere students as the Webbs: it is not to be disposed of in a cavalier manner. As a criticism of competition in production what may be drawn from Webb's whole discussion?

First, it directs attention to the acknowledged fact that the competitive order may not produce the satisfactions, because of the lack of "effective demand," which may be necessary for socio-economic interest as well as for other considerations. Whether it be due to the growth of humanitarianism or other forces, a social group finds it frequently impossible to await the development of effective demand by the slower but sounder method of creating higher wants which come spontaneously as a result of public education and the elimination of vice. The social group must therefore supplement, to some degree, the market place and the price mechanism.[60] Webb's emphasis upon the National Minimum is a contribution from this point of view.

Secondly, the growth of the producing unit undoubtedly foreshadows the development of productive organization in which the optimum size is such as to require organization either larger in magnitude or more intensive in coördination than even associative competition, of a private nature, can furnish. Again a growth in the number and kinds of natural monopolies will further socialization.

Thirdly, the socialists have directed attention to the need of an increasing amount of social control of produc-

[60] Hence the social group, as a state or municipality, exempts churches and schools from taxation; the social group, as individuals of common interest, supports symphony orchestras and civic operas, for which "effective demand" provides but a small fraction of the necessary expense.

tion not generated by the forces of competition. Webb's formulating of the Minority Report of the Poor Law Commission of 1905-1909 is in point. The governmental establishment and control of labor exchanges is the basis of their analysis in this report.[61]

Fourthly, the Fabians have emphasized a phenomenon to which they apply the term "unconscious socialism" and undoubtedly are correct in this emphasis. But their view that increase in social control will be municipal rather than national is a moot question.[62]

These criticisms of competition in production are well taken. The measures of social control which they suggest are fully in accord with economic competition. But to term increasing economic activities of the state, of the municipality, and of associations of consumers "socialism" is, in my opinion, merely phraseology. We now pass to an examination of the control of competition which the Fabian socialists deem desirable in exchange and value.

4

From the control based upon the conception of society as a fourfold democracy, utilizing its threefold form of public ownership, with its Democracy of Producers for each industry, and a Social Parliament for all industries—from this sort of control of competition in production we pass to a notable absence, in the socialists' program, of desired control of competition in exchange and value deter-

[61] Cf., S. & B. Webb, *The Minority Report of the Poor Law Commission, 1905-1909* (London: Longmans, 1909), Part 2, Chap. 5. Also S. & B. Webb, *English Poor Law Policy* (London: Longmans, 1910), Chaps. 6-8.

[62] An excellent brief statement on the development and extent of state and municipal enterprise is S. & B. Webb, "Can Industry be Organized by the National or Municipal Government?" *New Statesman*, V (No. 109, May 8, 1915), Special Supplement, pp. 1-32.

mination. But this is *not* to be understood that competition in exchange is productive of desirable results when uncontrolled competition exists in production. Relative to this, Webb has said:

> . . . there is no sort of assurance, ***even where business competition is supposed to prevail***, that the prices charged to the domestic consumer will, taken as a whole, automatically oscillate closely about the real or necessary costs of production, or that the public can rely on business competition as an effective safeguard against the extortion of an entirely unnecessary price. . . .[63]

This apparently is to be explained by what Webb claims the capitalist enterprise fails to do, namely, "fulfill a function in the social order." The socialistic organization, it is contended, aims at: first, producing in adequate quantity and quality that which the community needs; secondly, ensuring increasing efficiency of production; thirdly, maintaining prices at a point no higher than that which is sufficient to call forth the productivity required.[64]

The Fabians' solution to this has already, in part, been indicated in my examination of the control of competition in production. The Social Parliament would not only have "supreme control of the nation's economic resources" but it would also have

> . . . the financial co-ordination and direction of the nation's ways and means, including such arrangements as the currency, ***prices***, and ***charges***, the provision required for the future, the allocation of particular resources to particular needs, the equitable distribution of the national rent or surplus value, and, where necessary, the levying of taxation for the making up of deficits.[65]

The control of production and prices of the Social Par-

[63] S. & B. Webb, *Constitution for the Socialist Commonwealth of Great Britain*, p. 327. Italics mine.

[64] *Ibid.*, pp. 327-328.

[65] *Ibid.*, p. 119. Italics mine.

liament would extend, of course, only directly to those industries under national ownership. Production under control of local authorities or coöperative societies should, however, be provided with a "Chairman of the Finance Committee," just as the Social Parliament would have. In all cases the budget would depend "almost entirely on a fixing of fees and prices."[66]

Governmental bodies will find, however, says Webb, that "a simple adherence to the cost of rendering the service does not solve the problem." "A simple plan," he feels, is for each national industry or service to include an "overhead charge" in its prices to cover the whole expense of non-remunerative services.[67]

Another important aspect of price, concerning which one is interested in the socialistic control, is that which has to do not merely with price-fixing to cover "necessary costs" but with the provision of capital. Webb has a ready and direct answer. The National Board (and local boards) would allow in its budget each year for upkeep and extensions by a "loading" on the cost price.[68]

Such is the English socialists' view regarding the control over the price mechanism. What may be said of this doctrine?

First, it places an exaggerated faith upon accounting

[66] *Ibid.*, p. 338. In those industries still being conducted for private profit, says Webb, "the capitalist entrepreneur . . . will have to become a strictly regulated intellectual piece worker, remunerated according to results ascertained by accurate scientific measurement." (*Ibid.*, pp. 331-332.) This will be true because the Social Parliament will determine and enforce "Legal Maximum Prices" (*Ibid.*, p. 330).

[67] *Ibid.*, pp. 338-340. Webb's statement does not agree with what another leader of Fabian Socialism, Graham Wallas, says in his essay on "Property under Socialism" in the *Fabian Essays in Socialism*: "Under pure Socialism, to use the word in its narrowest sense, the State would offer no advantage at all to any citizen *except* at a price sufficient to pay *all the expenses* of producing it. . . ." (p. 144).

[68] *Ibid.*, p. 348.

and statistical technique for measuring of costs. While this may be merely a matter of technique, it is to be remembered, in the second place, that the Fabian program specifically states that adherence of price to cost "does not solve the problem." Matters of technique, therefore, become the infinitely more complex problem of matters of policy with regard to welfare. It is not to be denied that conscious, central control, with the criterion of welfare as a guide, should be given an increasing importance in our control of production of such goods and services as public education, health, and communication. This the increase of economic competition, as much so as socialism, necessitates.

In the third place, the Fabian socialists place a naïve reliance upon statistical control and "loading of prices" for the provision and direction of capital—to say nothing of using statistical-governmental control of the less objective forces of "progress" and "invention."

It is to be remembered, however, that English socialism makes no contention as to the extent to which government—either national or local—control of industrial capital shall go.[69] The ambiguous phrase coined by Sidney Webb during the exigencies of the Labour Party's first administration in 1924, namely, "the inevitable gradualness" of English socialism,[70] begs the same question and gives rise to the same ridicule as the Marxian explanation that a nation needs to be "ripe" for socialism when "the knell of capitalist private property sounds: the expropriators are expropriated."

How many industries, according to Fabian doctrine, are

[69] Cf. *supra*, pp. 234-235. See especially footnote 55, p. 234.

[70] Cf. Sidney Webb, "The Labour Party on the Threshold," *Fabian Tract No. 207* (1923).

to remain under private ownership and to what extent competition is therefore to be the determining force in exchange and prices, one cannot determine from any of the Fabians' writings. The Fabians' statement, apropos of the extent of private ownership, is obviously ambiguous. They say:

> What Socialists object to is the *perversion* of the institution of private property by the extension of the concept to things and rights which, in *their judgment*, are not *fit* objects of individual ownership. . . . The question of what things and what rights should be allowed to become private property is one *to be decided from time to time.*[71]

5

In the English socialists' reasoning concerning the limitations of competition in distribution, one argument is given almost sole attention. It is effectively and unequivocally stated by Sidney Webb in his Presidential Address to the Social and Political Education League:

> My thesis is that the necessary Basis of Society, in the complications of modern industrial civilisation, is the formulation and rigid enforcement in all spheres of social activity, of a National Minimum below which the individual, whether he likes it or not, cannot, in the interests of the well-being of the whole, ever be allowed to fall. It is this policy of a National Minimum which, in my judgment, is going to inspire and guide and explain the statesmanship and the politics of the twentieth century.[72]

The national minima, Webb holds, are those of leisure, sanitation, education, and subsistence. His view is not based on any conception of utopian egalitarianism or of Marxian class struggle. Though the process necessitates the observance of "inevitable gradualness," England now possesses

[71] S. & B. Webb, *Constitution for the Socialist Commonwealth of Great Britain*, p. 342. Italics mine.

[72] "The Necessary Basis of Society," *Contemporary Review*, XCIII (1908), 665.

the democratic state machinery—national and local—that may be employed to maintain a national minimum in the various phases of life. This should be particularly the function of local authorities.[73]

The establishment of a national minimum is to be made possible, of course, by means of the rents in all of their forms (obtained through the socialization of land and capital) going to social use rather than to increase the existing inequality of wealth. To what degree equality in wages is to be the guiding criterion in the Fabian program is quite impossible to determine from Fabian socialist doctrine. Although the *ownership* of instruments of production is to be vested in the "Democracies of Citizen-Consumers," the "Democracies of Producers" should exercise *control* (but not exclusive control) over

> . . . not merely their *pay*, their working *hours*, and their sanitation, safety and amenity of their places of employment, but also the character of the operations that they are called on to perform . . . and their practical freedom or opportunity to exercise their vocation in an efficient way.[74]

Inasmuch as there is to be a great variety of types of industrial organization (it is to be remembered that the industries to be nationalized—for the present at least—are but a half-dozen) with competition between them, a fair *guess* would be that inequality of wages would not be materially less than now. In the Fabian infrequent admission of this fact, it is implied that with the "moralization of society" exceptional pay for exceptional talent will be unnecessary.[75]

[73] S. & B. Webb, *op. cit.*, p. 321.

[74] *Ibid.*, p. 164. Italics mine.

[75] Cf. Graham Wallas in *Fabian Essays in Socialism*, pp. 142-143. Cf. also S. & B. Webb, *A Constitution for the Socialist Commonwealth of Great Britain*, pp. 336-337.

To what degree, or for how long a time, the English socialists would permit individual appropriation of rents arising from the exploitation of differential advantages in production is difficult to say. This, it seems to me, is true for two reasons: first, according to the "Basis" of Fabian Socialism there shall be "equitable consideration of established expectations"; and secondly, the transfer to the community shall only be "of all such industries as can be conducted socially."[76] Both of these obviously raise administrative questions upon which agreement is impossible. Add to this the policy of "inevitable gradualness," and the Fabian control of this aspect of competition in distribution becomes highly problematical.

The control in distribution to which the English socialists' doctrine points with regard to the social appropriation of rent is not, of course, unique to socialism. The advocate of an order of economic competition and the supporter of socialism merely differ, on this score, with regard to their opinion as to the *results* which will follow from the expropriation of land or capital which yields unearned incomes. The former (the advocate of an order of economic competition), in view of the difficulty of determining the portion which is *unearned* together with the difficulties of centralized control as against decentralized administration, does not believe expropriation would be productive of *net* advantage. In other words, the economic cost is too great; the result is unfavorable.

As to interest: The control which the socialists would exercise here is found in their contention that savings, after the establishment of social control of production, will be increased rather than decreased. Such savings will take the form of increased necessities of life for the poor, increased

[76] Cf. *supra*, p. 214.

insurance and also deposits in banks, "on which it may be quite permissible to pay interest, if such a stimulus to saving proves to be necessary or desirable."[77]

This is no attempt at all to cope with the problem of interest and the supply of capital. While the English socialists certainly do not follow Marx in an utter failure (or unwillingness) to comprehend the function of capital and of entrepreneurship, nevertheless their views concerning the supply of capital and of its direction over-simplify the problem to the point that their discussion is about as misleading in its simplicity as Marx's was fallacious in its narrowness.

6

To sum up: English socialistic criticism of competition represents a fusion of George's "idealism," Marx's revolutionary class doctrine, Fabian intellectual "permeation," and the "functional democracy" of the Guild socialists. While the influence of English socialism has been directly exerted on members of the Liberal Party and the Labour Party, it has shaped the thinking of critically minded people generally.

The English socialists' indictment of competition is unequivocally and emphatically stated. The reasoning upon which they arrive at their conclusion needs to be critically examined. Guild Socialism and the views of present-day English socialists are, in important respects, essentially different from Fabianism. The former will be considered in the following chapter.

The institutions which were England's caused English socialistic criticism of competition to be "Fabian" rather than "Marxian." The strongest force in the origin of the

[77] S. & B. Webb, *op. cit.*, p. 345.

Fabian movement was Henry George. He gave to English socialism its method—the use of existing governmental machinery; and he gave to it its text—the evils of competition are preventable by governmental action. And Sidney Webb gave to English socialists their program—immediately, reform measures; eventually, socialization of land and capital.

The propositions basic in Fabian belief are: Poverty is the inevitable outcome of private ownership of capital and land, private ownership of land and capital means exploitation; land and capital should be socialized, inequalities in income should be redressed (in part) by the State, a national minimum should be maintained, changes in the competitive order must be constitutional, and there should be taxation of unearned incomes of all forms.

The method, fundamental to the Fabian program, is the "permeation" of the electorate. In giving effect to this method the *Fabian Essays in Socialism*, the Fabian tracts and lectures have been employed with remarkable persistence and regularity.

The Fabian socialists' reasoning concerning the limitations of competition in production may be treated from: First, their statement of the case; secondly, the causes which give rise to these competitive evils; and thirdly, the remedies which they propose.

Regarding the first, production for private profit must be destructive of instruments of production, of natural resources, of quality, and of freedom. In view of the widespread influence of Fabian methods in general, and of their tracts in particular, it is strange that this sweeping and positive denunciation of Webb's has been given no critical examination.

In my opinion, Webb's condemnation of competitive

production rests, in the first place, on the assumption that market values are not measures of social values and hence are false directors of productive activity. The socialists should logically hold, in light of this assumption, that consumers' choice should not be free or that market price should not be uncontrolled. This they do not hold. Again, in refuting Webb's general denunciation of competition in production, it should also be emphasized that it has never been contended that competitive production is economically suitable to produce certain important utilities, as, for example, public education. Production of this sort must be carried on by the public; economic competition necessitates a positive governmental policy.

Webb's denunciation of competition rests, in the second place, on a labor theory of value. This, it is true, is not openly accepted. In the third place, he accepts the Marxian theory of capital, that is, in competitive productiveness capital is the mechanism of exploitation. And finally, the Fabian socialists make no attempt to distinguish that which is essential to the competitive order from that which is not.

Concerning the causes which give rise to competitive evils, the chief cause, the Fabians maintain, is found in private property of capital and land. Here their reasoning is fundamentally in error due to their confusion in the use of the marginal analysis. Also the socialists fail to see that the appropriation of unearned incomes is in accord with the competitive order. Moreover, they fail, to a remarkable degree, to comprehend (and in this the socialists are not alone!) the essence of "self-interest" and its social significance.

Another cause of the limitations of competitive production, the Fabian socialists assert, is found in the necessary destruction of small producers in a régime of large-scale production. Here they fail to distinguish ownership and management and, secondly, they relate competition to a particular *kind* (and size) of a competing unit.

Regarding the remedies proposed by the Fabian socialists for what they consider the unavoidable evils of competition in production, they are misled in their attack upon competition by viewing collective action, per se, as socialism. What is essential for an increase in economic competition, namely, collective action or a positive governmental policy, the socialists fallaciously hold means essentially the destruction of competition.

Their fundamental remedy, that is, public ownership of land and capital, is indefinitely qualified in the recently amended constitution of Fabianism. Further, the fourfold organization of "Democracies" and the twofold organization of Parliament, for which Fabian socialists contend, fall on the score that such organizations in a closely interrelated society are artificial and impossible. It is also to be noted that in the more recent Fabian economic doctrine "public ownership" means national, municipal, and coöperative ownership; and the first of these is to extend to but a mere "half-dozen" industries. With regard to public ownership and administration in general, there is a complete failure to consider the problems of civil service recruitment and administration.

The Fabian socialists' criticism of competition in production has in part, however, real merit. The measures of social control to which this criticism indirectly calls attention is in accord with the increase of economic competition.

In the Fabian socialists' program there is a notable absence of desired control of competition in exchange and, hence, in value determination. It is true that the Social Parliament shall see that prices are just sufficient to call forth "the productivity required." But the industries over which there is to be public control are presumably few. The "overhead charge," to carry on desirable non-remunerative services, and the "loading" on cost prices, as a means to create capital, place an utterly mistaken reliance on statistical control.

In the Fabian's reasoning relative to the limitations of competition in distribution one argument is paramount: society should enforce a "National Minimum" in all spheres of social activity. This should be particularly the duty of local authorities.

Fabian socialists' views on equality in wages cannot be determined. It seems that according to their *own* program practically the same inequality as exists today would continue. Neither can the degree of individual appropriation of rent, nor can the length of time of such appropriation, be determined from the Fabian doctrine.

The English socialists' statement that interest will be paid if such a stimulus to saving proves necessary or desirable gives no clue as to the degree to which control should be exercised on the competitive price paid for capital, or over the forces of demand for or supply of capital.

Suggestive as their criticism concerning the limitations of competition may be, sincere as their aspirations have always been, helpful as their educational work is in creating a social sensitiveness and a greater promptness in doing that which society may do in more equitably distributing the inevitable stresses and strains of economic changes, nevertheless, the Fabian socialists not only accepted most of the fallacious Marxian reasoning but also to this their analysis and program added much that was either misleading or erroneous.

VIII

LATER AND PRESENT-DAY ENGLISH SOCIALISTS: THE LIMITATIONS OF COMPETITION—THE PRAGMATIC ANALYSIS

Sec. 1. Guild Socialism; relation to earlier English socialism; development. p. 251.

Sec. 2. The philosophy of Guild Socialism. p. 254.

(1) The thesis.

Producers' control of industry.

"Functional" organization.

Public ownership *not* public control.

(2) The organization:

Ignores interdependence due to specialization.

(3) The control.

Of price; of wages.

Marxian doctrine.

Capital and entrepreneurship not comprehended.

Sec. 3. Most recent program of English critics of competition. p. 262.

The dilemma of competition; MacGregor's view; "rationalization."

Essentially differs from Fabian and Guild doctrine.

(1) Unemployment program.

National Labor Corps.

Hawtrey's control of price level.

Report of Colwyn Committee.

Trade union opposition.

Government planning of public work.

Fundamental weakness.

(2) "Conscious development" of national economic resources.

(a) Control of export of capital.

Report of Balfour Committee.

AS POINTED out in the preceding chapter, the current of English Fabian criticism of competition was distinctly affected by the emergence of Guild Socialism. The synthesis which followed has resulted in a view concerning the competitive order and also in proposals of control that are more aptly termed "later and present-day English socialism" than that of Fabianism. This has, in part, been indicated in the discussion of the preceding chapter concerning the organization of society which Fabian socialists have more recently deemed necessary in the control of competition in production. The conception of society organized on the basis of fourfold democracies, for example, has no relation to Fabian propositions or program. This, as well as many other important modifications in present-day Fabian or English socialistic views, represents, in very large part, the influence of Guild Socialism.

In this chapter, I shall first make a critical examination of the limitations of competition as expressed in the doctrine of the Guild socialists, and then turn to the consideration of the program of control of the competitive order which present-day English socialists advocate.

I

While differing on certain fundamental issues, Guild Socialism has nevertheless sprung from Fabianism, and they are at one as to method and general outlook. Identified as the former is to an important degree with Fabianism both with respect to personalities and views, it is, nevertheless, not to be confused with the Fabian philosophy. Nor is Guild Socialism to be regarded merely as an episode in the attack upon the present competitive order; it has been one of the important forces in changing the collectivists' attack upon competition. Also the energetic Guild socialists have undoubtedly been productive in shaping the views and issues of those present-day political parties who would decry socialism per se. Guild Socialism in its agitation against the limitations of competition has been, for example, a contributing influence in calling forth from the Liberal Party its support of an "Economic General Staff" and "Industrial Coöperation."[1]

The origin of this offshoot of Fabian thought, termed "Guild Socialism," occurred in 1906, based upon the contention that collectivism as such was incapable of solving the social problem.[2] The movement has been championed, says Bernard Shaw, "by the ablest and most industrious insurgents of the rising generation in the [Fabian] Society." It was given wide publicity from 1912 in *The*

[1] Cf., *Britain's Industrial Future: Being the Report of the Liberal Industrial Inquiry* (London: Ernest Benn, 1928), Book 2, Chap. 10 and Book 3, Chap. 17. Cf. *infra*, pp. 277-278, 280-281.

[2] A. J. Penty, *The Restoration of the Guild System* (London: Swan Sonnenschein, 1906), Preface, p. b. Cf. pp. 73, 95 ff. The Guild idea, as applied to modern industry, was first advanced by A. R. Orage's article "Politics for Craftsmen," *Contemporary Review*, XCI (1907), 782-794. Orage was the editor of the *New Age* for many years and used the journal for the support of the Guild movement.

The same thought as advanced by Orage, namely, the association "of industrial self-government with the existing structure of the British trade-union movement," was set forth by a former member of the Fabian Society, S. G. Hobson, *National Guilds: An Enquiry into the Wage-System and the Way Out* (London: G. Bell and Sons, 1919). This book appeared serially in *The New Age*, 1912-1913.

New Age, and also from 1913 in *The Daily Herald*, until after the War.

The mere course of events during and after the War gave prominence to workers' participation in industrial control. Guild Socialism and the National Guild League (founded in 1915 by G. D. H. Cole), however, were also undoubtedly, to some degree, responsible for this. But enthusiastic Guild socialists misinterpreted the necessary war expedient of employees' representation in administration. They saw in the Shop Steward system an entering wedge for the establishment of those Democracies of Producers or "functional" democracy, which to Guild Socialism is the *summum bonum*. In this view the laborers generally did not agree. They visualized in shop stewards and Whitley committees devices by which employers could further their control and disintegrate union organization.

Although the War furnished collectivism with the first large experiment in public organization, success or failure of such collectivism—directed, as it was, toward a single, abnormal, simple, wartime objective—certainly could throw no light on the efficacy of the Guild (or any other socialist) program for peacetime with its multitudinous objectives and problems. This, strangely enough, English socialists in general, and Guild socialists in particular, did not appreciate. When, therefore, wartime measures and trade union opposition put an end to the vision of national guilds, Guild Socialism as a *movement* did not survive.[8]

So much for a brief review of Guild Socialism as a

[8] Though a series of articles entitled "A Guildsman's Interpretation of History" continued to run in the *New Age* (the official organ of Guild Socialism) until Nov. 6, 1919, no further mention of Guild Socialism appears. It is interesting to note that the *New Age* has since then (Sept. 13, 1923 to Jan. 10, 1924) sponsored the "social credit" plan of social amelioration advanced by Major C. H. Douglass.

movement. Like that of early Fabian economic doctrine, the importance of Guild Socialism is not to be found in the organization or movement it generated. In the examination of the Guild socialists' attack upon the limitations of competition we shall see that the theory, although not the movement, of Guild Socialism remains an important influence in the criticism and program of present-day English socialists.

2

This section proposes to consider Guild Socialism with respect to, first, the central thesis it maintains; secondly, the organization it would set up to give effect to this thesis; and thirdly, the nature of the control over competition which would result.

The thesis of Guild Socialism may be stated in the following words of G. D. H. Cole, who says that the "central doctrine" of this socialism is that "the various industries and services ought to be democratically administered by those who work in them."[4] That such producers' control of industry *cannot* eventuate by means of collectivism, state socialism, or by whatever "ism" one wishes to term government ownership and operation of the industries, is the fundamental argument of all Guild socialists. Upon this (though not upon all other matters) there is absolutely common agreement among Guild socialists; and it is upon this central issue that Guild socialists parted company with the Fabians.

[4] "National Guilds Movement in Great Britain," *Monthly Labor Review*, United States Bureau of Labor Statistics, IX (No. 1, July 1919), 28. This article, in my opinion, is the best brief (8 pp.) survey of the subject in print.

To the founder of the modern Guild Socialism, A. R. Orage, collectivism was a false approach since the *political* necessities and demands of craftsmen were "very far from being the same as those of the artisan." Collectivism while satisfying the need of the latter might *aggravate* causes of complaint of the former.[5] To which his colleague, S. G. Hobson, added that "there is no blunder so profound as the assumption that the State is, or ever can be, an economic entity."[6]

In more recent years the Guild socialists' denial of collectivism has taken quite a different turn. The governing idea, according to G. D. H. Cole, the leader of this school (and formerly the leader of Fabian Socialism at Oxford) is that self-government in industry requires an organization of the economic life of the community on a "*functional*" basis.[7] Although Cole insists that Guild Socialism is not a "purely industrial theory" it seems that the "func-

[5] "Politics for Craftsman," *Contemporary Review*, XCI (1907), 790.

[6] "Guild Socialism," *The New Age*, XII (Nov. 7, 1912), 6. Cf. also A. J. Penty who represents another school of Guild Socialism which frankly desires the restoration of the medieval guilds. Collectivism, to Penty, is merely substituting the avarice of the individuals for the avarice of the many—"as if Satan could cast out Satan." ("The Restoration of the Guild System," *The New Age*, XIII (Aug. 21, 1913), 484; and *Ibid.* (Aug. 28, 1913), 512.)

[7] Cf. Cole's *Guild Socialism Restated* (London: Leonard Parson, 1920), *passim*, but especially Chap. 2; also his article in the *Monthly Labor Review* (*op. cit.*), p. 31.

Cole has been an exceedingly busy and versatile writer. Possibly, however, as a Guild leader his "Guild Socialism," *Fabian Tract No. 192* (1920) gives, very inadequately, more than any other *one* source the general reasoning of Guild socialists of the Cole school. That confining oneself, in an analysis of the Guild socialists, to a few sources (and possibly secondary ones) leads to utterly false views can be seen in Ernest Barker's widely used *Political Thought in England From Herbert Spencer to the Present Day*. Although reaching the conclusion that Fabian Socialism was the dominant form of socialism in England until the last few years and that it is now replaced (in part) by Guild Socialism, he nevertheless presents a brief analysis that contains serious errors. (See pp. 222-227.)

tional" organization idea expresses itself merely in that each person has several interests, two of which are the "economic" and the "human," and in each he should be self-governing.[8]

The more definite and important contention relates to control of industries. While agreeing with Fabian socialists on insisting upon public ownership (whether national, municipal, or coöperative), the Guild socialists are emphatic that this does *not* mean public control. That point, in fact, is the major premise of the Guild socialists. To use Orage's expression, the Collectivists' "colossal factory is a nightmare. The implications and the interstices of the vision are nothing short of revolting."

Upon what economic and social philosophy does the foregoing central thesis of the Guild socialist—society should have a "functional" organization which gives to workers the control of their industry—rest? The answer one finds in Cole's *Social Theory*:

> . . . our thesis that what occurs under Capitalism is a *perversion* of the true function of the State, and its use, not as a political instrument of the whole people, but as a secondary economico-political instrument by the dominant economic class. . . .
>
> It will be seen that the line of argument which I am adopting is an endorsement of a large part of the Marxian case.[9]

Indeed so completely is Marxian doctrine accepted, that class struggle and revolutionary methods are frequently held as necessary consequences of the workers not directly

[8] Cole, *Monthly Labor Review* (*op. cit.*), p. 31. As Cole uses the term "functional" in various places it suggests, it seems to me, that he may have adopted it from our writers in the field of scientific management, for example, Taylor and Emerson.

[9] (New York: F. A. Stokes, 1920), pp. 148-149. Cf., Cole, *Guild Socialism Restated*, pp. 18-19.

controlling the industries in which they are employed. To the Guild socialists, however, the slower transition by trade union methods is probably more generally accepted.

The organization which Guild socialists would set up to give effect to their doctrine centers, of course, about the national guilds. And here at once the difficulties of the Guild socialists' reasoning begin. It has been pointed out above that their contention is that each person has several interests and, in accord with a "functional" organization of society, in each of these interests the individual should be self-governing. It seems strange that Cole and his school have not seen (or at least have nowhere discussed) that which is clearly the logical conclusion of their reasoning, namely, *anarchism*. It is axiomatic that in an economic order of highly developed division of labor no economic activity of individual, trade, or nation stands alone. It follows that the producers' (call them "guilds" or what not) control over their industries must inevitably exercise control over other producers and *consumers*. The more these other producers are dependent upon a particular group of producers (who may be producing a basic raw material or service, e.g., coal and transportation) the more it is true that the latter cannot control their industry without necessarily controlling all others.

For Cole to set up four categories of human needs (domestic and personal, local or regional, national, and international) and to hold that there should be different self-governing guilds in each[10] is simply to ignore the essence of specialization by task, by occupation, by industry, and by territory in present-day production.

[10] *Self-Government in Industry* (3rd ed.; London: G. Bell and Sons, 1920), p. 12.

Or, to approach the same matter from another angle: The ultimate control of industry is, of course, consumers' wants. Representation of consumers in control of any one so-called guild seems obviously necessary. These consumers (except for a negligible number) are *producers* in the same and also in *other* industries from that of the guild (or guilds) in which they have representation as consumers. Hence it is inevitable that so far as consumers share control with producers in a particular industry the central thesis of Guild Socialism is vitiated. There is a surprising lack of discussion in Guild Socialism regarding "representation of consumers."[11]

Apparently considerable attention was given by Guild socialists to the technique of guild formation,[12] which, of course, does not meet the important, basic problems indicated above, namely, the relation of guild to guild and of producers to consumers. Added to these, it seems to me that another difficulty is almost insuperable. A highly dynamic condition of production is constantly conducive to industrial rearrangements (of which the trend toward integration is but one example). The result is that the concept of a national guild as being an association of all workers by hand and brain concerned in the "carrying on

[11] Cf., Cole, *Guild Socialism Restated,* p. 39.

[12] Regarding the question of guild formation and the number of guilds see S. G. Hobson, "Guild Socialism," *The New Age,* XII (Nov. 7, 1912), 6-7. Of the 1,200 different trades, crafts, and occupations in Great Britain, he would form 22 guild organizations. Cf., Hobson, *Ibid.* (March 6, 1913), 421-423. Here he speaks of 9 possible guilds. Also cf. (Editorial) "The Latest Utopia," *New Statesman,* III (No. 61, June 6, 1914), 267-269, in which 15 guilds are suggested.

Small producers were not to be "guildized" according to Cole, *Guild Socialism Restated,* p. 65.

As to occupations not considered amenable to guild routine, see S. G. Hobson, *op. cit.* (Nov. 14, 1912), pp. 29-31.

of a particular industry or service" is practically meaningless.[13]

One other point remains in the consideration of the organization the Guild socialists would set up in their control of competition: what changes will occur in the governmental organization? The Guild Socialists' reply is definitive:

> It will . . . at the least, "wither way" to a very considerable extent and I have no hesitation in saying that, in my belief, it will disappear altogether, either after a frontal attack, or by atrophy following upon dispossession of its vital powers.[14]

This, one can say, is not only inconsistent with the Guild socialists' own reasoning, but it also reflects that Marxian bias which is seen in other phases of the Guild doctrine.

The foregoing discussion may indeed give the reader the impression that Guild Socialism is a unified doctrine with regard to the organization which the Guild critics of competition would bring about. Such assuredly is not the case. The examination above has been confined to the economic reasoning of G. D. H. Cole, inasmuch as his school in leadership, in activity, in influence has been foremost. As a part of Cole's theory of "functional" democracy, the State is conceived as being a territorial association representative of consumers. It is supreme in this territory as producers' democracies are in theirs. We have in this philosophy a theory of balances or co-sovereignty in a two-power territory.

To a second school of Guild socialists, led by S. G. Hobson, such a theory of social-economic organization is un-

[13] Cole's "Congress of Industrial Guilds" to adjudicate difficulties, if it were really given sufficient authority to accomplish its purpose might, indeed, put the finishing touch to his volatile, functional democracy.

[14] Cole, *Guild Socialism Restated*, p. 123.

acceptable.[15] It would necessitate an almost perpetual joint session with inevitable delays and irritations. The joint session would become *ipso facto* the ultimate sovereign, and "functional democracy" would be non-existent. Hobson contends that economic functions are to be directed by Guilds *entirely* and consumers as such are to have no voice: National Guilds are to be absolute masters of their own house. In the Hobson school there is an even greater hiatus in the philosophy of the State than in that of Cole's.

To the third school of English Guild socialists, headed by A. J. Penty, the attack upon competitive organization has, it seems to me, at least the merit of greater logical consistency. This group objects to the emphasis upon quantity production and considers present-day industrialization more inimical to labor than is capitalism. The deduction is obvious: dispose of large-scale production; return to the blessing that was laborers'—the handloom and the cottage.[16]

Although my discussion of Guild Socialism will be confined to the Cole school, it is because this group's attack upon competition is more practical in the changes it sponsors and has had, therefore, the greatest influence. It is important to remember, however, that much of the spirit of the Penty and Hobson philosophy permeates the reasoning of Cole and his followers.

We now give attention to the control which the foregoing organization of "functional" democracy and national guilds is intended to bring to bear upon competition. With

[15] For Hobson's own view and a criticism of Cole see his articles "Guilds and Their Critics," *The New Age*, XXI (1917), 521-523; *Ibid.*, XXII (1917), 6; *Ibid.*, XXIII (1918), 5, 21, 38, 55, 69, 101.

[16] Cf. A. J. Penty, *Old Worlds for New: A Study of the Post-Industrial State* (London: Allen and Unwin, 1917), *passim.*

the producers' control of an industry, which the formation of a guild is intended to give, it would seem that the control of price and wages would be exceedingly great.

There is in fact a surprising lack of discussion upon this very important question. While it is clearly implied that each Guild is to have the right of determining the prices of their commodities and services, it is also occasionally suggested that consumers, by means of Consumers' Councils[17] or through the municipal or Parliamentary bodies, will treat with the guilds.[18] Precisely the same uncertainty exists regarding the payment of wages. To the Hobson school of Guild socialists "the acceptance of wages is in itself a servile act" and wages must be abolished.[19] To Cole, the question is uncertain. Apparently the union is to be the laborer's bargainer and paymaster. It would certainly seem to one looking at Guild Socialism from the *consumers'* angle, that the hideous "colossal factory" which the Guild socialists as *producers* despise in the collectivists' doctrine the Guild socialists themselves are advocating.

In brief, one may say that accepting the Marxian doctrine practically *in toto*, the reasoning of Guild Socialism is guilty of all the fallacies which pertain to the Marxian philosophy. And to these they add the further fallacies inherent in the particular organization of production, exchange, and distribution, which they sponsor. Imbued with the idea that "production should be for use and not for profit," they neither examine to what degree the latter is not a criterion of the former nor do they attempt

[17] Cf. Cole, *Fabian Tract No. 192*, p. 13.

[18] Cf. H. W. Macrosty, "Review of the Meaning of Industrial Freedom by G. D. H. Cole," *Economic Journal*, XXIX (1919), 72-73.

[19] *National Guilds: An Inquiry and the Way Out* (London: G. Bell & Sons, 1919), p. 235.

to advance a criterion which would serve as a better guide for "production for use."

The economic functions of capital and entrepreneurship are not comprehended. The complexity of the problem of directing production and assuming the responsibilities of organization is constantly increasing as a result of growing variability of human wants and of productive technique, on the one hand, and of increasing population and decreasing resources on the other. It seems impossible that control of industries by all of those employed in them will, in itself, set up the selective process more productive in giving leadership than is true of the present process.[20] But these are questions not at all considered by the Guild socialists.

3

Before leaving the analysis of the socialists' statement of the limitations of competition, it is well to consider briefly the most recent program of social control which English socialists offer. It is not to be understood that this program is intended to vitiate or supersede that which is fundamental in Fabian and Guild Socialism. Confining itself to the condition into which competition has brought production, this present-day program of the socialists concerns itself with *immediate* measures. Previous to making an examination of this program and these measures one

[20] This does not deny the truth of D. H. Robertson's well-stated contention that risks and responsibilities must involuntarily be assumed by the workman "when he throws in his lot with a particular business enterprise": capital does *not* assume them all. Poor management, shifting demand, trade depression strike workman and employer alike. (Cf. *The Control of Industry*, pp. 88-95.)

But, it appears to me, the essence of leadership is *making decisions*. This needs to be centralized for sake of economy and speed. To decentralize it into the hands of employees would necessarily magnify all those weaknesses inherent in committee control.

should see clearly the dilemma for the solution of which the most recent socialistic program is offered.

The dilemma of competition in production has recently been stated by D. H. MacGregor in these words:

> From any long point of view a perplexing problem is offered, because if on the one hand it is held that industrial joint-stock competition is becoming irrational in intensity, and will be destructive of itself as one industry after another reaches an advanced stage of capitalist organization, on the other hand monopolist tendency is also unstable in face of public criticism. Hence some dread, and others hope for, more attention to the third method, that of public control applied at any rate in some large instances.[21]

The answer, thinks MacGregor, is found in "rationalization," that is, the right of organization by an industry which is considered a "type of government" having for its end the interrelation of producers as to their policy and work. Such "rationalization" would have as the desired consequence the non-destructive elimination of the weak and the control over the entrance of new establishments.

And "rationalization," or in other words the application of rational or scientific principle to organization of production, furnishes the basis for the last pronunciamento of the English socialists.[22] "Socialism, as a matter of immediate practical politics, is bound to look different from the purely propagandist Socialism"; when a house is burning one should not grumble if only muddy water can be got!

More precisely, the State must control *policy* but as far as possible avoid administration. Says Cole:

> The more they [socialists] think about it in the light of particular

[21] "Rationalisation of Industry," *Economic Journal*, XXXVII (1927), 525.

[22] G. D. H. Cole, *The Next Ten Years in British Social and Economic Policy* (London: Macmillan, 1929). This book carries acknowledgments to (among others) Arthur Henderson and Sidney Webb.

instances requiring positive action the *less* they will be able to regard it mainly as a *change of ownership*, and the more they will come to envisage it as a change in control.[23]

Not the transference of capital and land to public ownership of Fabian creed, nor the producers' control over their own industries of Guild belief, but rather a "rationalization" that is made possible through public control of *policy*—this is what conditions of the moment necessitate.

So much for a general statement of the problem; now as to the program and measures which the limitations of competition necessitate.

In the public control of policy—"rationalization"—two proposals are advanced. These are: first, the policy concerned with the unemployed; and secondly, the "conscious development" of national economic resources, which may be said to include "conscious guidance" of new capital into those channels which will best furnish this development.

As to the first: Every unemployed worker, after his name has been registered at the Employment Exchange, should be given the option of enrollment in a nationally organized body of workers who are available to the government for "any useful form of service." Those who are unemployed due to purely seasonal conditions are to be excluded. Moreover, the scheme is voluntary, that is, the worker should be free to leave.[24] This nationally organized body of workers, designated as the National Labour Corps, should be given the work of "cleaning up England," which includes, for example, the pulling down of slums and erecting new tenements. Further, it is con-

[23] *Ibid.*, p. 142. Italics mine.
[24] Cf. *ibid.*, especially Chap. 3.

tended, the government should reserve such Corps to work that would *not* be done by other agencies.

It occurs to me that the critic who would facetiously inquire when, where, and to what degree is England unclean has, largely, disposed of the practicality of such a measure. Supposing it possible to meet this question by dependable, objective criteria rather than by following the dictates of local political influence, two other problems of major importance present themselves, namely, financing and trade-union opposition.

Regarding the former, the government's power of eminent domain, which would be used to obtain the property upon which the unemployed will be put to work, together with the government's tremendous credit, that may be quickly utilized in securing funds through the floating of short-term treasury certificates of indebtedness, may or may not be adequate in exercising a remedial effect. It is true that in so far as unemployment tends to be concentrated with particular severity in *certain* communities and trades, a program of strategically placed *direct* expenditure of the Government in the employment of the English socialists' Labour Corps (or in putting into effect a governmental unemployment relief program) would seem to be conducive of quick and direct relief. In so far as unemployment is *general*, it is doubtful whether such government expenditures would be a sufficient interjection into the credit and monetary mechanism to stimulate the needed recovery in the *general* productive activity.

If it is assumed to be desirable that government measures be taken in short-time programs for remedying the unemployment situation, it appears to me that Hawtrey's argument is more defensible. Not only may the extension of credit be used to stimulate production, but the general level of prices can and *ought* to be controlled by the manipulation of the rate of discount, made possible, of course, by the existing centralized banking organization.[25]

It is clear that in this approach to the unemployment remedy we take advantage of existing skilled, decentralized administration, that is, profit-seeking producers, rather than a politically influenced civil service. Moreover, since serious unemployment is general rather than local, credit expansion which stimulates general production is also more widespread in its effect of decreasing unemployment.[26]

Furthermore in connection with the present-day socialists' program of unemployment policy in their "rationalization" of industry, they do not consider the *possible* effect upon British capital which the added taxation (necessitated in order to meet the maturing short-term treasury certificates) *might* have especially in view of England's peculiar position in having large unexploited dominions, with a materially lower tax burden, offering a constant attraction to British capital and residents. Revenues needed to meet the added unemployment expenditure, so far as it cannot be secured by increased income tax (which cannot be evaded by foreign investment of capital), will tend, to a certain measure, to drive capital and residents abroad. To whatever degree this is true, to that degree the increase

[25] Cf. *Currency and Credit*, *passim*. And cf. *Monetary Reconstruction* (2nd ed.; London: Longmans, 1926), Chap. 2. Also expressed in his lectures while at Harvard University, 1928-1929.

Extension of credit becomes, of course, less efficacious with increasing magnitude and intensity of economic depression. A world-wide industrial collapse, coupled with international governmental difficulties such as we have experienced in the last five years, presents a whole group of social problems for which the manipulation of the rate of discount is obviously inadequate.

[26] *If*, it is to be reiterated, such an approach is thought desirable. As indicated in the discussion which follows, this assumption is to be questioned.

in employment brought on by the unemployment program will eventually be vitiated.

It is probable that the degree is much greater than the present-day English socialists have thought possible, imbued as they are with the doctrine of social appropriation of "rents" in all their forms. Turning to the recent Report of the Colwyn Committee on the National Debt and Taxation, apropos of the British tax burden in relation to business enterprise, it states:

> Very briefly we may say that, in business generally, the existing taxes tend to discourage a sanguine outlook. The Income Tax has little direct effect on public companies, and the death duties none. Private companies are much more susceptible to influence. . . . The enterprise of public companies receives some indirect check, so far as their reserves and the supply of capital from the public are diminished; in the case of private concerns, which depend on an internal supply of capital, the material basis for enterprise is more seriously affected, especially where there is a heavy liability to Super-tax. . . .[27]

The trade-union opposition to "rationalization" of industry and to the present-day English socialists' unemployment policy arises obviously from fear of disorganization which a National Labour Corps, in the nature of the case, would entail. In so far as trade unions are a political factor they would add to the already difficult task of the civil service administration.

In this first of their two proposals pertaining to "rationalization" of industry (that is, the policy concerned with the unemployed), the present-day English socialists' reasoning is—as elsewhere—fruitful in directing attention to problems whose solution cannot altogether await the action of competition. The government, as the largest buyer as well as the largest employer, certainly can anticipate or

[27] *Report of the Committee on National Debt and Taxation* (London: His Majesty's Stationery Office, 1927), p. 242.

retard its expenditure to a considerable degree and thereby exercise some remedial influence upon the unemployment situation.[28] But for the government to embark upon the organization of the millions of unemployed for the uncertain goal of "cleaning up England" is so different in degree as to make it an entirely different matter.

And not only does the unemployment proposal meet with the difficulties I have referred to above but furthermore it takes no step toward removing any of the various maladjustments to which unemployment is due. Such an unemployment program grants the assumption that it is desirable for the government to institute measures that are merely palliative in nature rather than to undertake the measures needed to correct the fundamental causes of unemployment. An assumption of this sort is frequently more false than true inasmuch as many of the short-time programs work in *direct opposition* to the remedies needed for the fundamental correction of the maladjustments to which unemployment at any one time is to be attributed. The fundamental correction of occupational redistribution may be distinctly hindered by a government unemployment program because not only is the needed correction

[28] Cf., F. W. Taussig, *Principles of Economics* (3rd ed.; New York: Macmillan, 1921), II, 367-368. Also see especially the views of O. T. Mallery (Chairman of the Committee on Public Works of the American Association for Labor Legislation), *Business Cycles and Unemployment* (Report of the National Bureau of Economic Research) (New York: McGraw-Hill, 1923) Chap. XIV, "The Long-Range Planning of Public Works." Of the great amount of material on this phase of unemployment this source is one of the most complete résumés in print of the experience of foreign governments and our own (federal, state, and local). This chapter is fully documented and brings together much data on the subject. The final conclusion is that "long-range planning of public works and of the purchase of supplies seems to be one of the simplest and most promising devices for stabilizing industry and employment." (p. 260). See too a note by the same author, "Advance Planning of Public Works to Stabilize Employment," *The American Labor Legislation Review*, XVII (1927), 210.

delayed, but also the danger of individual and public demoralization through the destruction of individual responsibility is ever present.

Now to turn to the second proposal in the "rationalization" program—the "conscious development" of national economic resources: Observing that industrial investment is almost wholly unregulated, Cole agrees with J. A. Hobson that there is no reason to assume that the right amount is saved, or that the rate of interest will fix itself at just the point to call forth capital to promote maximum well-being, nor that the preference of the investor leads automatically to the best distribution. To this is added the usual time-worn assertion that there is no necessary coincidence between the profits of the investor and the social good. Hence the old industries need complete reorganization, and since the risk is too great for the ordinary investor it must be performed by society.[29]

In criticism of Cole's reasoning, one need only say that his assertions, of course, beg the question. Whether the price paid for capital calls for the "right" amounts or whether the price paid for consumers' goods is in accord with their "social" usefulness, in the absence of objective measurements, must rest upon opinion. Productivity of capital and the price paid for it in its various uses as well as the price of consumers' goods rest at least on the opinion of the many in an order where freedom of consumers' choice prevails.

To give effect to this second proposal (that of "conscious development" of resources) in the "rationalization" program necessitates the "conscious guidance" of capital investment. This, Cole maintains, is provided for in the

[29] Cole, *The Next Ten Years in British Social and Economic Policy*, pp. 68-76.

Labour Party's program calling for an "Employment and Development Board," financed by a special grant from the Treasury.[80] That program, it is his view, is the "right line of advance but too timid." In addition, he asserts, the state should provide a Board of National Investment,

> . . . endowed with power to prohibit or license, according to the national interest, not merely public loans raised in this country for overseas use, but all loans so raised. . . .
>
> Indeed, there seems to be no reason why at an early stage a further step should not be taken, and all public appeals for capital, whether for use at home or abroad, require the sanction of the National Investment Board.[81]

This would be to the end that investments, which, under the direction of investment trusts, have gone into resources abroad rather than in stimulating home industries, may be directed into any of those domestic industries "that seem likely to succeed, and to provide employment on fair terms."[82]

This, it may be noted, raises two issues, namely, the policy of controlling the export of capital, and secondly, the federal control of capital investment. Cole's reasoning on these issues raises questions which are broad fields in

[80] The Labour Party's program with regard to the proposed Employment and Development Board is quite ambiguous. The Board, according to Cole, is entrusted with the task of "'bringing development schemes to the point of execution in readiness for the time when they should be pushed ahead in the interests of employment and trade.'" (*Ibid.*, p. 76.) This, of course, might mean much or little.

According to an organ of the Labour Party, the National Employment and Development Board would concern itself with six projects, namely, land reclamation, drainage, afforestation, slum clearance, roads, and transport. (Cf. "What Labour Would Do," *New Leader*, XVI—No. 131, Apr. 26, 1929.)

[81] *Op. cit.*, p. 77. Cole's plan is to give this Board jurisdiction over the entire field of capital investment excepting such capital as may be raised privately. It, indeed, goes far beyond what would seem to be the intention of the Labour Party with regard to its Employment and Development Board.

[82] *Ibid.*, pp. 79-87.

themselves. No attempt will be made, in this survey chapter, to present a critical examination of the validity of his argument. But some general statements can be made regarding the prohibition of loans raised in England for overseas use. In the first place, such governmental prohibitory measures would be to the disadvantage of those who had savings to invest inasmuch as domestic investment would mean a lower return to them. Secondly, considering the fact that England is to a large extent a producer of industrial materials and equipment, loans raised in England are to an important degree used in making purchases in England—purchases of those commodities (industrial products) not bought by work people. Prohibition of export of capital would *probably* be detrimental to the real income of the *working* classes. On the remarkably broad scope of investigation which makes the six-volume Report of the Balfour Committee on Industry and Trade a monumental piece of work, their conclusion with regard to the export of capital is as follows:

> It seems clear to us that full employment in our exporting industries, having regard to their *character* and extent, can *only* be attained in the near future if there is a *substantial increase* in the export of capital. . . . We are *not* prepared to recommend any general restriction of the amount of capital exported. We have considered also whether it would be *practicable* or *desirable* to control or direct the flow of British capital in order to prevent it from being used for particular purposes which are thought prejudicial to the best interests of this country, or to stimulate its use for purposes which are considered advantageous to British industry and trade. The practical difficulties attendant on such a scheme would be very great, and our opinion is that the disadvantages which would result from such an attempt to control or direct the flow would outweigh the advantages.[88]

[88] *The Balfour Committee Report on Industry and Trade* (London: H. M. Stationery Office, 1929). Final Report, pp. 44-45. Italics mine. The large number of organizations (each one of which was an association

And thirdly, it seems quite clear that export of English capital which goes toward the exploitation of resources, needed as they are, of course, for England's diversified manufacturing enterprises, must redound to the English laborers' advantage.

Upon the foregoing grounds alone, the contention of English socialists that there should be "rationalization" of industry through the policy of controlling the export of capital is largely refuted. In one respect, however, the argument against this policy of control is less conclusive. It must be remembered that the contention of English socialists for restricting the export of capital from England is frankly and expressly a *short-time* program for the particular circumstances in which post-war England finds herself. To the export of British capital has been attributable, at least in part, the failure of wages to rise in Great Britain since 1900, a period in which—due to expanding productive activity—an increasing money and real wage should have materialized.[84] To this unfavorable experience must now be added the present situation of a large amount of unemployment. It suggests the restriction of the export of capital as at least a short-time remedy. Retaining at home a good portion of that part of the £100,000,000 of foreign loans raised each year which is not left as credit in England for purchases but which flows abroad, this should add to bank reserves, extension of credit, stimulation of prices, wages, and production. Together with a proper control of the bank discount rate, there is no reason why short-time remedial effects upon unemployment could not be expected.

representing a great number of members) interviewed is given in Appendix 1, pp. 315-321.

[84] Cf., F. W. Taussig, "Great Britain's Foreign Trade Terms After 1900," *Economic Journal*, XXXV (1925), 1-10.

But, in my judgment, the immediate, short-time program is not the significant one. By giving attention to one industry at a time, the fundamental remedy which is needed becomes apparent. The present-day socialists themselves do not see in either public ownership, control, or any other measure a means by which unemployment in the British coal industry can be eliminated. In fact, they explicitly state that a large fraction of the unemployed workers in the coal industries will never find work in that industry again. Are not other manufacturing industries, especially in so far as they are dependent upon British resources, in precisely the same situation to a greater or less degree?

The important remedy, it seems to me, toward which increasing governmental action should be taken, is apparent: the mobility of British labor must be *tremendously* increased, a task made all the more difficult by a pernicious practice of employment doles.[85] But the necessary mobility is vertical as well as horizontal. British industries need a larger amount—in quantity and quality—of management. Mobility of this sort (into management) has been retarded in England by a tradition so established as to be a social institution. This "institution" needs to be "neutralized" if industrial unemployment is to be remedied. The tradition referred to is that of devoting educational institutions to

[85] Because of the moral hazard, on the one hand, and the great financial burden, on the other, the British unemployment insurance benefit must be kept down. (It is now—under the Unemployment Act of 1934—17 shillings for the man, and 15 for the woman, per week.) This makes the benefit a failure from either angle: although the benefit is small it has unquestionably caused considerable demoralization and increased the cost (for the fiscal year 1933-34, the benefit payments amounted to £40,290,000, of which the Government contributed £19,800,000; and in addition the Exchequer paid £52,250,000 of so-called "transitional" benefits) and still the benefit is so small as to make a self-respecting standard of living impossible.

preparation for social or governmental activities—*not* industrial leadership: Cambridge and Oxford men traditionally go, if not exclusively, at least largely, into the Civil Service.

The exceedingly difficult problem of neutralizing those social institutions which create and perpetuate immobility in England, is a problem with which local and national government should quickly, thoroughly, continuously cope. Nothing short of this will be adequate; anything short of this will more often be in direct opposition to the fundamental remedy and defeat its own purpose. And this is the very real sense in which a short-time program and the long-time program cannot be separated.

Again from another point of view the argument against the socialists' contention for controlling the export of capital is less conclusive. In so far as the exported capital is to be utilized for the development of foreign municipal or governmental ventures, the case for restriction of capital exportation from England seems to me to be in theory more favorable.

This is clearly stated in the Report of the Liberal Party Industrial Inquiry Committee on Britain's Industrial Future—a report which is, on the whole, particularly frank and sound. Of the £500,000,000 of annual new savings in England this Report estimates that £100,000,000 (as we have noted above) goes into investments abroad. Concerning this, the Committee says:

> So far as industrial, agricultural, and mining overseas enterprises are concerned, we think that the freedom of foreign investment has in the past greatly increased the national wealth and is increasing it now. We see no reason to do anything but encourage the trading, business, and pioneering private enterprise of British citizens abroad. We also think that in the Railway Age, the development of foreign and colonial rail-

way systems abroad out of British capital, when British materials, British savings, and British engineering enterprises were opening up the world for the supply of food and raw materials, was greatly in the interest of this country as well as of the world. But we are doubtful whether, *at the present time*, the existing machinery for investment necessarily preserves the correct balance between expenditure on *Public Utilities* at home and loans for *similar* purposes abroad to Government, Provinces, Municipalities, and other public bodies in foreign countries and in the Dominions. Our constructive proposals [are] . . . based on the assumption that the development and expansion of transport facilities, public utilities, industries, housing, and agricultural equipment *at home* should be a *first* charge on the national savings, and that only the surplus, after the satisfaction of all reasonable domestic requirements under these headings, should be made available to *public bodies abroad*. We think it possible—we cannot say more until the whole matter has been explored in detail from the practical point of view—that it *might* be to the advantage of the country if (say) £50,000,000 less were lent each year to *public bodies abroad* and £50,000,000 more were devoted to the development of the national resources and equipment at home.[36]

The question of the control over the export of capital, which English socialists would answer by the creation of a Board of National Investment, is a complex one. Together with the fact that a large proportion of the £100,000,000 of English capital exported annually goes to the furtherance of non-industrial uses which can increase the real income of the English only over a very long period of time (if at all) which is stressed by the Liberal Industrial Inquiry—together with this the question presents other issues. Export of British capital (that is, loans to foreigners) may indeed aid the expansion of foreign manufacturers with whom directly or indirectly British industries may be competing. Again the *great* length of time during which interest payments are continuing and before repayment of the capital occurs, as well

[36] *Britain's Industrial Future: Being the Report of the Liberal Industrial Inquiry*, pp. 109-111. Italics mine.

as the extent to which such loans cause gold movement with consequent changes in price levels and lagging changes in wage levels, are factors making it difficult to decide upon the soundness of supporting the free movement of capital on the same grounds upon which argument for the long-time beneficial results of free trade in general rests.

Pigou reaches the conclusion:

> Primâ facie it would seem that, if the policy of prohibiting or restricting the export of capital for new enterprises were introduced now and subsequently maintained in England, the effect in the first year or so would be *injurious*, after a few years beneficial, and, after the policy had continued in vogue for a long period, again injurious. But the issue is complicated by reactions which may take place in the emigration, and by political problems connected with international competition for "concessions" in backward countries and with the financing of foreign wars.[87]

So much for the policy of the national control of the exportation of capital. Now turning to the second issue raised by Cole's proposal of a Board of National Investment, namely, the extending of the control of such a Board to all public appeals for capital, whether for *use at home or abroad*. This, it will be recalled, is a phase of the second proposal with the view toward "rationalization" of industry.

With respect to the national control of domestic capital investment advanced by Cole as a measure of conscious development of national economic resources, this again would take us too far afield to treat adequately in this chapter. It is to be remembered that the Board of National Investment proposed by present-day English social-

[87] "Interest after the War and the Export of Capital," *Economic Journal*, XXVI (1916), 423. Italics mine.

ists is not to be confused with the more or less advisory governmental committees whose functions have very little of the far-reaching consequences of a Board of National Investment as Cole conceives it.

In the introduction to this chapter, I have suggested that Guild Socialism was one of the important contributing influences in calling forth from the Liberal Party some of its recent measures. This is no doubt true, but such measures are not to be misunderstood. In order to set in clearer relief the purpose of the Board of National Investment desired by English socialists of today (whose duty, as stated above, is to approve or deny "*all* public appeals for capital"), let us turn briefly to the proposal of the Liberal Party for a board which goes by the *same* name.

The Liberal Party Industrial Inquiry Committee writes:

> We think . . . the national efficiency would be increased if we were to take stock of the position annually and consider as a whole the capital expenditure which *is* being currently incurred under some form or another of *public authority*. We think that the funds *available for such purposes* should be pooled and that no desirable development should be postponed so long as a margin of savings exists to finance it. . . . With this object in view, we propose that there be established a Board of National Investment. This Board should take over the functions of the National Debt Commissioners and of the Public Works Loans Board and also certain additional duties. . . . It should be a subordinate department of the Treasury. . . .
>
> All *capital* resources *accruing in the hands of Government Departments* should be pooled in the hands of this Board, including, inter alia, the assets of the Post Office Savings Bank and of the Insurance Funds, and the repayment by way of amortisation of funds previously advanced. In addition the Board should be authorized to issue, when necessary . . . National Investment Bonds.
>
> Out of this pool there should be financed new capital expenditure by

all central, local, or ad hoc official bodies, by means of advances precisely on the lines of those now made from the Local Loans Fund.[38]

This, it would seem, is arguing for centralized and budgetary control of existing *governmental* revenues and expenditures. It is true that the Board is to be authorized to extend the work of *municipalities* by means of bond issues but it is not proposed to extend the control of such a Board to *all* capital commitments (that is, all investments making public appeal) as Cole would have it. What can be said of this phase of present-day socialists' "rationalization" of industry?

In an examination of this proposal, attention should be called to the findings of "the widest survey yet undertaken of British industrial and commercial conditions and prospects."[39] The Final Report of the Balfour Committee on Industry and Trade presented to Parliament in March 1929 has the conclusion:

> We do not believe that any of our principal basic industries have been so weakened, even by the long continued depression, as not to have the power within themselves to take the first measures towards their own regeneration, provided that they are thoroughly convinced that such measures are essential and unavoidable, and that they must be taken by themselves without reliance on any outside authority.[40]

To this conclusion a minority report disagrees and urges increased public control to the end that there be "scientific reorganisation and coördination of industry," that is, "rationalization." The minority report specifically calls for the establishment of two new bodies, namely, the National Economic Committee and the National Employment and Development Board. The first would have to do with

[38] *Op. cit.*, pp. 111-112. Italics mine.

[39] D. H. MacGregor's view of the Balfour Committee on Industry and Trade Report (Cf. *Economic Journal*, XXXIX—1929), 295-297.

[40] *Balfour Committee Final Report*, p. 299.

formulating general policy and publicity; the latter would be the executive of that policy.[41]

Whether to subscribe to the majority or to the minority report depends largely upon one's point of view. Upon one important criterion, there should be common agreement. The development of individual responsibility is essential for productive efficiency. An increase of such responsibility can only occur as a result of individual producers themselves assuming the risks and decisions involved in productive activity. This, of course, does not preclude an increase by the public in educative, informative, and statistical activities concerning production. This is true inasmuch as the responsibility for the use of such governmental service still remains with the individual.

While emphatically disagreeing with the Minority Report of the Balfour Committee as to either the desirability or the feasibility of a National Employment and Development Board, one might still unqualifiedly agree as to both the desirability and feasibility of a National Economic Committee with advisory and informative functions. The need of coördinating the ever increasing activities of each governmental department is perfectly apparent in view of interrelation of the complex services of the various departments and the detrimental social effect of working at cross purposes. Possibly our own United States Department of Agriculture and our United States Department of Commerce is a notable instance in point. Not only

[41] *Ibid.*, pp. 303-312. The National Economic Committee would formulate the rationalization plans and would, therefore, be a scientific and advisory body. The Employment and Development Board would see that such plans are undertaken by the industries concerned within the time limit which the Committee has set. If the plans have not been undertaken the Employment and Development Board would establish Control Boards for the industry (or industries) in question, if such industries are not "ripe for complete nationalisation" (p. 312).

is there a continuous increase of exceedingly extensive economic activities on the part of each but also these activities have not in certain important respects been coördinated, with the result of some duplication and more crossing of purposes.

Apropos of this, the "functional democracy" theory of Guild socialists (which caused them, as we have seen, to disagree sharply with the earlier Fabian doctrine) is, within limits, absolutely valid. And this has, as we have noted above, found expression in more recent Fabian Socialism in Webb's conception of a Social Parliament and a Political Parliament. We have considered the difficulties into which this led them.

The Liberal Party, it seems to me, has accepted the theory of the Guild socialists—or more accurately, the revision of this by the more recent Fabianism—and at the same time avoided the fallacies of the Guild-Fabian program. The problem of coördinating the vast economic activities of Government so as to avoid duplication and cross-purpose the Liberal Party would solve not by the present-day English socialists' Board of National Investment to sanction or deny *all* public investment appeals, but rather through the creating of an "Economic General Staff."

The Liberal Party Industry Inquiry Committee proposed this Staff's duties to be:

> (i) To engage in continuous *study* of current economic problems affecting national policy and the development of industry and commerce. (ii) To *co-ordinate* and, where necessary, to complete statistical and other information required by the Government and by Parliament. (iii) To act on its own initiative in calling the attention of the Cabinet . . . to important tendencies and changes at home or abroad. (iv) To *suggest* to the Government plans for solving fundamental economic

difficulties, such, for instance, as measures for stabilising trade conditions, avoiding unemployment, and developing national resources.[42]

In order that the finding of the Economic General Staff be used by the various departments of the Government with proper coördination, the further proposal is made of a Committee of Economic Policy. This would consist of the Prime Minister, The Chancellor of the Exchequer, The President of the Board of Trade, The Minister of Labor, The Minister of Health, and the Minister of Agriculture. To this Committee, the Economic General Staff would refer such of its findings as concern national policy.

This program would seem to accomplish the desirable increase in control of policy without the weaknesses inherent in "rationalization of industry." It accomplishes, first, the necessary development of public educative, informative, statistical activities; secondly, the coördination of the manifold positive activities which may follow; and thirdly, the creation of individual responsibility by leaving to the individual, to the corporation, and to the association the obligation of determining the direction of capital.

The foregoing examination of proposals for the "rationalization" of industry has said nothing of socialization or nationalization of industrial capital and land. We now turn to the consideration as to where the latter occurs in the present-day English socialists' program of "social control of policy."

Transfer of ownership, to the public, of capital and land has so long been associated with English Fabian socialists' discussion of the limitations of competition that it seems strange that they should now take the position they do. It

[42] *Britain's Industrial Future*, pp. 117-118. Italics mine.

is not to be taken for granted, says Cole, that the socialist wants "either *immediately* or in the *long run*, to nationalise, in the current sense of the term, any particular industry or service."[43] Rather the present-day English critics of the competitive order, hold:

> . . . what the Socialist does essentially set out to *nationalise*, or perhaps better to socialise, is . . . the *control* and direction of the economic life of the community. This will certainly involve the transference of a large number of enterprises now in private hands to various forms of public ownership and administration; but it does not involve either universal public ownership, or any one form of control or management in industry. As Socialism develops, the forms of socialisation are likely to be very diverse; and their diversity will be a source of strength.[44]

In English socialism today, therefore, *both* the industries to be socialized as well as the form such socialization is to take is an open question. If the Labour Government decides to socialize this or that industry its reasons will be *particular* and not general. The creed of early English socialism has given way to the belief that the state "must control policy, but as far as possible it must avoid assuming the function of administration."[45]

In another important respect present-day English socialism differs (or at least has taken more definite form) from the earlier movement. This is in regard to administration of public controlled services. Deviating again from Fabian and Guild doctrines, administration should be

[43] *Ibid.*, p. 133. Italics mine.

[44] *Ibid.*, pp. 130-131. Italics mine.

[45] *Ibid.*, p. 135. The leading economic problems with which the Labour Party has pledged itself to deal immediately and practically were unemployment, the provision of work, and the increase of unemployment payments, the relief of congestion in the labor market by keeping children at school for an additional year and by adequate pensions for the old, the reorganization of the coal industry, and the placing of housing under public control. [Cf. the official organ and the Labour Party, *The Labour Magazine*, VIII (No. 1, May 1929), 24-27 (editorial)].

placed in the hands of independent and responsible commissions and not assigned to Parliament or to the Civil Service, which are already overweighted. These commissions should not be responsible to Parliament but to "some public authority capable of coördinating their several activities."[46]

In my opinion this amounts to a complete repudiation of the socialist position. A control of policy without public ownership, and regulation by independent commissions, rather than the civil service administration—these measures are nothing more or less than the measures which all governments have undertaken. With regard to our own Government we have the instances of the Interstate Commerce Commission, Federal Trade Commission, and the Federal Radio Commission. There is possibly one important element of difference. Although holding, it is true, that "Socialists of today will be making a great mistake if they set out on the practical work of Socialism in the same attitude of mind" [as early socialists], the present-day English socialists, no doubt, contemplate a *much* more rapid increase in public control of governmental commissions than that contemplated by one who is an exponent of economic competition.

The Labour Party today faces, of course, tremendous pressure to put into practice its socialist doctrine and remedy the "evils of competition."[47] In the two industries

[46] *Op. cit.*, p. 136.

[47] This pressure came, of course, primarily from the left wing of the Labour Party in general, and from the Independent Labour Party in particular. The latter (the I.L.P.) has demanded public ownership of land, transport, mining, electrical generation, Bank of England, and complete public control of importation of foodstuffs and raw material. The immediate demands are for a living wage with a minimum standard of life and employment, extension of the Trade Board Act, adequate wages in agriculture, and until nationalization of mines is accomplished the work day for miners be reduced to seven hours, old age pensions granted, the

where action might be expected, present-day socialists have this to offer. In the mining industry, existing owners shall be offered a scheme of reorganization which they will be invited to carry out under state supervision and with state financial assistance. Public ownership is needed only in those cases of "recalcitrance or inefficiency." A full-time Mining Commission shall exercise authority over marketing, prices, output, and allocating quotas.[48] In regard to the railroad, again there is no advantage of public ownership, and what is desired is public *control*.

The question which seems to be particularly significant is the *extent* to which present-day English socialists desire to carry their "rationalization," or public control of policy. We have seen that the two proposals of rationalization (the policy concerned with the unemployed and the conscious development of resources) go a considerable distance, or at least one can say the potentialities of these proposals are very great. To these two proposals is added the direct control of policy by means of commissions in various industries of which mines, railways, power, transport, and the cotton industry are specifically mentioned. Of course, in *practice* the rate of growth in the public "control of policy" will be dictated by political expedience; what *principles* should govern the application of public control of policy, it is less possible to determine in later English socialism than it is in earlier socialistic doctrine. It is remarkable that one finds no consideration by

---

school age raised, school maintenance provided, the regulation of recruitment to the mining industry, transference and migration of miners, and increased unemployment allowance. Cf. the I. L. Party's weekly organ *The New Leader*, XVI (No. 131, Apr. 26, 1929). Also *Ibid.*, XVI (No. 157, Oct. 25, 1929) for the demands made upon the then Minister of Labour, Miss Bonfield, for increased maintenance.

[48] *Ibid.*, pp. 138-141.

present-day socialists in their writings, concerned as it is with the limitations of competition, of the principles which in a competitive order have determined the need of public control (or ownership), such as the significance to society as a whole that every individual be a "consumer" at least to a minimum degree of certain commodities or services (as, for example, education, public health, living conditions); the need of standardization or uniformity greater than that which could be obtained at the hands of many producers (as in "public service" industries generally); the conditions, such as large fixed costs, which give rise to "natural" monopolies; and the need of certain services or commodities to increase the productive efficiency of society in the aggregate although individual consumers may not be "effective demanders" (as, for example, highways and poor relief).[49]

The present-day English socialists, in their reasoning concerning the "public control of policy," give no consideration, so far as one can determine from their writing, to principles such as the foregoing. As difficult as it may be to apply objective tests to these principles in their actual application, it is unquestionable that upon the basis of these principles there will be an increasing amount of public control (and ownership).

With our advancing efficiency in production, our rapidly rising standard of living has not been experienced to nearly the same degree among the various classes of society. This is but one of many forces which will call for increased public action. Again with growing associative competition, added public control, either positive or nega-

[49] Cf., F. W. Taussig, *Principles of Economics* (3rd ed.; New York: Macmillan, 1921), II, Chap. 64. Also H. Sidgwick, "Economic Socialism," *Contemporary Review*, L (1886), 625-627.

tive, will undoubtedly increase. And this is entirely in accord with accentuated economic competition.

4

To summarize: In this chapter, we have been concerned with a critical examination of the economic doctrine of later and present-day English socialists as well as with an examination of the program proposed by these critics of competition in their effort to rectify the limitations of the competitive order. The emergence of later and present-day English criticism of competition may be said to be marked by the development of Guild Socialism which has merged with Fabian criticism to modify both the spirit and program of the present-day attack on competition.

The central thesis of Guild Socialism is that industries and services should be administered by those who work in them. And such control of industries cannot eventuate by means of government ownership and operation. In this thesis the Guild critics of competition differ from the earlier, or Fabian, critics. To this turn from collectivism has been added the Guild socialists' argument for the organization of society on a "functional" basis. These "functions" coincide with the various interests each person has, and in each function or interest the individual should be self-governing. The implications of this thesis the Guild socialists have not developed. The economic conclusion they draw is that there should be public ownership (national and local) but *not* public control.

The organization that Guild socialists would set up to give effect to "functional" democracy is the "guild." The argument for "self-government" of each guild clearly overlooks the inevitable inherent interdependence brought on by modern specialization. Again they fail to consider that consumers' wants are the ultimate control of industry. Throughout their writing there is insistence upon producers' control, and also one may note the fundamental error of not recognizing the significance of consumers' demands.

The highly dynamic state of production, with consequent industrial rearrangements, is entirely ignored by the Guild critics of the competitive order. This state of production would of necessity alter the relation of guild to guild—inasmuch as each guild, according to the argument, is to be self-governing—and also the relation of producers to consumers.

More clearly than elsewhere the Marxian bias in the reasoning of the Guild socialists is seen in their attitude toward the State. Under an order of competition, the State is an instrument of the "dominant class"; it will (must) disappear by atrophy or destruction.

The control that Guild socialists would bring to bear upon competition with respect to wages and prices is uncertain. While it is clearly implied that each guild would determine both, nevertheless consumers and government are (whether inadvertently or intentionally it is quite impossible to determine) frequently recognized.

We find in Guild Socialism not only the fallacies of the Marxian doctrine but also the further fallacies of inconsistent organization. Again, as in early English socialism, it is especially true that the economic functions of capital and entrepreneurship are not comprehended.

The last program of the present-day English critics of competition calls for "rationalization" of industry. The fundamental thesis here is that the State must control *policy* but avoid administration. In the "rationalization" program two proposals are advanced.

Regarding the first—unemployment—the proposal is for a National Labour Corps to be employed in any work involved in "cleaning up England." This presents three principal difficulties, namely, the objective criteria in selecting such work, the financing method and burden, and trade-union opposition. In addition to these objections it may also be regarded as doubtful whether increased governmental expenditure furnishes relief for *general* unemployment. Hawtrey's argument that the general level of prices can and *ought* to be controlled by the rate of discount is a sounder approach. It avoids most, if not all, the difficulties involved in the administration of large (and temporary) expansions in governmental expenditures. It also eliminates the problem of the increased taxation necessitated by the extended governmental program. This problem, in light of England's circumstances, is the possibility of driving capital and residents abroad—a possibility greatly increased by the existence of England's attractive, unexploited dominions. And much more important is the objection to this first proposal in the "rationalization" program that not only does the unemployment program *not* remove the maladjustment causing unemployment, but also governmental unemployment measures may work in direct *opposition* to the necessary remedies.

Regarding the second proposal in the "rationalization" program ("conscious development" of national economic resources and the control of capital investment): This calls, according to the present-day English critics of competition, for a Board of National Investment. This Board should be empowered to restrict exportation of capital and also sanction (or deny) appeals for capital in the market for domestic use. In my analysis we have seen that the proposal for such a Board has indeed some merit. It does not, however, concern itself with the important remedy, namely, increasing the vertical and horizontal mobility of British labor in *all* of its classes and stages. This clearly calls for neutralizing certain English institutions—a task toward which both local and national governments should energetically direct their efforts.

In this second proposal the Board of National Investment should not be confused with the Board of the same name sponsored by the Liberal Party today, together with its "Economic General Staff." One can readily agree with the Liberal Party program, as well as with the Minority Report of the Balfour Committee (calling for a National Economic Committee), and still deny the validity of the present-day English Socialists' National Board of Investment or the National Employment and Development Board of the Balfour Minority Report.

The early English, Fabian, socialistic attack upon the competitive order calling for nationalization of capital and land is *distinctly* modified today. Nationalization of *control* of the community's economic life is now desired. Deviating from both Fabian and Guild doctrine, neither the control by the existing Parliament nor by a "Social Parliament" is desired, but rather administration by controlling commissions whose activities are coördinated by specialized public authority. This amounts to repudiation, at least for the present, of socialism as an attack upon competition; it is a recognition of the practice of our public utility commissions as a method of "rationalization" of industries.

Two important points of difference in the attitude of

the present-day English critics of competition distinguish it from the attitude of an advocate of economic competition. With respect to the former, in the first place, the contemplated rate of increase of public control of policy is, under the pressure of the left wing of the Labour Party, much more rapid. And, secondly, no apparent consideration is given to those principles which have to a greater or less degree dictated the increasing public control in our own competitive organization of production, exchange, and distribution.

IX

CONCLUSION

THE purposes of the preceding chapters of this book have been four in number. These are: first, the statement of the problem presented by the diversity of usage of "free competition" in economic philosophy; secondly, the analysis and statement, as I conceive it, of the nature of free competition in the *economic* sense, or the essence of economic competition; thirdly, the critical examination of the use of "free competition" in the writings of leading economists; and fourthly, the presentation and evaluation of the programs of control of competition proposed by those writers who are concerned primarily—if not entirely—with the limitations of competition. In closing this volume, this chapter will present the conclusions which we now arrive at with respect to each of these four phases of the work.[1]

[1] This chapter is not intended to be a general summary. The book has covered a field too broad in scope and in material to bring into one chapter a summary of the whole work. And, furthermore, this seems unnecessary since the last section of each chapter contains a summary.

This final chapter presents such conclusions with respect to each phase of the work so as to give the reader the direction of the analysis as a whole.

I

The problem presented by the vague and diverse usage of the term "free competition" is quite apparent in several fields of economic thought. The connotations of "free competition" vary with different writers on the same subject, with the same writer on different subjects, and, indeed, with the same writer on a particular subject. The conclusions arrived at, therefore, by various writers on an economic problem involving the competitive relations of employee to employee, of employer to employer, of capitalist to labor, and of producer to consumer—such conclusions must not only be uncertain, but furthermore (and more important) the reason for the divergence of opinion cannot be traced, due to the fact that the concept of "free competition" has been used tacitly with essentially different connotations.

And the problem is even more clearly seen when one reflects on the prevalence of the use in economic discussions (either interchangeably or at least with entirely inadequate distinction) of such terms and ideas as "laissez faire," "individualism," and the "competition" of business parlance. While the problem of analyzing the unexpressed sense in which "free competition" is used comes to the front most clearly in economic controversies on such subjects as socialism, trusts and combinations, the problem is not limited to these fields.

It is my conviction that much of the disagreement and consequent unrest caused by the critics of competition has been due to the failure, by such critics, of comprehending what is the essence of competition *in the economic sense*; that which is *essential* to competition and the competitive order is not distinguished from that which is non-essential.

And now as to the conclusion with respect to the second phase of my analysis.

2

Three groups of general distinctions are preliminary to an analysis and statement of the nature of "free competition" in the economic sense (or economic competition).

The first of these distinctions is competition as to form and competition as to results. This is but another way of saying that one must distinguish the means from the end. Changes in technology, in wants, and, in fact, in the whole of human environment call for constant changes in the form which competition takes. The desired result remains the same, namely, the greatest satisfaction of wants with a given expenditure of human energy. It has not been sufficiently emphasized—although, as we have seen above, it is alluded to by Cunningham, Liefmann, and Marshall —that the form and manner of competition (as well as other social institutions) *are relative to time and place.* The result of economic competition—the greatest social utility—has necessitated a constant change of competitive relations and organization. We have passed far from personal competition, and the form of competition is rapidly becoming "associative." In light of such objective criteria as economies of large-scale production, it can readily be demonstrated that competition has not been "destroyed," but in terms of *results* competition has vastly increased. And again, it may also be held that increasing division of labor and technological development have meant increased competition of producer with producer, as well as an increased competitive relationship of producers to consumers.

The second group of distinctions in the use of "free competition" which must be made is the use of competition in the sense of a postulate, of a precept, and of an institution. The first is dictated by the needs of scientific methodology, the second is an expression of the belief in a government policy (generally termed "laissez faire"), and the third is an application to economic reasoning of the analogy of evolution in biological life with progress in social life. Needless to say these three uses of competition have no necessary relation to each other. Nevertheless, one finds in *much* economic thinking and writing that it *is* expressly or tacitly held that such a relation exists.

The third group of distinctions in the use of "free competition" which must be made is in the application of competition to each of the four main departments of economic activity, namely, consumption, production, exchange, and distribution. To what degree the conclusions arrived at with regard to competition in one phase of economic relations hold for the other economic activities is not only frequently left unexpressed but, moreover, the question is usually not considered. Unanimity of opinion in favor of "free competition" in consumption (consumers' choice); complete diversity of opinion as to the desirable degree of competition in production; almost complete disagreement as to either desirability *or* practicability of restricting competition in exchange; and a marked difference of opinion as to what really constitutes "free competition" in distribution as expressed by Mill on the one hand, that both laws and conditions of distribution were matters "of human institution solely," and on the other hand, the opinion of Henry Clay that in no department of economic activity is "free competition" so complete as in "distribution of wealth"—these views clearly demonstrate the need of distinguishing the sense in which "free competition" is employed in conclusions made concerning competition in economic activities.

Such are the conclusions with regard to those preliminary distinctions which must be made in the use of the idea of "free competition" in economic philosophy. Now as to the propositions and prerequisites upon which the analysis of economic competition is based.

In the analysis and statement of the nature of economic competition as set forth by me, two propositions are fundamental. These are, first, that economic terminology should be defined in accord with the general purpose of economic science, and secondly, we assume that individuals are rational and striving for maximum economic return. The necessary corollary is that, given mobility of labor and capital, equality of returns and also maximum social returns tend to follow.

The essence of economic competition is, therefore, mobility of the factors of production or, to speak with greater exactness, proportional variability. For the existence of such mobility (or proportional variability) there are five fundamental prerequisites. Anything which extends or increases these prerequisites necessarily brings about an increase in economic competition. These prerequisites are: first, the phenomenon of scarcity (not "rarity"); second, a utilitarian outlook on life; third, knowledge of present and potential economic differences; fourth, divisibility of the factors of production; and fifth, neutralizing or eliminating those social institutions which retard unrestricted movement of the factors of production to places and activities where return is the greatest.

Such are the distinctions, the propositions, and the prerequisites which are basic in the analysis and statement of the nature of economic competition.

We now pass to the conclusions relative to the third phase of this volume—that phase which is concerned with the critical examination of the use of "free competition" in the writings of leading economists.

3

With regard to the concept of competition in the philosophy of the classical writers, it is highly important to bear in mind three general considerations in our analysis of "free competition." The considerations are, first, the economic conditions under which the writing occurred; secondly, the political and social circumstances of the time; and thirdly, the nature of the general problem in which the different writers were interested. With respect to each of these, Smith, Ricardo, McCulloch, and Mill differed to a marked degree—a fact frequently ignored when we approach these writers as a "School." These considerations explain the marked differences in the use of the idea of "free competition" in the writings of the classical economists.

Smith wrote on the eve of the Industrial Revolution, in a political environment of restraint and repression, and with the problem in view of attacking and eliminating certain types of governmental restrictions. Not only is there not in Smith a *carte blanche* adherence to "free competition" (to laissez faire, or to a natural order) but on the contrary there is recognition of the limitations of the principle of natural liberty and suggestion of the need of regulating free competitive relations.

The forty-one years which passed between Smith's and Ricardo's writing brought those social and economic changes which marked the second stage of the Industrial Revolution. The latter indeed differed from Smith on all three considerations noted above. While interested primarily in elucidating the ultimate consequences when the force of competition had run its course, Ricardo also saw the immediate and temporary effects of competition. With the latter in mind, his writing specifically called for regulation of competition.

McCulloch and Mill, writing a whole generation after Ricardo, again differed with respect to the latter on each of the three general considerations to which I have called attention. Contrary to the view often held, McCulloch explicitly states that government is "obliged to interfere" with unrestricted competition "in [to use his own words] an infinite variety of purposes." He specifically makes reference to the fact that no solution, applicable at all times and under all circumstances, is possible for the problem of what duties the state ought to perform.

Mill (and McCulloch, as well) truly saw what may be termed the third stage of industrial development, a stage which was a product of all those forces brought to a focus by 1848. Political and social conditions had developed a new outlook and the general problem in which Mill was interested. The key to Mill's reasoning concerning competition is found in that which he claimed distinguished his work from previous economic writing, namely, that modes of distribution of wealth, unlike laws of production, depended on human will. Not only does his reasoning clearly allow for the non-existence of "free competition" but, more than that, he held that the competitive order was based on social expediency. While Mill was quite dissatisfied with a competitive order (as his extensive discussion of laborers' associations and coöperative societies indicated), he nevertheless regarded competition a necessary stimulus at the present time. It is true Mill saw the authoritative interference of government in the competitive order as decidedly restricted but he did so on general philosophical grounds (as seen in his *Essay on Liberty*) rather than on economic reasoning as such. Indeed when his reasoning is the latter, he asserted "there is scarcely anything really important to the general interest, which it may not be desirable, or even necessary, that the government should take upon itself."

With Cairnes the concept of competition acquired more definiteness. His writing falls distinctly into two fields of inquiry. In the first, that of economic method, he sharply separated the science of economics from its application and unequivocally held that the use of competition as a postulate of economic science had no bearing on free competition as a precept of government practice (laissez faire). In his second field of inquiry, that of economic doctrine, Cairnes clearly elucidated the limits which must be placed upon the assumption of free competition in economic philosophy. He particularly emphasized the failure of such competition to operate with respect to labor and to the use of land.

In Marshall's writing, the broadened scope of economic inquiry, the interdependence of social relations, and the unity of economic phenomena are, in general, the striking characteristics of his economic philosophy. Concerning "free competition" his reasoning was based upon the two principles which pervade the Marshallian structure, namely, the principle of continuity and the principle of substitution. Continuity—equilibrium—is the "Fundamental Idea"; substitution is the process which gives it effect. To clearly emphasize that competition and the competitive order do not preclude coöperative and governmental action but, on the contrary, competition necessarily calls for a widened scope of such action—to emphasize this,

Marshall used the terms "Economic Freedom" and "Free Enterprise." Throughout his reasoning it is indicated that competition, or substitution, is not perfect.

Whatever further denial is needed of the commonly held view, that not only the reasoning of the economists of the so-called "Classical School" was based upon free competition but also that these writers were supporters of the precept of free competition ("laissez faire"), is furnished by Marshall.

In general, one characteristic appears to be true of Marshall's use of "Economic Freedom" or competition. Its nature and *extent* are uncertain or unexpressed to an inexplicable degree. For example, to determine what Marshall's views are on non-competing groups is next to impossible without reading unauthorized, relative weights into his different passages upon the subject scattered throughout his books and articles. It is true that he has, in part, supplied this unknown quantity in his doctrine by calling attention to the fact that in the application of the principle of continuity the element of time is the center of difficulty. And for the solution of the difficulty he has furnished his exceedingly useful concept of quasi-rent.

We shall now give our attention to the conclusions we may draw concerning the fourth phase of this volume, which is concerned with the elimination of competition and the programs of control of competition the English critics of the competitive order have advanced.

4

Pigou's theoretic analysis of the limitations of competition proceeds from the basis that the equalizing of the marginal "social net products" of the different industries will not tend to occur where production is guided by self-interest (competition) though competition does equalize marginal *private* net products. The former equalization is essential if welfare is to be maximized; marginal private net product and marginal social net product cannot in the absence of regulation be harmonized. Pigou, therefore, logically establishes a *primâ facie* case for governmental intervention.

Upon examination of government intervention in the competitive order which Pigou considers, one finds that although he unequivocally holds that the disadvantages of government control are largely diminished by the use of commissions, nevertheless when he considers a fourfold program of control he also unquestionably holds that each program of control of competition promises to be ineffective.

The theoretic attack by Pigou on the limitations of competition, it is important to note, is limited to the field of production excepting for an examination of wages. Here again with regard to wages, what seems feasible in principle he feels will be bungled in practice.

Finally, the interferences in a competitive order with the end in view of transferences from the rich to the poor are advocated only to the extent that the transferences will differentiate against idleness. The transferences for which there is economic justification are those necessary for the establishment of a National Minimum. And here we can come to no definite conclusion, from Pigou's argument, with respect to what the content of such a minimum should be and to what degree it would alter the functioning of competition.

The limitations of competition and the program of control of the competitive order which furnish a counterpart to Pigou's theoretic analysis is the pragmatic analysis of the earlier and of the present-day English socialists.

Concerning the former—that of the Fabians—we find with reference to indictment and to economic doctrine much that is Marxian, although with regard to competitive control it is the employment of existing democratic government agencies for public ownership or control of the agencies of production which is desired.

The important conclusion relative to this earlier English socialistic criticism of competition is that there was a distinct change from nationalization, as the remedy first suggested, to "socialization" with a threefold form of public ownership of which "national ownership" became decidedly subordinate. The reasoning upon which the program of control is developed reflects a curious misconception of the necessary relation of private ownership, as such, and unearned incomes. This misconception is largely, if not entirely, due to an erroneous rent analysis.

Surprising as it may seem, one finds nowhere in either the earlier or more recent Fabian proposals which they advance, much, if any, consideration of such questions as the population problem, motivation in economic life, selection of leadership, and the standard of living. Unless we assume that the critics of the competitive order are indifferent to the standard of living, it is clear that the broad problems of population and motivation need careful analysis. The need of this analysis is apparent when one considers that their reasoning concerning the limitations of competition and the programs of reform of the competitive order built upon such reasoning certainly points to far-reaching changes in social organization.

From the Fabian attack upon competition at least one constructive result has followed. With the constant emphasis upon a "National Minimum" a greater social sensitiveness has evolved to the end that the "lag" is diminished between the existence of such actual need for social control as may arise and the actual prosecution of such control.

Later and present-day English criticism of competition takes a distinctly different turn from that of Fabianism. This turn—at the hands of the Guild socialists—was the emphasis upon producers' control of their own industries and *not* socialization of ownership. That stream of criticism of competition converged with the main current of Fabianism to produce the program of control of competition sponsored today by the English pragmatic critics of the competitive order.

In this program a second distinct divergence from the early, Fabian criticism of competition is made. Neither nationalization of ownership, nor producers' control of industries ("functional democracy"), but rather, "social control of *policy*" is now demanded. The present-day program, termed "rationalization" of industry, proposes unemployment measures and "conscious" development of national resources.

The question might well be raised whether we do not find, finally, in the present-day program of control advanced by the critics of competition and the competitive order, a complete repudiation of socialism. Have they not seen what is, after all, essential to an order of "economic competition"? Does not an order of "economic competition," with the readjustments necessitated by the increasing displacement of the decentralized, corporative form of competition by centralized, associative form of competition, call for an ever widening scope of positive action on the part of the government?

BIBLIOGRAPHY

BIBLIOGRAPHICAL NOTE

IN THE first two phases of this book, concerned with the statement of the problem and with the analysis and elucidation of the nature of "economic competition," the works which have been useful are exceedingly scattered and diverse in character. My bibliography contains only those which are cited in the foregoing pages and in addition such sources as have been directly consulted for the purpose in hand. With respect to those which were found helpful, although not cited, I have specifically indicated in my bibliography the parts, chapters, or pages within each of these sources that have special bearing on the problem of my investigation. I have not indicated the part, chapter, or page references in the bibliography of sources to which citations are made in the foregoing chapters inasmuch as such references are already given in the footnotes; to repeat them would not, of course, serve any purpose.

In the third main phase of this book, concerned with the critical examination of the sense in which "free competition" was employed in the writings of leading economists, the sources used and included in the bibliography are only the important economic treatises of each of the writers considered. Because of the broad scope covered, it seemed more advisable to confine myself to such treatises and examine them more intensively than to treat a larger number of sources and cover them extensively. Furthermore, I am convinced by an examination of the sources other than the important economic treatises of each of the leading economists considered, that, on the whole, in so far as those other writings are important in the economic philosophy of the writer, it is incorporated in some form in his leading economic treatise; if it is not so incorporated it adds little, if anything, to the writer's view on competition and the competitive order. This, for example, is illustrated in the case of Cairnes. The analysis of his political essays in various periodicals does not add to our understanding of the sense in which he used "free competition." And again, with Mill: his writings outside of his *Principles* were often based upon *general* philosophical views and intended for general social purposes. I have not brought these sources together since they have thrown no added light upon his economic philosophy.

To come to the bibliography of the third main phase of this book—that concerned with the limitations of competition and the competitive order: The sources given in the bibliography are quite inadequate. The 242 Fabian Tracts published up to date present an important record of the development of English critical thought regarding competitive relations. It is my opinion that the historical and theoretical value of this material has not been sufficiently recognized. Unfortunately, at least Nos. 2, 3, 4, and 6 of the tracts have been withdrawn by the Fabian Society; and Nos. 8, 10, 11, 16, 17, 18, 27, 43, 46, 53, and 59 are also out of print. Many others undoubtedly are now unavailable.

Besides these tracts, other pamphlets have appeared either individually or in series. They too will have increasing value with the passing of time. While my bibliography contains only such pamphlets which have borne directly upon the subject under examination I wish to emphasize, however, that much of the pamphlet material, to which I have alluded above, is exceedingly important in giving the general course of English critical thinking on the theory of competition and on the limitations of the competitive order.

To one other point I wish to call the reader's attention in this bibliographical note. That part of this volume which is critical, rather than historical, necessarily takes the discussion into fields which are not only broad in scope but also distinct in content from the subject of the present inquiry. This is clearly the case in Chapter VIII where, for instance, the problem of the export of capital is raised. In such cases where my analysis is not based upon generally accepted economic theory, I have supported my criticism by the use of a few important sources.

BIBLIOGRAPHY

BOOKS

Bagehot, Walter. *Economic Studies* (London: Longmans, 1880).

Balfour Committee. *Report on Industry and Trade* (London: His Majesty's Stationery Office, 1927), Final Report.

Barker, Ernest. *Political Thought in England: From Spencer to the Present Day* (London: William and Norgate, 1919?).

Beer, M. *A History of British Socialism* (London: G. Bell and Sons, 1921).

Belloc, Hilaire. *The Servile State* (London: T. N. Foulis, 1912), Introduction.

Black, J. D. *Introduction to Production Economics* (New York: Henry Holt, 1926).

Blackmar, F. W. *Justifiable Individualism* (New York: Thomas Y. Crowell, 1922), pp. 41-142.

Blease, W. L. *A Short History of English Liberalism* (New York: G. P. Putnam's Sons, 1913).

Bonar, James. *Philosophy and Political Economy* (London: G. Allen and Unwin, 1922), pp. 255-265.

Boyle, James. *What Is Socialism?* (New York: Shakespeare Press, 1912), Chap. 10.

Brasol, B. L. *Socialism vs. Civilization* (New York: C. Scribner's Sons, 1920), Introduction by T. N. Carver.

Brown, H. G. *Earned and Unearned Incomes* (Columbia, Mo.: Missouri Book Co., 1918), Chaps. 3 and 6.

Bukharin, Nikolai. *Historical Materialism* (Translated from 3rd Russian ed.; New York: International Publishers, 1925), Chap. 2.

Cairnes, J. E. *Essays in Political Economy: Theoretical and Applied* (London: Macmillan, 1873).

Cairnes, J. E. *Political Essays.* (London: Macmillan, 1873).

Cairnes, J. E. *Some Leading Principles of Political Economy Newly Expounded* (New York: Harper, 1874).

Cairnes, J. E. *The Character and Logical Method of Political Economy* (2nd ed.; London: Macmillan, 1875).

Campbell, C. G. *Common Wealth: A Study in Social Philosophy* (London: Century, 1925), Chap. 6.

Cannan, Edwin. *The Economic Outlook* (London: T. F. Unwin, 1912), Chap. 7.

Carter, G. P. *The Tendency Toward Industrial Combination* (London: Constable, 1913).

Carver, T. N. *Essays in Social Justice* (Cambridge: Harvard University Press, 1925).

Carver, T. N. *Principles of Political Economy* (Boston: Ginn, 1919), Part 7, Chaps. 46, 47.

Carver, T. N. *Principles of Rural Economy* (Boston: Ginn, 1911).

Carver, T. N. *The Present Economic Revolution in the United States* (Boston: Little, Brown, 1926), Chap. 2.

Carver, T. N. *This Economic World and How It May Be Improved* (Chicago: A. W. Shaw, 1928).

Chalmers, Thomas. *Political Economy in Connexion with the Moral State and Prospects of Society* (Edinburgh: Sutherland and Knox, 1832), Vol. II.

Chamberlin, E. H. *Monopolistic Competition* (Harvard University Press, 1932).

Clapham, J. H. *The Economic Development of France and Germany 1815-1914* (London: Cambridge University Press, 1923).

Clark, J. M. *Social Control of Business* (Chicago: University of Chicago Press, 1926).

Clay, Henry. *Economics for the General Reader* (New York: Macmillan, 1924), Chap. 24.

Clayton, Joseph. *The Rise and Decline of Socialism in Great Britain 1884-1924* (London: Faber and Gwyer, 1926).

Cole, G. D. H. *A Short History of British Working Class Movement* (London: G. Allen and Unwin, 1925), Vol. 3.

Cole, G. D. H. *Guild Socialism Restated* (London: Leonard Parson, 1920).

Cole, G. D. H. *Self-Government in Industry* (3rd ed.; London: G. Bell and Sons, 1920).

Cole, G. D. H. *Social Theory* (New York: F. A. Stokes, 1920).

Cole, G. D. H. *The Next Ten Years in British Social and Economic Policy* (London: Macmillan, 1929).

Colwyn Committee. *Report of the Committee on National Debt and Taxation* (London: His Majesty's Stationery Office, 1927).

Cooley, C. H. *Personal Competition: Its Place in the Social Order and Effect Upon Individuals* (New York: Macmillan, 1889), Chap. 2.

Cossa, Luigi. *Introduction to Political Economy* (London: Macmillan, 1893).

Davenport, H. J. *Economics of Enterprise* (New York: Macmillan, 1916), Chap. 28.

Dell, Robert. *Socialism and Personal Liberty* (London: L. Parsons, 1921), Chap. 2.

Dickinson, G. L. *Justice and Liberty* (New York: McClure, 1908), pp. 55-132.

Donisthorpe, Wordsworth. *Law in a Free State* (London: Macmillan), Chap. 2.

Ely, R. T., Hess, R. H., Leith, C. K., and Carver, T. N. *The Foundations of National Prosperity* (New York: Macmillan, 1920), Chap. 5.

Ferris, A. J. *Pauperizing the Rich* (Philadelphia: T. S. Leach, 1899), Chap. 22.

Fisher, Irving. *Elementary Principles of Economics* (New York: Macmillan, 1912), Chap. 25, Sec. 5.

Garver, F. B., and Hansen, H. H. *Principles of Economics* (Boston: Ginn, 1928), Chap. 32.

George, Henry. *Progress and Poverty* (25th anniversary ed.; New York: Doubleday, Page, 1925).

George, Henry. *Social Problems* (New York: Doubleday, Page, 1911), Chap. 2.

Gide, Charles. *Principles of Political Economy* (New York: D. C. Heath, 1924), Book 3, Chap. 2.

Hadley, A. T. *Economics* (New York: G. T. Putnam's Sons, 1896).

Hadley, A. T. *Freedom and Responsibility* (New York: C. Scribner's Sons, 1903), Chap. 6.

Hake, A. E., and Wesslau, C. E. *The Coming Individualism* (Westminster: A. Constable, 1895), Chaps. 1 and 2.

Haldane, Lord. *The Problem of Nationalization* (London: Allen and Unwin, 1921).

Harvey, John, et al. *Competition, a Study in Human Motive* (London: Macmillan, 1917).

Hawley, F. B. *Enterprise and the Productive Process* (New York: G. P. Putnam's Sons), Chap. 13.

Hawtrey, R. G. *Currency and Credit* (3rd ed.; London: Longmans, Green, 1928).

Hawtrey, R. G. *Monetary Reconstruction* (2nd ed.; London: Longmans, 1926).

Hawtrey, R. G. *The Economic Problem* (London: Longmans, 1925).

Haynes, E. S. P. *The Case for Liberty* (New York: E. P. Dutton, 1919), Chap. 9.

Henderson, H. D. *Supply and Demand* (New York: Harcourt Brace, 1922).

Herbert, Auberon. *The Right and Wrong Compulsion by the State* (London: William and Norgate, 1885), pp. 1-73.

Hirsch, Max. *Democracy versus Socialism* (London: Macmillan, 1901).

Hobson, S. G. *National Guilds: An Enquiry into the Wage-System and the Way Out* (London: G. Bell and Sons, 1919).

Hobson, J. A. *The Industrial System* (Rev. ed.; London: Longmans, Green, 1910), Chaps. 7 and 9.

Hobson, J. A. *The Science of Wealth* (London: William and Norgate, 1911), Chaps. 6 and 9.

Hobson, J. A. and Mumery, A. F. *The Physiology of Industry* (London: J. Murray, 1889), Preface and Chap. 2.

Hollander, J. H. *Economic Liberalism* (New York: Abingdon Press, 1925).

Hunt, E. E. *Recent Economic Changes in the United States* (New York: McGraw-Hill, 1929).

Hutchins, B. L. and Harrison, A. *A History of Factory Legislation* (2nd ed.; rev.; London: P. S. King, 1911).

Ingram, J. K. *History of Political Economy* (London: Macmillan, 1894).

Jandus, William. *Social Wrongs and State Responsibilities* (Cleveland: H. Carr, 1913), pp. 57-68.

Jevons, W. S. *The State in Relation to Labor* (London: Macmillan, 1887), Chap. 8.

Johnson, A. S. *Introduction to Economics* (Boston: D. C. Heath, 1909), Chap. 20.

Jones, Eliot. *The Trust Problem in the United States* (New York: Macmillan, 1921).

Keynes, J. N., Editor. *Official Papers by Alfred Marshall* (London: Macmillan, 1926).

Keynes, J. N. *Scope and Method of Political Economy* (2nd ed.; London: Macmillan, 1897).

Kidd, Benjamin. *Social Evolution* (New York: Macmillan, 1898).

Knight, F. H. *Risk, Uncertainty, and Profit* (Boston: Houghton Mifflin, 1921).

Kyrk, Hazel. *A Theory of Consumption* (Boston: Houghton Mifflin, 1923), Chap. 2.

Lennes, N. J. *Whither Democracy?* (New York: Harper, 1927), Chaps. 4 and 7; also pp. 330 ff.

Liberal Industrial Inquiry Committee. *Britain's Industrial Future: Being the Report of the Liberal Industrial Inquiry* (London: Ernest Benn, 1928).

Macassey, Lynden. *Labour Policy: True and False* (London: Thornton Butterworth, 1922), Chap. 14.

Mackay, T. *A Plea for Liberty* (New York: D. Appleton, 1891), Introduction.

Macrosty, H. W. *The Trust Problem in British Industry* (London: Longmans, Green, 1907).

Malthus, T. R. *Principles of Political Economy* (Boston: Wells and Lilly, 1821).

Marriott, J. A. R. *Economics and Ethics* (London: Methuen, 1923), Chaps. 12 and 17.

Marshall, Alfred. *Industry and Trade* (3rd ed.; London: Macmillan, 1920).

Marshall, Alfred. *Money, Credit and Commerce* (London: Macmillan, 1923).

Marshall, Alfred. *Principles of Economics* (8th ed.; London: Macmillan, 1920).

Mathews, B. C. *Our Irrational Distribution of Wealth* (New York: G. P. Putnam's Sons, 1908).

McCulloch, J. R. *Principles of Political Economy* (4th ed.; Edinburgh: A. and C. Black, 1849).

McKechnie, W. S. *The State and the Individual* (Glasgow: J. MacLehose, 1896), Chaps. 12, 14, and 15.

Menger, Anton. *The Right to the Whole Produce of Labour* (Translated from the German by M. E. Tanner; London: Macmillan, 1889), pp. CV-CX.

Mill, John Stuart. *A System of Logic* (New Impression; London: Longmans, 1925).

Mill, John Stuart. *Autobiography* (London: Humphrey Milford, 1873?).

Mill, John Stuart. *Essay on Liberty* (London: Longmans, 1874).

Mill, John Stuart. *Principles of Political Economy* (Ashley ed.; London: Longmans, Green, 1926).

Mill, John Stuart. *The Irish Land Question* (London: Longmans, 1870).

Money, L. G. G. *Riches and Poverty* (1st ed.; London: Methuen, 1905), Chaps. 9, 11, and 12.

Montague, F. C. *The Limits of Individual Liberty* (London: Rivingtons, 1884), Chap. 7.

Montgomery, B. G. *British and Continental Labour Policy* (London: K. Paul, Trench, Trubner, 1922), Chaps. 11, 12, 16, and 17.

National Bureau of Economic Research. *Business Cycles and Unemployment* (New York: McGraw-Hill, 1923).

Nicholson, J. S. *Principles of Political Economy* (London: Macmillan, 1901).

Nicholson, J. S. *Strikes and Social Problems* (London: A. and C. Black, 1896), Chap. 7.

Palgrave, R. H. I. *Dictionary of Political Economy* (London: Macmillan, 1894), II, 756 ff.

Pareto, V. *Cours d'economie politique* (Paris: Pichon, 1896).

Pease, E. R. *The History of the Fabian Society* (London: A. C. Fifield, 1916).

Penty, A. J. *Old Worlds for New: A Study of the Post-Industrial State* (London: Allen and Unwin, 1917).

Penty, A. J. *The Restoration of the Guild System* (London: Swan Sonnenschein, 1906).

Pigou, A. C. *Essays in Applied Economics* (London: P. S. King, 1923).

Pigou, A. C. *Industrial Fluctuations* (London: Macmillan, 1927).

Pigou, A. C. *Memorials of Alfred Marshall* (London: Macmillan, 1925).

Pigou, A. C. *The Economics of Welfare* (2nd ed.; London: Macmillan, 1924).

Price, L. L. *A Short History of Political Economy in England* (11th ed.; London: Methuen, 1922).

Ray, John. *Contemporary Socialism* (London: Swan Sonnenschein, 1890).

Read, H. E. *The Abolition of Inheritance* (New York: Macmillan, 1918), Chaps. 30 and 32.

Ricardo, David. *Principles of Political Economy and Taxation* (Everyman's Library edition; New York: E. P. Dutton, 1911).

Robertson, D. H. *Banking Policy and the Price Level* (London: King and Son, 1926).

Robertson, D. H. *The Control of Industry* (New York: Harcourt, Brace, 1923).

Ross, E. A. *Social Control* (New York: Macmillan, 1901), Chaps. 31-33.

Russell, Bertrand. *Political Ideals* (New York: Century, 1917), Chap. 4.

Russell, Bertrand. *Proposed Roads to Freedom* (New York: Henry Holt, 1919), Chap. 2.

Ryan, J. A. *A Living Wage* (New York: Macmillan, 1920), Chap. 10.

Schäffle, A. E. F. *The Quintessence of Socialism* (Translation from 8th German ed. by Bernard Bosanquet; New York: Humboldt, 1894).

Schumpeter, Joseph. *Theorie der Wirtschaftlichen Entwicklung* (Leipzig: Duncker and Humbolt, 1912).

Shaw, G. Bernard. *The Intelligent Woman's Guide to Socialism and Capitalism* (New York: Brentano, 1928).

Sidgwick, Henry. *Principles of Economics* (3rd ed.; London: Macmillan, 1901).

Skelton, O. D. *Socialism: A Critical Analysis* (Boston: Houghton Mifflin, 1911).

Smart, William. *Studies in Economics* (London: Macmillan, 1895), Chap. 10.

Smart, William. *The Distribution of Income* (London: Macmillan, 1899), Part 2, Chaps. 1 and 28.

Smith, Adam. *Wealth of Nations* (Everyman's Library Edition; New York: E. P. Dutton, 1910), Vols. I and II.

Smith, J. H. *Economic Moralism* (New York: Macmillan, 1917), Chap. 1. Also pp. 121 ff.

Spargo, John. *Social Democracy Explained* (New York: Harper, 1918), Chap. 10.

Spargo, John. *Syndicalism, Industrial Unionism and Socialism* (New York: B. W. Huebsch, 1913), Chap. 5.

Spencer, Herbert. *Principles of Sociology* (London: William and Norgate, 1893), Vol. I, Chap. 2.

Spencer, Herbert. *Principles of Sociology* (London: Williams and Norgate, 1897), Vol. III, Part 8, Chap. 2.

Spencer, Herbert. *Social Statics* (New York: D. Appleton, 1892), pp. 120 ff.

Spencer, Herbert. *The Man versus The State* (New York: D. Appleton, 1884).

Taussig, F. W. *Principles of Economics* (3rd ed.; New York: Macmillan, 1921), Vols. I and II.

Taylor, H. C. *Agricultural Economics* (New York: Macmillan, 1919).

Thornton, W. T. *On Labour* (2nd ed.; London: Macmillan, 1870).

Todd, A. J. *Theories of Social Progress* (New York: Macmillan, 1918), Chaps. 13, 14, and 15.

Toynbee, Arnold. *Lectures on the Industrial Revolution of the 18th Century in England* (London: Longmans, 1884—9th Impression 1927).

Trevelyan, G. M. *History of England* (London: Longmans, 1926).

Veblen, Thorstein. *Theory of Business Enterprise* (New York: C. Scribner's Sons, 1904), Chap. 7.

Veblen, Thorstein. *The Place of Science in Modern Civilisation* (New York: Huebsch, 1919).

Walling, W. E., Editor. *Socialism of Today* (New York: Henry Holt, 1916), pp. 50, 257-259.

Ward, A. W., Prothero, G. W., and Leathes, S., Editors. *The Cambridge Modern History* (London: Macmillan, 1910).

Webb, Mrs. Sidney, Editor. *The Case for the Factory Acts* (London: Grant Richards, 1902).

Webb, Sidney and Beatrice. *A Constitution for the Socialist Commonwealth of Great Britain* (London: Longmans, 1920).

Webb, Sidney and Beatrice. *English Poor Law Policy* (London: Longmans, 1910).

Webb, Sidney and Beatrice. *Industrial Democracy* (London: Longmans, Green, 1897), Vol. II.

Webb, Sidney and Beatrice. *The Decay of Capitalist Civilisation* (London: George Allen and Unwin, 1923).

Webb, Sidney and Beatrice. *The Minority Report of the Poor Law Commission, 1905-1909* (London: Longmans, 1909).

Wells, H. G. *What Is Coming* (London: Cassell, 1916).

Willoughby, W. W. *Social Justice: A Critical Essay* (New York: Macmillan, 1900), Part 2, Chaps. 8 and 9.

Wilson, Woodrow. *The New Freedom* (New York: Doubleday, Page, 1913).

JOURNALS

Adams, H. C. "The Relation of the State to Individual Actions." *American Economic Association* Publications, I, No. 6 (1886), 7-85.

Ashley, W. J. "The Present Position of Political Economy." *Economic Journal*, XVII (1907), 467-489.

Ayres, C. E. "The Function and Problems of Economic Theory." *Journal of Political Economy*, XXVI (1918), 69-90.

Bascom, John. "Competition, Actual and Theoretical." *Quarterly Journal of Economics*, XIV (1900), 537-542.

Cairnes, J. E. "Political Economy and Land." *Fortnightly Review*, VII (1870), 41-63.

Cannan, Edwin. "Pigou's Economics of Welfare." *Economic Journal*, XXXI (1921), 206-214.

Carver, T. N. "The Theory of Wages Adjusted to Recent Theories of Value." *Quarterly Journal of Economics*, VIII (1894), 377-403.

Clapham, J. H. "Of Empty Economic Boxes." *Economic Journal*, XXXII (1922), 305-314.

Clark, J. B. "Monopolies and the Law." *Political Science Quarterly*, XVI (1901), 463-475.

Clark, J. B. "The Future of Economic Theory." *Quarterly Journal of Economics*, XIII (1898), 1-14.

Clark, J. M. "The Changing Basis of Responsibility." *Journal of Political Economy*, XXIV (1916), 209-229.

Clarke, William. "Socialism in English Politics." *Political Science Quarterly*, III (1888), 549-571.

Clay, Henry. "Review of Sidney and Beatrice Webb's, 'The Decay of

Capitalist Civilisation.'" *Economic Journal*, XXXIII (1923), 215-220.

Clay, Henry. "The Authoritarian Element in Distribution." *Economic Journal*, XXXVII (1927), 1-18.

Clay, Henry. "The Public Regulation of Wages in Great Britain." *Economic Journal*, XXXIX (1929), 323-344.

Cohn, Gustav. "Government and Laissez Faire." *Economic Journal*, XVII (1907), 180-191.

Cole, G. D. H. "British Labor Movement." *American Economic Review*, VIII—Part 2 (1918), 485-504.

Cole, G. D. H. "National Guilds Movement in Great Britain." *Monthly Labor Review*, United States Bureau of Labor Statistics, (No. 1, July 1919), 24-32.

Cooley, C. H. "Political Economy and Social Process." *Journal of Political Economy*, XXVI (1918), 366-374.

Cunningham, W. "The Relativity of Economic Doctrine." *Economic Journal*, II (1892), 1-16.

Dunbar, C. F. "The Academic Study of Political Economy." *Quarterly Journal of Economics*, V (1891), 397-416.

Dunbar, C. F. "The Reaction in Political Economy." *Quarterly Journal of Economics*, I (1887), 1-27.

Ely, R. T. "The Past and Present of Political Economy." *Johns Hopkins University Studies* in Historical and Political Science, Second Series, March 1884, pp. 5-64.

Foxwell, H. S. "The Nature of Industrial Struggle." *Economic Journal*, XXVII (1917), 315-329.

Furnivall, J. S. "Organization of Consumption." *Economic Journal*, XX (1910), 23-30.

Grant, I. F. "The Survival of the Small Unit in Industry." *Economic Journal*, XXXII (1922), 489-505.

Gray, H. L. "War-Time Control of Industry." *Economic Journal*, XXIX (1919), 224-226.

Hadley, A. T. "Interest and Profits." *Annals of the American Academy of Political and Social Science*, IV (1893), 337-347.

Hansen, A. H. "Economics of Unionism." *Journal of Political Economy*, XXX (1922), 518-530.

Hayes, E. C. "The Social Control of the Acquisition of Wealth." *American Economic Review*, VIII—Part I (1918), 194-211.

Hobson, S. G. "Guilds and Their Critics." *The New Age*, XXI (Oct. 18, 1917), 521-523.

Hobson, S. G. "Guilds and Their Critics." *The New Age*, XXII (Nov. 1, 1917), 6-8.

Hobson, S. G. "Guilds and Their Critics." *The New Age*, XXIII (May 2, 1918—June 13, 1918), 5, 21, 38, 55, 69, and 101.

Hobson, S. G. "Guild Socialism." *The New Age*, XII (Nov. 7, 1912), 6-7.

Hobson, S. G. "The Restoration." *The New Age*, XIII (Aug. 7, 1913), 421-423.

Hoxie, R. F. "The Demand and Supply Concepts." *Journal of Political Economy*, XIV (1906), 337-361.

Jenks, J. W. "Economic Aspects of Decisions on Trusts." *Journal of Political Economy*, XX (1912), 346-357.

Jewkes, J. and Campion, H. "The Mobility of Labor in the Cotton Industry." *Economic Journal*, XXXVIII (1928), 135-137.

Knight, F. H. "Some Books on Fundamentals." *Journal of Political Economy*, XXXI (1923), 342-359.

Knight, F. H. "The General Theory of Price." *Journal of Political Economy*, XXXVI (1928), 353-370.

Labour Magazine. "Editorial Notes." *The Labour Magazine*, VIII (No. 1, May 1929), 24-27.

Liefmann, Robert. "Monopoly or Competition." *Quarterly Journal of Economics*, XXIX (1914), 308-325.

MacGregor, D. H. "Final Report of the Committee on Industry and Trade." *Economic Journal*, XXXIX (1929), 295-297.

MacGregor, D. H. "Motives and Standards in Industry." *Economic Journal*, XXXIII (1923), 6.

MacGregor, D. H. "Rationalisation of Industry." *Economic Journal*, XXXVII (1927), 521-550.

Macrosty, H. W. "The Meaning of Industrial Freedom by G. D. H. Cole." *Economic Journal*, XXIX (1919), 72-73.

Mallery, O. T. "Advance Planning of Public Works to Stabilize Employment." *The American Labor Legislation Review*, XVII (1927), 210.

Marshall, Alfred. "The Social Possibilities of Economic Chivalry." *Economic Journal*, XVII (1907), 7-29.

Moses, Bernard. "Certain Tendencies in Political Economy." *Quarterly Journal of Economics*, XI (1897), 372-387.

New Leader, Editorial. "Stop the Persecution." *The New Leader*, XVI (No. 157, Oct. 25, 1929), pp. 1-2.

New Leader, Editorial. "What Labour Would Do." *The New Leader*, XVI (No. 131, Apr. 26, 1929), Supplement, p. iii.

New Statesman, Editorial. "The Latest Utopia." *New Statesman*, III (No. 61, June 6, 1914), 267-269.

Orage, A. R. "Politics for Craftsmen." *Contemporary Review*, XCI (1907), 782-794.

Patten, S. N. "The Interpretation of Ricardo." *Quarterly Journal of Economics*, VII (1893), 345 and 346.

Patten, S. N. "The Theory of Social Forces." *Annals of the American Academy of Political and Social Science*, Supplement to Vol. VII (1896), Chap. 4.

Penty, A. J. "The Restoration of the Guild System." *The New Age*, XIII (Aug. 21, 1913), 483-485.

Penty, A. J. "The Restoration of the Guild System." *The New Age*, XIII (Aug. 28, 1913), 511-512.

Pigou, A. C. "Empty Economic Boxes: A Reply." *Economic Journal*, XXXII (1922), 458-465.

Pigou, A. C. "Interest after the War and the Export of Capital." *Economic Journal*, XXVI (1916), 413-424.

Pigou, A. C. "Marshall's Principles of Economics, 5th Edition." *Economic Journal*, XVII (1907), 532-535.

Pigou, A. C. "The Unity of Political and Economic Science." *Economic Journal*, XVI (1906), 372-380.

Pigou, A. C. "Wage Policy and Unemployment." *Economic Journal*, XXXVII (1927), 355-368.

Price, L. L. "The Practical Aspects of Economics." *Economic Journal*, XI (1909), 173-189.

Reynard, Helene. "The Industrial Situation." *Economic Journal*, XXIX (1919), 290-301.

Rignano, Eugenio. "A Plea for a Greater Economic Democratisation." *Economic Journal*, XXIX (1919), 302-308.

Robbins, Lionel. "The Representative Firm." *Economic Journal*, XXXVIII (1928), 387-404.

Robertson, D. H. "A Constitution for the Socialist Commonwealth of Great Britain by Sidney and Beatrice Webb." *Economic Journal*, XXXI (1921), 61-65.

Seligman, E. R. "Social Elements in the Theory of Value." *Quarterly Journal of Economics*, XV (1901), 321-347.

Sidgwick, H. "Economic Socialism." *Contemporary Review*, L (1886), 620-631.

Taussig, F. W. "Great Britain's Foreign Trade Terms After 1900." *Economic Journal*, XXXV (1925), 1-10.

Thompson, J. G. "Mobility of the Factors of Production as Affecting Variation in Their Proportional Relation to Each Other in Farm Organization." *Journal of Political Economy*, XXIX (1921), 108-137.

Veblen, Thorstein. "The Preconceptions of Economic Science." *Quarterly Journal of Economics*, XIII (1889), 396-426.

Viner, Jacob. "Adam Smith and Laissez-faire." *Journal of Political Economy*, XXXV (1927), 198-232.

Wagner, Adolf. "Marshall's Principles of Economics." *Quarterly Journal of Economics*, V (1891), 319-338.

Webb, Sidney and Beatrice. "Can Industry be Organized by the National or Municipal Government?" *New Statesman*, V (No. 109, May 8, 1915), Special Supplement, pp. 1-32.

Webb, Sidney and Beatrice. "Can the Organization of Industry be Based exclusively on Associations of Producers?" *New Statesman*, II (No. 45, Feb. 14, 1914), Special Supplement, pp. 1-31.

Webb, Sidney and Beatrice. "The Co-operative Movement." *New Statesman*, III (No. 60, May 30, 1914), Special Supplement, pp. 1-34.

Webb, Sidney. "Socialism in England." *American Economic Association Publications*, IV, No. 2 (1889), 7-73.

Webb, Sidney. "The Difficulties of Individualism." *Economic Journal*, I (1891), 360-381.

Webb, Sidney. "The Necessary Basis of Society." *Contemporary Review*, XCIII (1908), 658-668.

Young, A. A. "Pigou's Wealth and Welfare." *Quarterly Journal of Economics*, XXVII (1913), 672-686.

PAMPHLETS

Allen, C. R. *Fabian Tract No. 82*—"The Workmen's Compensation Act." (London: The Fabian Society, 1897.)

Cassel, Gustav. *League of Nations, International Economic Monographs*—"Recent Monopolistic Tendencies in Industry and Trade." (Geneva: League of Nations, 1927), Preface, p. 2.

Cole, G. D. H. *Fabian Tract No. 192*—"Guild Socialism." (London: The Fabian Society, 1920).

MacDonald, Ramsay. *Fabian Tract No. 64*—"How to Win an Election." (London: The Fabian Society, 1895).

Phillips, W. L. *Fabian Tract No. 1*—"Why are the Many Poor." (London: The Fabian Society, 1884).

Shaw, G. Bernard, Editor. *Fabian Essays in Socialism.* (London: The Fabian Society, 1889).

Shaw, G. Bernard. *Fabian Tract No. 41*—"The Fabian Society." (London: The Fabian Society, 1892).

Shaw, G. Bernard. *Fabian Tract No. 70*—"Report on Fabian Policy." (London: The Fabian Society, 1896).

The Fabian Society. *Fabian Tract No. 7*—"Capital and Land." (London: The Fabian Society, 1896).

The Fabian Society. *Fabian Annual Report*—"The Fortieth Annual Report of the Fabian Society." (London: The Fabian Society, 1923).

The Fabian Society. *Fabian Annual Report*—"The Forty-First Annual Report of the Fabian Society." (London: The Fabian Society, 1924).

United States Department of Labor. *Bulletin No. 380*—"Post-War Conditions in Germany." (Washington: U. S. Printing Office, 1925), pp. 90-93.

Webb, Sidney. *Fabian Tract No. 8*—"Facts for Londoners." (London: The Fabian Society, 1899).

Webb, Sidney. *Fabian Tract No. 9*—"An Eight Hour Bill." (London: The Fabian Society, 1889).

Webb, Sidney. *Fabian Tract No. 51*—"Socialism: True and False." (London: The Fabian Society, 1894).

Webb, Sidney. *Fabian Tract No. 207*—"The Labour Party on the Threshold." (London: The Fabian Society, 1923).

Webb, Sidney. *Toward Social Democracy?* (London: The Fabian Society, 1916), p. 3.

INDEX

INDEX

(See also the analytical table of contents)

www.ingramcontent.com/pod-product-compliance
Lightning Source LLC
LaVergne TN
LVHW011821200926
848484LV00005B/1267

9781512805581